International Conflict Management

International Conflict Management

J. MICHAEL GREIG, ANDREW P. OWSIAK,
AND PAUL F. DIEHL

polity

First published in 2019 by Polity Press

Polity Press
65 Bridge Street
Cambridge CB2 1UR, UK

Polity Press
101 Station Landing
Suite 300
Medford, MA 02155, USA

ISBN-13: 978-1-5095-3052-6
ISBN-13: 978-1-5095-3053-3(pb)

A catalogue record for this book is available from the British Library.

Library of Congress Cataloging-in-Publication Data
Names: Greig, J. Michael, author. | Owsiak, Andrew P., author. | Diehl, Paul F. (Paul Francis), author.
Title: International conflict management / J. Michael Greig, Andrew P.
  Owsiak, Paul F. Diehl.
Description: Cambridge, UK ; Medford, MA : Polity Press, 2019. | Includes
  bibliographical references and index.
Identifiers: LCCN 2018054233 (print) | LCCN 2019016696 (ebook) | ISBN
  9781509530557 (Epub) | ISBN 9781509530526 (hardback) | ISBN 9781509530533
  (pbk.)
Subjects: LCSH: Conflict management–International cooperation. |
  Peace-building–International cooperation. | Diplomatic negotiations in
  international disputes. | Pacific settlement of international disputes.
Classification: LCC JZ6368 (ebook) | LCC JZ6368 .G74 2019 (print) | DDC
  327.1/7–dc23
LC record available at https://lccn.loc.gov/2018054233

Typeset in 10 on 13 pt Swift by
Servis Filmsetting Ltd, Stockport, Cheshire
Printed and bound in the United Kingdom by TJ International Ltd

For further information on Polity, visit our website: politybooks.com

Contents

List of Figures

List of Tables

List of Boxes

About the Authors

J. Michael Greig is Professor of Political Science and University Distinguished Teaching Professor at the University of North Texas. He is the co-author of *International Mediation* (2012) and numerous articles in leading international relations journals. His recent research examines the onset and termination of civil conflict, peacekeeping, and diplomacy.

Andrew P. Owsiak is Associate Professor of International Affairs at the University of Georgia. He is the author of numerous articles in leading international relations journals. His areas of expertise include interstate conflict and conflict management processes—including diplomacy, territorial disputes, rivalries, war, and non-violent conflict management strategies.

Paul F. Diehl is Associate Provost and Ashbel Smith Professor of Political Science at the University of Texas-Dallas. He is the co-author most recently of *The Puzzle of Peace* (2016) and Past President of the International Studies Association and the Peace Science Society (International) respectively. His areas of expertise include the causes of war, UN peacekeeping, and international law.

1

Introducing International Conflict Management

The Korean War ended in 1953. Nevertheless, the threat of renewed war on the Korean peninsula has persisted constantly between then and now. More than forty militarized disputes (involving the threat, display, or use of military force) related to the conflict have occurred in this period. Although nuclear concerns date back to 1993 when North Korea first threatened the Nuclear Non-proliferation Treaty (NPT), the risk of nuclear war stemming from the peninsula's conflict has accelerated since North Korea began nuclear tests in 2006.

It is fortunate that none of the post-1953 Korean confrontations has escalated to full-scale war. Some of this "success" results from the myriad conflict management efforts of the international community. Over the past seven decades, various actors have employed a wide range of approaches to manage the conflict. Military intervention under United Nations (UN) auspices first attempted to control and end the conflict in 1950, even as it later expanded, perhaps prolonged, the war, and contributed to the stalemate of 1953. Subsequent negotiations between the United States, South Korea, and North Korea dealt with a variety of issues, from lower-order concerns (e.g., reuniting families) to mid-level concerns (e.g., humanitarian aid) to issues central to the conflict (namely, the acquisition of nuclear weapons by North Korea). On occasion, these negotiations have even been facilitated by third-party mediators, as when ex-US President Jimmy Carter acted as a go-between in the 1994 nuclear negotiations.

Conflict management efforts have not, however, been confined to diplomacy alone. The UN and individual countries have imposed economic sanctions on North Korea and its leadership at various junctures and to various degrees. These coercive tactics are designed to discourage North Korea from further advancing its nuclear program and, ideally, to encourage it to abandon its desire to possess nuclear weapons at all. Importantly, they also follow failed attempts at consensual conflict management rooted in international law. One hundred and ninety-one countries have voluntarily accepted the NPT, with non-nuclear states promising to use nuclear power only for peaceful purposes and to foreswear any weapons development. International legal agreements have consequently received credit for limiting the number of new nuclear states (Fuhrmann and Lupu 2016), as well as proving effective in restraining North Korea.

The enduring conflict in Korea provides a window into the myriad approaches available for international conflict management, along with the conditions affecting their successes and failures. This book reviews the most prominent of these approaches, used widely to manage both interstate and civil conflicts. At one end of the spectrum sit the more coercive means of compelling protagonists to cease their violent or otherwise undesirable behavior; military intervention and sanctions fall into this category. The rest of the spectrum contains a variety of less hostile conflict management approaches, under which disputants cede various degrees of control over the conflict management process and outcome to third-party actors. Negotiation and mediation, for example, require the cooperation of disputants to begin the conflict management process, reach a settlement on the disputed issues, and enforce any settlement terms. Peacekeeping and peacebuilding activities, on the other hand, still rely on cooperation to a significant degree, but their outcomes rely extensively on the effectiveness of the third parties that conduct the peace operation. Somewhere between mediation and peacekeeping lie the legal approaches (adjudication and arbitration) in which the disputants permit a third party (court or arbiter) to settle their disputed issues, usually through formal, legal processes over which the disputants have little control.

This is a book about conflict management. As such, we begin with defining conflict *management* and distinguishing it from another process—conflict *resolution*—with which it is often confused.

Conflict Management vs Conflict Resolution

Conflict management and conflict resolution are often used interchangeably in the media and scholarly analyses (for an overview of the field's development, see Kriesberg 1997). Both occur in contexts where a significant likelihood of armed conflict exists. Violence or even full-scale war might be manifest, but short of that extreme, conflicting positions on important issues or explicit threats of violence raise the specter of violence in the near future. Preventive measures appear in the early stages of conflict, prior to the onset or threat of violence; management and resolution needs then expand during active violence (e.g., an ongoing war); and disagreements might need to be managed or resolved in the aftermath of any militarized conflict. The management and resolution concepts therefore occur during multiple conflict stages and capture a broad range of pre-, intra-, and post-conflict activity.

The two processes also share the penultimate goals of stopping ongoing violence and preventing its onset or renewal. Yet they do this in slightly different ways. Both processes seek—at a minimum—to achieve what is often termed "negative peace," usually defined as the absence of violence (or war specifically). Conflict resolution, however, goes slightly further, with a greater focus on "positive peace" as well. Positive peace requires not only the end of violence, but also the achievement of social justice and the removal of the root causes of violence (see Galtung 1969; on types of peace, see Kacowicz and Bar-Siman-Tov 2000, or the discussion in Goertz et al. 2016). Its achievement often requires negative peace as a foundation on which to build. As this distinction in peace types demonstrates, conflict management and conflict resolution are not the same processes, nor do they necessarily produce the same results. Fundamental differences distinguish them from one another.

Maoz (2004) identifies a series of goals for conflict management, three of which are fundamental. The first is to control or limit violence in the dispute. Note that this does not necessarily eliminate all violence or end the possibility of it. Rather, conflict management tries to lower the level of violence to some predefined limit or merely relative to the status quo. A second goal is to contain the geographic scope of any conflict. That is, conflict management works to prevent violent conflict or potential unrest from spreading to new areas, because this expansion would increase the conflict's negative consequences and perhaps complicate resolution. Finally, a third, related goal is to restrict the number of participants involved in the conflict. Much as firefighters try to confine a blaze to its original structure, conflict managers seek to confine conflict to as narrow a set of locations and actors as possible, which then makes battling the original conflict easier. This also includes limiting the consequences so that civilians are not killed or otherwise adversely affected by the conflict.

Although conflict obviously involves disagreement, conflict management assumes that disputants share some common interest(s) in limiting the conflict and its effects. This does not suggest that all disputant preferences are compatible, but only that some or all of the disputants would like to limit the conflict. These limitations might be temporary (e.g., a ceasefire during a war) or (quasi-) permanent (e.g., a desire to prevent conflict escalation, which produced support for a peacekeeping force in Cyprus [1964–present], even as the underlying issues at the root of the conflict remain unresolved). It is possible, and indeed at times common, for this assumption to be incorrect. There are instances in which some disputants do not want to stop fighting or to place limits on the conflict. If a side is winning battles, for example, then limiting conflict stalls its momentum and potential for victory. For example, in 1997, once the Alliance of Democratic Forces for the Liberation of Congo (AFDL) took the city of Kisangani, they refused to negotiate with the government in Zaire until President Mobutu resigned, despite previously pressing for negotiations with the government. Similarly, conflict management that freezes the status quo can disadvantage the disputant seeking to revise it (e.g., a government seeking to oust insurgent groups from any territory it holds or a rebel group desiring to overthrow a government). In these circumstances, conflict management efforts are prone to failure, largely because of the revisionist side's lack of cooperation.

Conflict resolution, in contrast, goes beyond conflict management. In its ideal form, conflict resolution works to remove the issues under contention or the underlying bases of dispute from the relationship (Burton 1987). In other words, it renders the risk of conflict escalation moot because there is no longer a reason to fight. Consistent with this logic, some (e.g., Luttwak 1999) take an expansive view of conflict resolution that includes military victory for one of the warring sides, a situation in which resolution is achieved through brute military force. More commonly, though, conflict resolution resolves the underlying, disputed issues through non-violent mechanisms. For example, if an interstate territorial dispute ends with a mutual agreement to draw a border, then the prospects for war may fall and the groundwork for cooperative activities in other areas may strengthen. This occurred after the Vatican mediated a resolution of the Beagle Channel dispute in 1985; since that agreement, Argentina and Chile have greatly expanded trade with each other and are now considered friendly with one another.

Conflict resolution efforts begin with a more optimistic assessment of the prospects for dealing with the conflict. Except for wholly naive or misguided attempts, third parties must believe that there exist outcomes that will satisfy all disputants. This often means finding non-zero-sum settlements, although settlements heavily weighted toward the interests of one side may still be acceptable to the loser. The International Court of Justice, for example, ruled in 2015 that Costa Rica had full sovereignty over a disputed island, and Nicaragua has indicated that it will abide by that ruling. Conflict resolution therefore requires, beyond limiting the violence, that disputants have "overlapping bargaining spaces" (one or more settlement options acceptable to all disputants), as well as some willingness to end the conflict and accept a settlement. Importantly, conflict resolution also need not be all or nothing. Disputants can agree to settle some disputed issues while leaving others to future resolution efforts, or merely agree to disagree.

Conflict management and conflict resolution are not fully separate but are interrelated in numerous ways. First, many of the conflict management approaches discussed throughout this book can be used for either process. Bringing disputants to the table for direct negotiations or mediation, for example, may produce outcomes that either manage or resolve a conflict—or both (e.g., an agreement to manage the conflict in the short term, while implementing provisions of a comprehensive agreement in the long run). Some agreements even include provisions for conflict management *following* resolution. After disputed issues are resolved, for example, the possibility arises that disagreements will reoccur over those issues or that new sources of dispute will emerge; conflict management mechanisms cannot ensure that disagreements will not arise, but they can provide peaceful mechanisms to address those disagreements. The World Trade Organization (WTO), for example, has a Dispute Settlement Body that provides for resolving (future) trade disputes, ideally through consultations with the parties and, if necessary, via quasi-judicial panel hearings and awards.

Second, conflict management approaches can be precursors to conflict resolution. Stopping a war or limiting the scope of violence often constitutes the first step in a broader peace process. Traditional peacekeeping forces operate on this principle; they usually deploy following a ceasefire to ensure compliance with it, thereby creating a more suitable environment for negotiations between the combatants. In other instances, actors hope that progress on conflict management will produce a cascade of cooperation that makes conflict resolution more likely; according to this logic, a step-by-step cooperative process, starting with the concerns easiest to address, lays the groundwork for more expansive settlements, including those that resolve the most contentious issues. The Oslo Accords (1993 and 1995) between Israel and the Palestinians relied on this idea. Interim arrangements secured the withdrawal of Israeli forces and Palestinian governance in occupied territory; the final resolution of issues such as borders and the status of Jerusalem, however, was deferred for future negotiations. In other circumstances, conflict management from one approach tries to achieve conflict resolution through another, subsequent approach. For example, negotiations may produce an agreement to halt provocative actions toward claims (e.g., territorial ones) and to submit the dispute to an international arbiter or court (see, e.g., the Colombia–Venezuela or Ethiopia–Eritrea border disputes).

Third, some approaches facilitate conflict management and conflict resolution efforts, although they may themselves produce neither. Economic sanctions offer an illustration. They often attempt to bring a recalcitrant disputant to the negotiating table, where management and resolution could occur. The sanctions against South Africa eventually convinced it to end apartheid and permit majority rule. Similarly, global sanctions on Iran encouraged the multiparty negotiations that produced a deal in which Iran suspended nuclear weapons development in return for the lifting of those sanctions.

Finally, the original pursuit of either management or resolution might produce the other. A process designed for conflict management, for example, could yield resolution. The opposite, however, is more likely, as outcomes fall short of aspirations. Parties in an international or civil war might sign a ceasefire but fail to find the common basis needed for a comprehensive peace agreement; the end of fighting in the Korean War illustrates this idea.

The chapters that follow focus on conflict management and the various approaches used to achieve it. Conflict management is a necessary (but insufficient) condition for resolution. Starting from the premise that a violent conflict exists or there is a significant risk of it, management will take precedence over resolution because resolution is unlikely to proceed in the face of violence or its threat. Nonetheless, as noted above, one cannot always distinguish between conflict management and conflict resolution. The descriptions and, to some extent, the processes and outcomes, of these two approaches may therefore be the same or similar for both.

Overview of the Book

In the following chapter (Chapter 2), we set the stage for our analysis of individual conflict management approaches in several ways. First, we identify a series of key ideas about conflict management and its success found in numerous works; these reappear frequently as threads that connect the logics of conflict management across different approaches. This is followed by a specification of some patterns in conflict over time, as the conflict context is an important variable in determining which conflict management approach is selected as well as when success is achieved. Nevertheless, some conflicts are never managed, even when their importance and negative consequences suggest that they should have been; we will cover some of the occasions when conflict management has been absent and examine the reasons why. The chapter concludes with an overview of how conflict management success might be judged as well as some indicators that might be used to measure that success.

We devote a separate chapter to each distinct conflict management approach: intervention, sanctions, negotiation, mediation, legal approaches, and peacekeeping (see Table 2.2 below). These chapters follow a similar format. We first establish a foundation by defining the approach, discussing its key concepts and characteristics (often in relation to other approaches), describing how the conflict management process unfolds, and providing information on the logic or strategic considerations underlying how the approach facilitates conflict management. We next identify the actors that most commonly employ the approach, along with some historical patterns (when appropriate). Finally, we devote the main parts of each chapter to specifying the conditions under which actors select the given approach and the approach succeeds, based on the extensive scholarly research available. The book then concludes with a chapter that explores how approaches interact with one another. This is an important consideration not only because approaches can occur simultaneously or sequentially, but also because they are often theoretically and practically interdependent. One approach may have downstream consequences for another.

Within each substantive chapter (Chapters 3–9), we also include extended discussions of conflict cases that illustrate the chapter's major concepts and conclusions. Chapters 3–8 contain two cases each: one a relative success (e.g., negotiation that leads to a lasting peace agreement) and the other a relative failure (e.g., unsuccessful negotiations in which disputes continue).

Chapter 9 includes one illustration of the conflict management trajectory concept, which contains a series of successes and failures. These cases collectively represent different types of disputes (e.g., civil and interstate), disputants (e.g., major and minor powers), and geographic regions.

We begin with conflict management approaches on the more coercive end of the scale, starting with military intervention—the sending of troops into a dispute's theater to engage a disputant militarily, protect civilians, or deliver humanitarian aid (Chapter 3). This might, at first glance, appear to be contradictory to conflict management—using military force to limit military force. Indeed, external actors occasionally become a direct party to the conflict, which runs counter to common conceptions of conflict management. Nonetheless, intervention aims to mitigate armed conflict or its effects. Third parties may still be serving their own self-interest in the process. Our focus, however, is not on military interventions designed *exclusively* to further the interests of the intervening party (e.g., the US invasion of Iraq in 2003), but rather on those attempting to promote the cessation of hostilities or end human rights abuses, even as the intervention might favor one protagonist over others. The amount of coercion desired and needed to achieve these goals will vary; the advent of the United Nations and the proliferation of numerous regional organizations, for example, means (multilateral) intervention trends toward less coercion and less frequent use of traditional military force over time. Nonetheless, the goal remains to change the disputants' calculus about whether violence will help them achieve their goals, and to assist civilians experiencing unacceptable costs from violence.

Outside parties can also exert leverage over disputants through economic sanctions (Chapter 4). Sanctions impose economic costs and limit policy options as a way to compel disputants to comply with third-party demands. They can, for example, inflict sufficient economic pain on belligerents to end a conflict (that is, incentivize a shift from violent to non-violent conflict management) or change a conflict-prone policy (e.g., the abandonment of a nuclear weapons program). They also may limit the resources, such as weapons, that disputants need to continue fighting. More recently, "smart" sanctions target specific sectors of an economy or decision-makers' assets; the goal is to impose high costs on specific actors (e.g., political leaders or military forces) that have the greatest influence over policy, while minimizing any effect on the broader population.

Whatever their exact form, actors frequently employ sanctions because they are viewed as a less risky, lower-cost, and more humane conflict management approach than outright military intervention. Important questions, however, persist about both the application and effectiveness of sanctions as a conflict management tool. The conflicts in which actors use sanctions tend to be those with highly salient issues at stake for the disputants and, therefore, those most likely to produce intense fighting. Under such circumstances, only extremely high costs will change disputant behavior, and sanctions rarely inflict them. Moreover, third parties often apply sanctions not because they expect them to succeed at managing a conflict, but rather because sanctions provide a low-cost *appearance* of doing something. In light of these considerations, understanding the conditions under which sanctions will most likely be effective gains in importance.

Of the more cooperative forms of conflict management, negotiation is perhaps the most familiar (Chapter 5). In the negotiation process, disputants' representatives meet directly with one another—without the assistance of a third party—and pursue agreements designed to halt existing violence, lessen the likelihood of future violence, and decrease hostility between them. This behavior theoretically carries similarities across diverse contexts (e.g., arms control, labor disputes, etc.), and research focuses on determining the conditions under which negotiations occur and produce agreements. One set of concerns, which we might label micro-level influences, concentrates on the attributes, behavior, and interactions of those conducting the negotiations. Some disputants, for example, do not agree to negotiate for "sincere" reasons, choosing to use negotiations as an opportunity to regroup for later violence instead; understanding why and how actors come to the negotiating table therefore has downstream consequences for their ability to reach agreements during talks and implement agreements after negotiations occur. In contrast, macro-level factors, such as the relative power of the involved actors and international norms, reflect the contextual influences under which the negotiations take place. These, too, alter the prospects for reaching and implementing agreements, since even when negotiations produce agreements, many fall apart when the parties renege on promises or fail to implement key provisions in the agreement.

Mediation (Chapter 6) shares many similarities with negotiations, but refers broadly to a wide range of distinct, third-party behaviors designed to mitigate or resolve conflict, including the facilitation of negotiations (i.e., good offices) and the proposal of potential settlement terms (i.e., conciliation). The third parties involved may be private individuals (e.g., Jimmy Carter) or representatives of states (e.g., Norway or the Pope), international organizations (e.g., the United Nations), or non-governmental organizations (e.g., the Quakers). They engage in mediation when disputants prove incapable of managing their conflict alone and, therefore, require help. Disputants permit this third-party involvement because it offers them both assistance with and significant control over the conflict management process and its outcome. Mediation is an entirely voluntary process, meaning the disputants must accept the mediator, the process, and the outcome; disputants can walk away at any time and are not bound to accept any agreement the process produces, even one proposed by the mediator. This distinguishes it markedly from legal approaches (which are binding) and coercion.

Many of the theoretical and empirical interests in mediation mirror those found in negotiation studies (e.g., conditions for effectiveness), and sometimes these sets of studies are indistinct from one another. Nevertheless, mediation studies frequently focus on the attributes (e.g., impartiality) and strategies of the mediator as important factors in mediation's occurrence and success (that is, the "supply side" of conflict management), in addition to disputant characteristics and contextual factors (that is, the "demand side"). This occurs because the involvement of a third party necessarily changes the bargaining dynamic and, therefore, the theoretical expectations for when mediation will occur and succeed, thereby differentiating it further from negotiations.

Under legal approaches, disputants cede greater control over their conflict's management (Chapter 7). In particular, disputants place their conflict in the hands of a third party—a standing, formal judicial institution (e.g., the International Court of Justice) or an ad hoc quasi-judicial body that follows pre-established procedures, applies international legal principles (or other pre-approved considerations), and issues a binding award that resolves the disputed issues with legal finality. The exact legal process in operation adheres to the policies, rules, and procedures of the body hearing the case, with significant differences between various international courts. Nonetheless, these processes often progress through a phase in which the third party decides whether it has jurisdiction (or accepts the case), reviews evidence and arguments submitted by the disputants (e.g., written and oral proceedings), deliberates, and issues a ruling. Arbiters and international courts typically do not themselves implement their rulings, although they occasionally hear appeals that a disputant is in non-compliance (see International Court of Justice).

Because disputants agree to adhere to a ruling before the legal process begins and because the third party's policies, rules, and procedures guide the process, disputants lose significant control under legal approaches. The use of legal approaches therefore usually indicates that disputants recognize direct negotiation or mediation has been or will be unsuccessful. In some cases, it may also suggest disputants' preference for avoiding negotiation or mediation to resolve their dispute, a preference that arises frequently when leaders want to settle a disputed issue, but do not want to be responsible to their constituents for the concessions that might be required to do so. As a final topic, we then explore the key debates surrounding the use of legal approaches, including whether they effectively resolve disputes and, relatedly, whether disputants actually comply with legal rulings.

Between legal approaches and coercion lie peace operations, which are cooperative but require significant third-party commitments (Chapter 8). Peace operations have changed significantly over the past fifty years. Traditional peacekeeping missions (stationing a small contingent of lightly armed forces or observers to separate and monitor combatants) proved helpful during many conflicts but seemed inadequate to address the many civil conflicts proliferating after the Cold War ended. Third parties therefore expanded mission mandates, ultimately producing peacebuilding missions. Such missions aim to prevent conflict recurrence, introduce and strengthen government institutions (e.g., election monitoring or a revised judicial system), and return displaced persons to their homes. This profusion of tasks suggests that a variety of logics underlie peace operations. The complexity of the logics builds further when we consider that a variety of actors authorize and participate in peace operations, each of which has distinct motivations for doing so (e.g., United Nations vs African Union vs Australia). Such considerations, along with the conflict context and disputant characteristics, affect how, why, where, and when peace operations occur. Moreover, given the variety of mandated tasks, determining the effectiveness of peace operations can be challenging. Traditional measures of success (e.g., no recurrence of fighting), for example, may be inappropriate or incomplete indicators of some missions' success (e.g., a peacebuilding mission), while other mandated tasks (e.g., support for confidence-building measures) may be difficult to assess at all.

Finally, after considering each approach in isolation (Chapters 3–8), we next entertain their interactions (Chapter 9). This represents a key advancement in recent research. Attempts to manage a dispute rarely occur in isolation. Rather, most disputes see a constellation of conflict management attempts, often involving different approaches (e.g., mediation and peacekeeping) and third parties. For a variety of reasons, conflict managers are aware of one another's efforts and incorporate information about these previous efforts into their decisions about what to do next. The same third party, for example, often tries to manage a dispute via multiple efforts; it will know what it previously did. Similarly, because international disputes (and their management) are high-profile events, potential third parties (e.g., the United Nations) monitor conflict management efforts. This means that we should expect conflict management efforts within the same dispute to be interrelated. Recent research has begun to theorize about this interdependence more explicitly, even advancing the concept of a conflict management trajectory: a "path" of conflict management within a given dispute that can be theorized, tracked, and studied empirically. After introducing this concept in greater detail, the chapter explores the potential theoretical connections between various conflict management approaches and explains what we know about how actors select among and sequence the approaches presented in earlier chapters.

2

Key Ideas and Frameworks

It is evident that conflict management approaches differ in many important ways (e.g., some are more coercive, whereas others are consensual). Nevertheless, our understanding of these different approaches can often derive from common elements. In this chapter, we examine some of those commonalities with respect to important concepts, the conflict context for management, and the standards used to judge success or failure.

Cross-Cutting Concepts

Although there are a variety of conflict management approaches, some concepts cut across them and form the basis for whether and when approaches succeed. Many of these concepts developed originally within negotiation studies, the research milieu with the longest pedigree, but they extend well beyond that subfield. They therefore feature prominently in the chapters that follow.

Timing and Related Ideas

One of the most prominent ideas in conflict management holds that the "timing" must be right in order for conflict management to succeed. One might interpret the term "timing" literally, and indeed, early research focused on whether conflict management occurred during the early, middle, or later stages of a conflict. "Timing," however, indicates something broader than this. Good timing means that the conditions required for a given conflict management attempt to succeed are manifest. It is therefore a mistake to consider the attempt in isolation; desirable outcomes result from a concatenation of different factors, of which the conflict management approach is only one.

This view suggests that conflict management attempts will succeed at some points in time but not others, and the approach itself is not necessarily at fault. Much depends on whether the other requisite conditions are present. Thus, conflicts are often labelled as "ripe" or "ready" for management or resolution if these other conditions are present. Theoretically, mediation, negotiation, and other approaches should be tried at such moments. For example, peacekeeping forces are better able to limit violence after a cease-fire, or even better after a peace agreement, than they are during ongoing wars; a conflict is "ripe" for peacekeeping after these agreements.

Mitchell (1995) identifies four different models of "ripeness." All or parts of these appear in various forms throughout discussions of conflict management approaches, and most were developed within the context of mediation and negotiation specifically. Perhaps the most well-known is the "mutually hurting stalemate."

Mutually Hurting Stalemate

The term "mutually hurting stalemate" (MHS) entered the lexicon of international studies through the work of I. William Zartman. First introduced over three decades ago (Zartman and Berman 1982; Touval and Zartman 1985), MHS is a perceptual condition "in which neither side can win, yet continuing conflict will be very harmful to each" (Zartman 2003). The existence of this condition supposedly encourages disputants to go to the negotiating table and possibly to reach a settlement.

MHS has three essential components. The "stalemate" component signifies an impasse in the conflict such that no disputant can envision achieving its goals through continued fighting. The "hurting" element denotes that the parties are paying costs by fighting, costs that can eventually become significant enough for disputants to consider changing their behavior or relationship. Finally, the "mutually" component indicates that *each* party experiences the first two components. A one-sided hurting stalemate creates a situation in which the non-hurting side may continue fighting and reject any settlement attempt. A sufficient level of pain must therefore be experienced by each disputant, although this need not mean that the pain has to be equal across disputants, or from the same source (Zartman 2001, 2007).

When disputants experience a MHS, they look for an opportunity to switch from violent to non-violent pursuit of their goals. This is based on a cost–benefit calculation, consistent with a rational choice model of decision-making. In particular, the switch makes sense if disputants see a potential catastrophe down the road (e.g., paying unacceptably high costs without achieving their goals) and therefore work through non-violent means to avoid that catastrophe. Otherwise, rational actors should not reach a MHS absent incomplete information, uncertainty, or failed institutions precipitating the MHS; a fully rational actor would negotiate and settle its dispute before the MHS could occur.

According to Zartman (2001), a MHS is merely a necessary condition for de-escalation and negotiation. Other elements must therefore be present for an improvement in the belligerents' relationship to occur, including "a way out" (that is, a viable alternative to the status quo) or a "mutually enticing opportunity" (see the discussion of these elements below; Zartman 2000, 2007). If these are also present, then the conflict is "ripe" for settlement.

Imminent Mutual Catastrophe

The model based on imminent mutual catastrophe (IMC) builds on the idea of a MHS. IMC goes beyond the costly stalemate concept to argue that the prospect of even greater, disastrous costs lying on the horizon if conflict continues will push disputants into conflict management. Inertia and internal politics (within a country or group) may lead a disputant to resist conflict management, even when a MHS exists. A major shift in the cost–benefit calculations is therefore required before disputants will be open to management and resolution (i.e., for the conflict to be "ripe" for settlement). The looming, disastrous costs create that shift.

Mitchell characterizes the IMC as an extreme version of the MHS. The costs of conflict remain critical to the IMC, but these costs must be significant and occur in the near future rather than in the present. The argument therefore relies on the perception of costs, as opposed to actual ones—and both sides must face such a catastrophe.

What kinds of catastrophic costs might alter disputants' willingness to pursue and accept a settlement? This is more difficult to determine empirically than in the abstract. The prospect of nuclear war offers a likely situation, encouraging disputants to step back from the brink (e.g., India and Pakistan); yet this occurs rarely. Mitchell (1995) mentions the end of World War II as an example: the Japanese surrendered after having two atomic bombs dropped on them, while the Allies were willing to settle rather than pay the costs associated with invading the Japanese homeland. But even this does not quite fit. Japan had already experienced catastrophe, though it could have experienced more. Moreover, Japan's calculations resulted in an unconditional surrender; albeit negotiated, this is not the symmetrical outcome that most conflict management approaches envision. Perhaps a better example might be the Cuban Missile Crisis, in which the United States and the Soviet Union backed away from possible annihilation. These (limited) cases demonstrate that the IMC model remains more hypothetical than empirically based.

The Entrapment Model

A third variation on the idea of timing and ripeness is the "entrapment" model (ENT). The MHS and IMC rely on rational cost–benefit calculations: when the costs of conflict become much greater than its prospective benefits, (non-violent) conflict management has a greater likelihood of producing its desired outcome. The entrapment model employs a different logic.

The ENT model essentially rests on the notion of "sunk costs" (i.e., the accumulated costs—financial and otherwise—of conflict), which then influence decision-making. Rational disputants should consider future costs in determining whether to continue violence; the sunk costs paradox, however, posits that, as a disputant pays higher (accumulated, past) costs, it is more likely to continue fighting and will resist conflict management efforts. In this sense, it might be considered the inverse of the two previous models of ripeness. Disputants believe that they must defeat their opponent to justify past expenses and suffering. This logic parallels human behavior in many other contexts, such as gambling or a greater willingness to continue standing in line at a restaurant because of the time already spent waiting rather than how long the remaining wait might be. This logic seemingly implies that conflict management might be best early in the conflict before costs accumulate, although that turns out not to be the case.

Can disputants ever escape this trap? Mitchell (1995) suggests so. Initially, disputants focus on their goals and justify any costs paid in terms of achieving those goals. As the conflict drags on, they will next focus on maximizing relative gains (that is, punishing the opponent in addition to obtaining goals) and minimizing losses. Once they exhaust resources, disputants then search for a way out. This process implies the need for conflict management much later in a conflict's lifespan, after a key transition point where decision-makers experience a psychological shift from a sunk-costs orientation to one based on loss minimization. It is unfortunately not clear what precipitating events or conditions bring this shift about. Furthermore, there are no known cases in which an actor has completely exhausted its resources prior to accepting conflict management.

The Enticing Opportunity Model

The final variant of "ripeness" is the "enticing opportunity" model, which stresses the available alternatives to conflict instead of the costs associated with continued conflict. This model also relies on a cost–benefit analysis, but emphasizes the benefit component; it therefore focuses attention on what conflict management can offer the disputing parties. Ripeness occurs when an attractive alternative appears that disputants find clearly superior to continued violence.

It is unlikely that a brand-new conflict management opportunity will suddenly arise, but more likely that existing alternatives appear in a new light (Crocker 1992). Throughout a conflict, all disputants usually know both a variety of prospective settlement outcomes, as well as the conflict management approaches available to achieve them. Clever, new proposals can arise, but this would be rare. The key, then, is not to expand or enhance the menu of settlement options, but to make the existing alternatives to violence more attractive to disputants.

What will accomplish this goal? First, leadership changes among one or more disputants often produce different policy priorities and preferences. A disputant might therefore become more willing to accept conflict management and to settle a conflict under terms it previously regarded as unacceptable (of course, the reverse can be true as well). Second, conflict management efforts can manipulate the relative costs and benefits of violence and non-violence. If they raise the costs of continued violence, then they theoretically encourage the use of non-violent alternatives; economic sanctions attempt this. Alternatively, if they raise the benefits of non-violent alternatives, then they increase the likelihood that disputants will abandon violence. Peacekeepers that guarantee a negotiated settlement's terms, for example, ensure that the benefits promised in the agreement accrue to the disputants; this is the essence of the credible-commitment concept discussed below.

Enticing opportunities can occur during the early, middle, or later stages of a conflict. Indeed, they might be considered as a "way out," one of the elements that moves a MHS to a desirable settlement outcome (Zartman 2000). Sudan experienced this logic. After decades of civil war, a plebiscite on independence was not only attractive to South Sudanese forces, but also became so to the central Sudanese government.

Credible Commitment

A second general idea that explains why conflict management succeeds or fails concerns credible-commitment issues. Credible commitments refer broadly to the durability of potential settlement outcomes, in particular disputants' perceptions about how likely their opponents are to cooperate honestly in conflict management efforts and to implement any agreement reached. A specific application of this broad concept produces the "commitment problem," which arises when a settlement will fundamentally change disputants' relative power (Powell 2006). This possibility opens opportunities for the strengthening state to renege on the agreement after it is signed and to exploit the weakening one to obtain better terms for itself. As a result, the actors that will be weakened refuse to reach a settlement, and conflict management stalls. Rebel disarmament after civil war offers the quintessential illustration, although the problem appears in interstate disputes as well. Rebel groups must disarm after civil war—to restore the government's monopoly on the organized use of force within the state—and disarmament terms therefore appear in many agreements that end civil wars. If disarmament occurs, however, the now unarmed rebels face an armed government, which can then renege on the agreement previously reached and compel the rebels through force (the threat of death or imprisonment) to further make concessions on disputed issues. This creates a familiar impasse: the government refuses to negotiate without disarmament, while the rebels refuse to disarm because they will lose substantial bargaining leverage.

The credible-commitment logic rests on three assumptions. First, successful conflict management requires the cooperation of two or more disputants.

This is uncontroversial for most of the conflict management approaches examined throughout this book. Negotiation and mediation, for example, are voluntary processes that cannot operate without disputant consent. Similarly, traditional peacekeeping operations involve the consent of one or more disputants, largely because their mandated tasks demand disputant assistance (e.g., maintaining a ceasefire or holding free and fair elections).

Second, disputants lack trust in their opponents. Intense hostility and a history of violence erode trust, leaving disputants with little reason to believe that their opponents sincerely want peace. Moreover, an enemy that cheats on an agreement can threaten a disputant's security or existence. A rebel group can *promise* to disarm and disband after a peace agreement, but most governments would find this promise alone unacceptable. Failure to disarm and disband places the state at risk, and government supporters would therefore find this approach untenable. The South African government, for example, only accepted a peace deal for the independence of Namibia after securing a peacekeeping force to monitor the disarmament process in the country. In a similar vein, rebel disarmament in the face of government promises not to kill or imprison (former) rebels often proves insufficient; the possibility of government cheating places rebels' individual security at risk.

Credible-commitment concerns can sabotage conflict management in numerous ways. Negotiations and by extension other conflict management approaches proceed through three broad stages (Walter 2002). Disputants first entertain conflict management and decide whether to "come to the (bargaining) table." They then bargain in pursuit of an agreement to change their behavior or resolve disputed issues. The form of this agreement varies by approach; negotiation and mediation produce a ceasefire or substantive agreement, while peacekeeping typically secures an agreement to deploy a peace operation. Finally, if an agreement emerges, disputants enter an implementation phase, in which they execute the provisions of the agreement (e.g., to enact the terms of a negotiated or mediated agreement, to uphold an international court ruling, or to conduct elections as promised in a peace agreement).

Credible commitments appear most acutely in the final stage of negotiations, but ripple backwards to affect the others (Fearon 1998). If, for example, a disputant strongly believes that its enemy will not implement any agreement reached, why would it participate in conflict management? The process would offer it little foreseeable benefit. In this way, implementation concerns undermine the possibility of even getting to the table. With little promise of implementation (stage three), disputants do not expect to reach an agreement, regardless of what they do (stage two); they therefore never attempt to bargain in the first place (stage one). Note that this is not identical to saying that disputants must believe an agreement is imminent if they participate in conflict management; disputants know that managing conflict over highly salient issues will be challenging. Nevertheless, they must believe that their enemies are participating in good faith, that is, pursuing conflict management with sincere intentions to resolve the dispute and implement agreements (on the question of insincere motives, see Chapter 5). Otherwise, why bother?

Third parties can short-circuit this logic. If the third party ensures that enemies keep their promises, then commitments become more credible. A third party does this in several ways. The first involves monitoring and verifying the conflict management process and outcome. Returning to the example of rebel group disarmament and demobilization, a third party (e.g., peacekeepers) can certify this occurs and is complete; because the government trusts the third party more than rebel leaders, such a certification increases credibility and allays government fears. A second way uses third-party reward (or "carrots"). For example, a third party might provide financial or other aid in exchange for a disputant successfully implementing a peace agreement; if the added incentive for compliance outweighs any benefits from cheating, then the third party instills confidence that disputants will honor their commitments. Finally, and relatedly, third parties can punish non-compliance (i.e., use "sticks"). For example, threats of military force and sanctions (two forms of conflict management discussed in later chapters) reinforce other conflict management approaches (e.g., mediation or peacekeeping) by encouraging compliance.

Spoilers

There is a tendency to focus almost exclusively on the primary disputants and the third-party managers when trying to account for conflict management success and failure. This myopic approach, however, ignores the behaviors of other actors that can influence conflict management outcomes. The oversight grows when we assume that all involved actors—primary disputants, third parties, and omitted actors—*want* conflict management. In reality, many actors, including primary disputants and third parties, possess motives to slow, damage, or wreck the conflict management process. These actors, whether within or outside the conflict management process, are considered "spoilers" (Stedman 1997; Nilsson and Kovacs 2011).

Spoilers are "leaders and parties who believe that peace emerging from conflict management threatens their power, worldview, and interests, and use violence to undermine attempts to achieve it" (Stedman 1997: 5). Hamas offers an example. After Israeli Prime Minister Netanyahu proclaimed that he would not negotiate with the Palestinians until terrorist or other attacks stopped for an extended period, Hamas militants launched rockets and sponsored suicide bombers to ensure that such negotiations never occurred.

The definition above is relatively narrow, suggesting that spoilers come from one or more of the warring parties, that negotiations are underway or envisioned, and that violence is the means for spoiling. Relaxing each of these specifications, however, allows us to understand spoiling behavior better (for a review of these and related issues, see Nilsson and Kovacs 2011). We leave aside any normative judgments about whether the spoiling behavior is justified or morally desirable. Although usually framed in negative terms, instances exist in which spoiling might be morally defensible, for example, if an agreement might result in human rights abuses, authoritarian rule, or other undesirable characteristics that spoilers' actions can stop.

First and foremost, spoilers can arise from within or outside of a peace process. Primary disputants do not always want peace, and their actions can directly undermine conflict management efforts. If, for example, a disputant is winning a war, then stopping the violence forestalls its victory and interferes with its ability to achieve its goals. Serbian forces experienced this early in the Bosnian War of the 1990s. Disputants might also object to prospective management or settlement terms, and use spoiling behavior to exercise leverage over or rearrange conflict management priorities. This seems most likely in a multiparty negotiation, where agreements disproportionately serve the interests of some disputants, but not others. In other circumstances, spoilers come from outside the conflict management process. Informal negotiations to secure a ceasefire in the Syrian civil war, for example, did not include the Islamic State (ISIS); they had no interest in halting hostilities or encouraging others to stop attacking one another, because this would allow these other actors to devote greater resources and attention to combating ISIS. These various considerations suggest that finding (potential) spoilers requires a careful analysis of who has an interest in continued violence and why.

Second, spoiling behavior does not only occur during negotiations or only at the negotiation table specifically. All conflict management approaches can be spoiled. Trading with a sanctioned state, for example, renders economic sanctions less effective. Similarly, reinforcing military positions or ignoring judicial awards (e.g., China's actions in the South China Sea) undermines legal approaches, while not participating in elections or refusing to accept electoral outcomes damages a peacekeeping mission tasked with arranging and monitoring democratic elections. In addition, spoiling can occur in the pre-negotiation (e.g., refusing to come to the table), negotiation (e.g., issuing unrealistic and insincere demands), and implementation stages (e.g., ignoring agreement terms). If we focus only on the negotiating table, we therefore miss much potential spoiling behavior.

Third, violence is not the only spoiling mechanism. To be sure, violence derails a peace process. Armed attacks, by definition, undermine negative peace. They also precipitate violent responses, and the consequences of the resulting action-reaction cycles complicate efforts to restore a ceasefire or to achieve a more enduring, peaceful outcome. Nevertheless, violence is not the only way to ruin conflict management efforts. Nilsson and Kovacs (2011), for example, catalog a series of other actions that constitute spoiling, such as: refusing to negotiate, reneging on agreements, refusing to demobilize, or establishing roadblocks against peacekeepers seeking to monitor a given area. In short, spoilers need only interfere with conflict management efforts; how exactly they do so varies widely.

Many motives underlie spoiling behavior, and these can produce opposition to all forms of peace, to a particular conflict management effort, or to a single component of a conflict management outcome. Within a given conflict, every interested party likely holds a motivation to spoil at one time or another. Whether the spoiling behavior occurs and has its intended effects, however, varies; this substantially depends on the capability of the party and the opportunities available to it. A small, well-armed group can attack a peacekeeping force or renew fighting with a group engaged in a peace process. An isolated group without this capacity, in contrast, faces significant limitations when attempting the same. Similarly, a country that trades substantially with a sanctioned state in valuable goods holds greater potential for spoiling those sanctions than a country with limited trade ties involving non-strategic goods. One can look at a party's resources, number of supporters, and the like for assessing its spoiling capability. Yet one must also consider the party's opportunities for spoiling as well. Even with capability, a party may not be able to stop negotiations or a judicial process, especially if those conflict management attempts have already begun; a state that cannot bypass a sanctions regime to engage in trade with a sanctioned state likewise cannot undermine sanctions, even if the resulting potential trade might do so.

Stedman's (1997) typology of spoilers provides a useful framework for understanding the origins and motivations of spoilers. Total spoilers reject the basic principle of any settlement or accommodation with the opposing side. Limited spoilers seek to derail the implementation of an agreement for narrower reasons, believing that some subset of issues of concern to them have been unsatisfactorily addressed by the terms of agreement. Greedy spoilers oppose a settlement and seek to continue conflict, not because they have opposing views on the settlement of the issues at stake in the conflict, but because they benefit materially from the chaos produced by the conflict itself.

Beyond providing a framework by which to categorize spoilers, Stedman's typology also distinguishes the ways in which different types of spoilers are most effectively dealt. Because greedy spoilers are motivated by material concerns, they tend to be most susceptible to inducement, most often in the form of side payments to buy their support for the agreement. Limited spoilers, because they do not at root oppose a peace process, can sometimes be effectively managed by offering them revised terms of agreement that speak to their specific areas of concern or by socializing them to recognize the benefits of the agreement for them. Total spoilers can be more problematic. Nevertheless, Stedman (1997) proposes that one way to overcome a total spoiler problem is through a "departing train" strategy, in which conflict management moves forward whether the spoiler participates in it or not. The idea is that a total spoiler who realizes that they will not derail the process will eventually stop. George Mitchell used this strategy in the talks leading up to the 1998 Belfast Agreement on Northern Ireland. The talks began in 1996, but excluded Sinn Féin because of continued violence by the Irish Republican Army (the Mitchell principles precluded violence). When it became clear that the violence would not undercut the peace process (i.e., that the train was departing without them), and Sinn Féin realized it was better to be in the negotiations than not, it renounced violence, and Mitchell admitted them to the talks in 1997. The threat of an agreement being decided without them (i.e., not being on the train) brought them on board.

Conflict Patterns Since World War II

Conflict management cannot operate independently of conflict itself. How conflict manifests in the international system therefore determines, in part, the demand for conflict management approaches. In general, dramatic differences exist between the issues, actors, and other conflict characteristics found in conflicts exclusively between states (interstate), those exclusively internal to the state (civil), and those that combine these two types (internationalized civil conflict, which has belligerents both within and outside the state). Mindful of this, Figure 2.1 tracks the prevalence of each of these types of conflict over time, focusing on conflicts involving twenty-five or more battle-deaths, using data from the Uppsala Conflict Data Program.

Figure 2.1 reveals several trends that have implications for conflict management. First, the number of conflicts that might or should be managed has increased over time. Some of this derives from the dramatic increase in the number of independent states in the international system; immediately after World War II, states numbered just over fifty, whereas nearly 200 exist today. This means that there is greater "opportunity" for conflict over time, both within these new states (civil conflict) and as they interact with one another (interstate conflict). Nonetheless, this opportunity has not translated into a rise in the number of interstate conflicts, which has remained relatively low on a year-to-year basis since 1945.

Civil conflict increased gradually over time, peaking in the 1990s, and then declining somewhat thereafter, although it remains at levels much higher than the other two conflict types. Beyond the sheer number of states, subnational actors now have greater access to arms and other support that permits them to

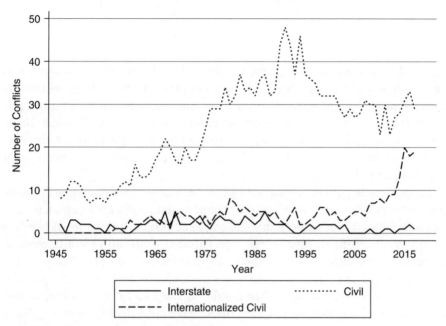

Figure 2.1 Patterns of Conflict, 1946–2016
DATA SOURCE: Uppsala Conflict Data Program.

challenge existing governments more readily. The international community increasingly recognizes these internal conflicts as a threat to international peace and security writ large, and therefore as something that international conflict management should address. As we note in several chapters, this recognition has resulted (in part) from changing international norms on sovereignty. The international community now asserts a greater right to intervene in the internal affairs of states, particularly when grave threats to human rights occur. Moreover, civil conflicts produce significant "negative externalities" in the form of refugees, fighting across borders, and the like, making the consequences of civil wars extend beyond the confines of any one state. Most evident from Figure 2.1, however, is the increase in international-ized civil conflict, especially since 2005. Civil conflict, as in the Congo and Afghanistan, increasingly involves not only internal combatants, but external states as well.

Overall, both the number and configuration of violent conflicts have changed. Conflict managers therefore not only face a growth in conflict situa-tions generally, but also must address conflicts of growing complexity, at least in terms of the number and type of belligerents involved. Interstate conflict remains an important facet of international conflict management, but the predominant threats to peace now (and likely in the near future) arise from internal conflicts between governments and rebel groups—civil conflicts that might also attract the involvement of other states.

Why are Some Conflicts Never Managed or Resolved?

As we discuss conflict management approaches throughout this book, it is easy to lose sight of the fact that most conflicts are *not* subject to conflict management. Nearly 85% of militarized interstate disputes, for example, experience *no* third-party attempts at conflict management (Owsiak 2014). This raises a critical question: why do disputants and third parties not avail themselves of the various approaches available to manage and resolve their disagreements peacefully?

Theoretical arguments about timing (i.e., "ripeness"), credible commitments, and spoilers offer some answers; they suggest that conflict management may not be appropriate or succeed in some contexts. One of these contexts involves high-severity conflicts. Ideally, the international community would manage a conflict early, before violence becomes imminent or occurs. This prevents bloodshed and the damage associated with violence. Moreover, the promise of long-term resolution rises when conflict management is conducted before feelings of loss and victimhood, casualties, and diminished trust set in. This is similar to a doctor treating a disease before serious symptoms appear or the disease progresses too far. Early on, leaders experience fewer constraints from domestic audiences; once positions harden, however, their ability to make concessions evaporates. Reconciliation efforts also face less difficult hurdles before family members are killed or driven from their homes. This makes early conflict management attractive to policymakers. Why, then, are early "golden opportunities" for conflict management missed?

First and foremost, the international community lacks an effective "early warning" system to identify nascent conflicts at risk of escalation. Pre-violence initiatives, however, presume these well-developed and effective early warning systems exist. Without them, one cannot accurately predict when and where armed conflict is likely. The UN has early warning capacities in issue areas like famines, earthquakes, and tsunamis, yet it unfortunately lacks a similarly robust structure for predicting the onset of violent conflict. Furthermore, the UN Secretariat's monitoring activities remain limited in both scale and scope, and rarely motivate early conflict management.

Some assume that the UN could easily acquire early warning capabili-ties by relying on regional organizations, non-governmental organizations (NGOs), and the global flow of information generally. This is not necessarily true. The European Union has perhaps the best-developed early warning systems, but even these prove inadequate. Its Global Conflict Risk Index (GCRI), for example, tracks the risk of violent conflict for each country over the coming one to four years, based exclusively on quantitative indicators from open sources. Yet most of the indicators used (e.g., GDP per capita or the homicide rate) show little variation over time and will therefore be unable to detect changes in risk levels. Moreover, rapid changes to these indicators in the days, weeks, or months leading up to an impending crisis are likely to be missed by the aggregate data (e.g., often, yearly measures) or known only after the fact. And the EU system is not designed to make specific "predictions." It tracks only the underlying conditions for conflict, not particular triggers; accordingly, it is of limited value for use in early warning.

The belief that the wealth of information available through online databases and contained in global communications will prove sufficient for an early warning system is similarly illusory. More and better data do not automatically produce better predictions. Multiple streams of information—some of them contradictory—and the need to analyze them bring both computational and interpretive burdens. This information and data must also be inserted into models with a good track record of successfully predicting conflict. Despite doing well at predicting some natural phenomena (e.g., droughts), early warning models struggle to predict human behavior; few models (if any), for example, predicted the Arab Spring uprisings. We still need a greater understanding of the precise triggers for violent conflict before we can construct good early warning predictors.

Second, the international community often lacks the political will to act. Early warning would not fix this. States at risk for armed conflict, for example, may be offended if labeled as such (especially for civil conflict), and some potential conflict management approaches (e.g., intervention) raise serious sovereignty issues. Early warning systems are also bound to produce a number of "false positives," or instances where the system predicted the need for a conflict management effort that was not, in fact, needed. Because they suggest the system "does not work," these false positives threaten to create member resistance and resentment, and undermine the credibility of the UN in the long run. They also necessarily stretch limited resources across a broader range of efforts.

The international community, including organizations such as the UN, is also notoriously crisis-driven, taking action only when serious problems manifest. With limited resources and attention, third parties allow problems to linger and potentially fester, especially if the risk of violence is not immediate. This is not necessarily a foolhardy strategy. Most disputes do not escalate to war, and if preventing the latter is the singular or primary goal of conflict managers, then they can often achieve it without acting. Failures to act, however, carry notable, negative consequences. Relations between disputants will sour (e.g., less trade, cooperation, and trust), and there remains the risk that unmanaged disagreements will escalate at some point in the future. Nonetheless, given limited resources and a lack of violence, it may be difficult for the international community to muster the political will or support needed to manage a conflict.

Low-level conflicts are therefore less likely to generate conflict management. Somewhat paradoxically, so too are high-severity conflicts. Full-scale wars, for example, should be the greatest priority for conflict managers, given their destructive power; yet they are often ignored. This arises not from indifference, but is, rather, a deliberate strategy. Intense conflicts may *not* be receptive to many conflict management approaches (e.g., adjudication or peacekeeping); if so, one must wait for the conflict to dissipate before any approach can be used effectively. Waiting, however, necessarily carries consequences. It means a significant loss of life, property, economic activity, and resources, but it also means that conflict management will not be doomed to fail if tried, preserving options for the future.

Somewhat independent of the severity of the conflict, third-party interests also determine whether conflict management occurs. If members of the international community do not see their interests affected by the dispute at hand, then they may choose not to act. UN Secretary-General Boutros Boutros-Ghali captured this idea best when he chastised the international community for ignoring the "poor man's wars" in Somalia and Rwanda while focusing all its attention on Bosnia.

Who are the third parties that ignore conflicts because the violence does not affect them? Any actor in the world might qualify. State interests, for example, will be most directly affected when violence spreads across international borders, such as when conflict produces refugees, rebel groups that cross borders, and other negative externalities. If the violence remains within a state's borders, however, these factors never trigger other states' interest in the conflict. Major states' calculations get more complicated, however. They have more expansive, global interests and greater capabilities (e.g., the United States and European Union countries). They consequently receive criticism for inaction, especially because they have the resources to intervene militarily, impose meaningful sanctions, exercise leverage in mediation, or authorize peace operations; indeed, efforts will likely fail without the cooperation of such states. Nevertheless, many conflicts in the world (e.g., South Sudan) take place at great distances from these major states and do not disturb their security or economic interests. In short, although conflict management can be motivated by altruism (see the discussion of the "Responsibility to Protect" in Chapter 3), conflict managers often must see something in it for themselves when they decide to manage a conflict.

Identifying Conflict Management Success

All approaches to conflict management are designed to improve a situation—to decrease violence, even if the threat of it is not fully eliminated. This improvement might be labeled "success," but what does that look like in practice? In this section, we consider how to identify conflict management success and then explore some indicators that would demonstrate it.

Some Considerations

Scholars, policymakers, the media, and the public often deem conflict management efforts a success or failure without elaborating on the criteria used to reach their assessment. These criteria can sometimes be derived from an accompanying discussion, but explicit, *a priori* conceptualizations of success and operational indicators of it are frequently absent. This undoubtedly occurs because defining conflict management success is not easy. Three main challenges arise (for a detailed discussion, see Diehl and Druckman 2010).

The first consideration is: success for whom? Conflict management involves several stakeholders: the international or regional community, the third-party conflict managers, the primary disputants, the peripheral disputants (e.g., external spoilers), and the local population. Interests among these various stakeholders may overlap. Many stakeholders, for example, want to limit both the violence and the other negative externalities that accompany conflict (e.g., human rights violations, refugee flows, and disrupted trade). Their reasons for and willingness to pursue this goal, however, may vary, and their interests are not always completely coterminous.

The wider community—a collection of regional and international actors—strives to obtain long-term stability and uphold certain collective norms that violent conflict undermines (e.g., the peaceful resolution of disputes, democratic governance, and respect for human rights). Yet it recognizes that there exist material costs to violent conflict as well. Violence disrupts the interactions among the wider community's increasingly interdependent actors, creating effects (e.g., on trade) that reverberate through its network. Some of these effects are unintended consequences that threaten to broaden the scope of a conflict by bringing in additional disputants. For example, the United Nations reports that the Syrian conflict has created approximately 5.5 million registered refugees as of October 2018. These refugees reside primarily in Turkey (3.5 million), as well as Lebanon, Jordan, and Iraq, which gives each of these host states a concrete interest in managing the Syrian conflict—to stop the further inflow of refugees, allow those being hosted to return home, and prevent a souring of relations between the host state and the state from which the refugees fled (i.e., halt the spread of the conflict; see United Nations 2018). The last of these can be a significant threat; in April 2018, for example, the *Washington Post* reported that Turkey had soured on the Syrian refugees' presence. Turkey now wants these refugees to leave, largely because the Turkish population fears that the refugees are taking jobs and social services resources away from them (Cunningham and Zakaria 2018). If these sentiments intensify, then Turkish–Syrian relations will be negatively affected. Given such varied interests, the wider community generally sees limiting violence as a success, but desires other outcomes as well, including the return of refugees, the restoration of trade, a decline in human rights violations, and the use of non-violent conflict management techniques.

Limiting violence also motivates many third-party conflict managers (for a detailed discussion of third-party motivations, see Chapters 3–9). This motivation might spring from a desire for peace generally, but more likely it arises from the third party's self-interest (see Princen 1992). A third party, for example, may wish to stop the negative externalities associated with conflict, thereby aligning its interests with the broader community interests discussed above (e.g., Turkey in the Syrian conflict). Yet a third party may also seek to gain a reputation as a conflict manager (e.g., Norway's mediation in the Middle East), to protect their relationship with one or more disputants (e.g., alliance integrity; see the United States involvement in Greece–Turkey disputes), and to pursue specific substantive outcomes (e.g., the promotion of democracy). These not only determine which third parties manage a conflict, but how they perceive what a successful conflict management effort looks like.

Primary disputants have a more diverse set of motivations. At times, they want violence to cease—either because they are making a good-faith effort to pursue a less violent tack or because, more nefariously, they want breathing space to regroup for more conflict (Richmond 1998). At other times, they want the conflict to continue, especially if they believe they can obtain a better substantive outcome for themselves through fighting. Disputants' interest in limiting violence will therefore seem more volatile than that of other stakeholders. This results, in part, from their worry about the substantive issues underlying the conflict, such as who governs the state or how to control as much territory as possible. Limited violence may not offer them a way to maximize these goals, so for primary disputants success might focus more on the substantive issues under dispute, rather than the level of violence itself.

In contrast to primary disputants, spoiler interests are more unified. A spoiler wants the conflict to continue and (often) uses violence to undermine any effort that might halt the violence or bring the conflict to a close (see Stedman 1997). This motivation arises when an agreement on substantive issues begins to form but the spoilers do not like its emerging terms. For example, when the 'Real' Irish Republican Army (RIRA) split from the Irish Republican Army (IRA) in 1997, it did so because it thought the IRA had abandoned the movement's core goal—the pursuit of a united Ireland (through an armed struggle). The IRA agreed to a ceasefire, which permitted Sinn Féin to join the ongoing peace process. This brought the Irish Republican voice into the peace process, but tacitly endorsed partition (e.g., by legitimizing the Unionist position). The RIRA therefore interpreted the ceasefire as an unacceptable compromise, assumed the mantle of the Republican movement, and worked to undermine the peace process. For them, success involves continued violence, a failed peace, a British withdrawal from Ireland, and the unification of the Irish isle.

Finally, the local population constitutes a distinct stakeholder, as its interests differ from those of the political elites that coordinate and drive violent conflict. The local populace often desires a return to normalcy; that is, they may simply want adequate access to their homes, food, and medical care. Ongoing violent conflict interferes with meeting these needs, and limiting violence is therefore a prerequisite for obtaining them. Nonetheless, the local population is unlikely to view the mere cessation of violence as a successful outcome. Success occurs for them when basic needs are met; halting the violence allows progress to be made toward meeting basic needs but does not in itself meet such needs.

As this discussion highlights, stakeholder interests may overlap. Yet they need not, and even when they do, the overlap occurs for disparate reasons. Each stakeholder therefore employs a different standard of what constitutes success. Judgments of success then vary according to the standard used. This means that success for one stakeholder might constitute failure in the eyes of another. In Bosnia, for example, a peace force (the United Nations Protection Force) that could not protect the local population undermined the human rights goals of the world community, but also actually benefitted Serb forces, which were able to seize territory and "cleanse" local areas. More broadly, some actors will want to limit violence (e.g., the wider community, third-party conflict managers, and some disputants), while others will not (e.g., some disputants, as well as those who want the conflict to exhaust a disputing rival, who are selling materiel to the disputants, or who want to spoil conflict management momentum).

A second consideration notes that success depends on whether one adopts a short- or long-term perspective. Achieving goals during the conflict management process—such as alleviating starvation or improving medical care during a military intervention, holding democratic elections under a peace operation's auspices, or signing a mediated agreement—constitutes one form of success. Alternatively, success might demand an achievement after conflict management ends. This longer-term perspective might prioritize the absence of violent conflict for several years following an intervention, or, as in the case of Afghanistan, the consolidation of a fully functioning democratic government (a condition that has not been met).

Both the short- and long-term perspectives have utility. Nevertheless, they often lead to a different assessment of an approach's success or failure. A negotiated ceasefire agreement, for example, can be one type of short-term success. If the ceasefire temporarily halts bloodshed on the battlefield and saves civilian lives, this is yet another form of short-term success. Finally, if the ceasefire fails to hold and no further agreements emerge, then conflict management ultimately failed in the long term. Depending on when the assessment takes place and what perspective it employs, conclusions about how a conflict management approach fared will vary.

Most stakeholders prioritize long-term goals, but these are often the most difficult to assess. For example, how long a time frame should one use when assessing long-term goals? Conflict management might have consequences that extend for decades (e.g., peace operations that try to build the rule of law or democratic institutions, or legal approaches that draw international borders). Extraordinarily long time frames, however, make it impossible to assess a recently concluded conflict management approach. If we must wait decades to know if a peace operation successfully laid the foundation for a consolidated democratic government, then we cannot assess the operation's success in the interim. Furthermore, the longer the time period between the end of the management effort and the assessment, the more difficult it will be to draw a causal conclusion about the impact of that effort; intervening forces are likely to have had as great or a greater impact on the outcome as the management attempt itself. Finally, long-term assessment will likely be unsatisfactory for policymakers, who cannot wait years to judge the value of an initiative. Decisions on whether to continue a policy or pursue an alternative means of conflict management often require some evaluation even before an initial approach ends.

A third consideration is how to develop a baseline or standard against which to assess conflict management. One possibility is that initiatives be judged against a situation in which no conflict management occurred. This "better than nothing" standard, however, biases judgments. Decision-makers rarely choose between a given conflict management approach and taking no action; rather, they select from a broader menu of complementary and substitutable options (e.g., mediation, economic sanctions, or intervention). Moreover, any improvement in the situation following a conflict management approach will likely be considered a success, especially when the costs involved are ignored. Positive assessments therefore appear in more cases than they might otherwise.

An alternative standard compares the conditions prior to conflict management with those found during and after it. This standard brings a key advantage: adjusting the baseline to the conflict context. Moderate levels of violence during conflict management, for instance, may be considered progress in some contexts (e.g., in the midst of a full-scale civil war, as in Bosnia), but backsliding in others (e.g., following a ceasefire, as in the Ethiopia–Eritrea conflict). Yet this standard still risks regarding any improvement as successful and ignoring long-term goals.

One might also measure effectiveness across the same conflict management approach (e.g., comparing one mediation effort with others). This baseline compares "apples to apples" in terms of approaches, but overlooks the fact that dissimilar contexts exist and alter outcomes as well. Is it reasonable to compare the work of a UN mediation team sent to war-torn Congo or Sudan with one deployed to Cambodia or elsewhere that arrives after a comprehensive peace settlement emerges? Such an approach also fails to provide an absolute baseline for assessment. What, for example, is the general, expected level of success for mediation efforts? These comparisons will not tell us.

Indicators of Conflict Management Success

With the above considerations in mind, there are some indicators that conflict management has been successful. We first digress briefly, however, to discuss some oft-used metrics that might be misleading. The first is an "agreement" between disputing parties. These agreements range from a ceasefire to more sweeping provisions for conflict management (e.g., an agreement to arbitrate) to the resolution of disputed issues (e.g., how exactly to govern after a civil war). They are often hailed as a definitive indicator of conflict management success, and there is a logic to this. The main purpose of negotiations, for example, is to produce agreement, and a signed agreement supplies a tangible indicator of disputants' commitment to the conflict management process.

Nonetheless, there are limitations with this as a sole indicator. Legal approaches highlight them well. Once started, the legal process can almost always produce an award (i.e., a court ruling); in fact, it is designed to do just that, even with recalcitrant disputants (see Chapter 7). Judging legal approaches by whether they hit this benchmark is therefore a very low bar. This matter aside, however, signing an agreement and implementing it are distinct matters (see above). Numerous instances exist in which disputants sign an agreement (or legal approaches issue an award), but fail to follow up on the provisions contained therein. Despite repeated arbitration between Colombia and Venezuela in the nineteenth and twentieth centuries, for example, the two states developed a rivalry that persisted into the twenty-first century and worsened over time. Similarly, a substantial number of peace agreements that end civil wars are followed by renewed warfare within several years (Hartzell 2016). The absence of a peace agreement might therefore be considered a conflict management failure, but the achievement of an agreement does not necessarily herald conflict management success. We must look for changes in the disputants' behavior as a barometer of that success, rather than relying solely on promissory actions.

One such behavioral change is conflict abatement. Conflict management approaches attempt to discourage and reduce violent conflict (e.g., war or attacks on civilians), perhaps as a prerequisite for broader and deeper forms of peace and cooperation. Progress along this dimension might be measured by tracking the number of combatant and civilian casualties, episodes of violence, or, most commonly, the number of days or months without renewed conflict (i.e., "peace duration"). The latter requires an appropriate "starting point." This might be the deployment of a peacekeeping operation, the award date for legal approaches, or the end of the bargaining period for negotiations and mediation.

Alternatively, one might assess a conflict's spread, where containment—a form of conflict abatement—signals success. Containment prevents a conflict from expanding to include additional disputants or geographic areas. Indicators of success for this criterion include the number of parties involved in the conflict, the extent of arms and financial flows to the combatants, and the geographic location of violent episodes.

Although conflict abatement indicators apply to several of the conflict management approaches covered in this book (e.g., negotiation, mediation, arbitration, adjudication, and peacekeeping), they make little sense in the context of other approaches, at least in the short term. Military intervention might have the ultimate purpose of stopping violence or its spread, yet in the short term (and perhaps longer) violence and death may *increase* as the intervening force engages with the military units of the disputant(s). Furthermore, by definition, military intervention increases the number of actors involved in the conflict, and if the intervener is a neighboring state, the geographic scope of the fighting might expand as well. Sanctions likewise do not often directly affect active fighting. They aim to change disputant behavior, but usually this involves changing a policy (e.g., apartheid, or the pursuit of nuclear weapons), rather than pushing disputants toward non-violence (although an arms embargo pursues this more directly; see Chapter 4). The connection between sanctions and conflict abatement is therefore less apparent than for other approaches, especially at the outset.

Other indicators of conflict management success are unique to the specific conflict management approach used. Table 2.1 illustrates some of these distinctive benchmarks.

For military interventions motivated by humanitarian concerns, for instance, stopping or preventing genocide is an important indicator of success; its use has been advocated in Syria and Sudan, among other locations,

Table 2.1 Distinctive Indicators of Conflict Management Success by Approach

Conflict Management Approach	Distinctive Success Indicator
Military intervention	Halting genocidal actions
Sanctions	Reversing objectionable policy
Negotiation and mediation	Implementing agreement
Adjudication and arbitration	Complying with legal ruling
Peacekeeping	Free and fairly supervised elections

and it is the centerpiece of the emerging "Responsibility to Protect" norm. One might measure the success of economic sanctions by the degree to which the sanctioned state reverses the policies that prompted the sanctions; Iran's willingness to suspend its nuclear weapons development in return for the lifting of sanctions offers an example. Negotiation and mediation success might look beyond the achievement of an agreement to the prompt and full implementation of that agreement by the signatories. The exact indicator used will depend on the agreement, but could involve factors such as the disarmament of rebel groups following a civil conflict (part of a majority of post-civil-conflict peace agreements). The Irish Republican Army's behavior illustrates this indicator in action. After the 1998 Belfast Agreement, IRA decommissioning dragged on (officially) until 2005; many regarded this as a short-term failure but a long-term success (as it *eventually* occurred). Similarly, disputant compliance with judicial awards signals the attainment of effective legal conflict management. Finally, measuring peacekeeping success depends on the individual mission's mandate; when supervising elections in a post-civil-war context, for example, having those elections certified as free and fair represents a job well done. This was the case when peacekeepers oversaw the election process in Cambodia in 1993.

Success indicators will also vary according to the conflict context in which they operate. Securing a ceasefire is paramount above all other goals when conflict managers enter an ongoing war. This is not relevant, however, when conflict management tries to prevent violent conflict from breaking out or escalating—as was the purpose of Nelson Mandela's mediation efforts in Burundi, sponsored by the African Union and operating in the shadow of ethnic conflict that could have resembled that found in its neighbor, Rwanda. Furthermore, some conflict managers are tasked with multiple functions, necessitating indicators of success that are crafted for each of their activities. Given the wide range of activities carried out in peacebuilding operations, for example, there may be indicators to track whether an operation successfully supervised elections, facilitated troop withdrawal and disarmament, created civil society institutions, promoted human rights, and so on.

Table 2.2 summarizes the different conflict management approaches along a number of dimensions. We highlight these dimensions throughout the individual chapters, as they form the basis for analysis within and comparison across approaches. The discussion of how approaches interact also relies upon the information in the table. It will therefore be a useful reference as we cover the international conflict management terrain.

Table 2.2 Characteristics of International Conflict Management Strategies

	Negotiation	Mediation	Legal approaches		Peacekeeping	Coercive approaches	
			Arbitration	Adjudication		Sanctions	Intervention
Third-party involvement	No	Yes	Yes	Yes	Yes	Yes	Yes
Third-party type	Not applicable	States, IGOs, NGOs, private individuals	States, IGOs (esp. standing bodies)	IGOs (international courts)	States, IGOs (e.g., UN)	States, IGOs	States, IGOs
Consensual/voluntary	Yes	Yes	Often	Yes, consensual between parties, but not by individual dispute	Yes (if host state consents)	No	No
Mechanism	Direct talks	Facilitated talks, information exchange/gathering, cost–benefit calculation change	Due process, application of relevant international legal principles	Due process, application of international law	Observation, separation, reporting, restoration of order and institutions, civilian protection	Coercion (cost–benefit calculation change)	

Table 2.2 Characteristics of International Conflict Management Strategies (*cont.*)

	Negotiation	Mediation	Legal approaches			Coercive approaches	
			Arbitration	Adjudication	Peacekeeping	Sanctions	Intervention
Control dimension	Greater disputant control	←——————————————————————→				Greater third-party control	
Control of process	Disputants	Disputants/third party	Third party (with disputant input)	Third party	Third party	Third party	
Control of outcomes	Disputants	Disputants	Third party	Third party	Third party	Disputants (as manipulated by third parties)	
Disputant preference for non-violence	Yes	Yes (assumed) during most active conflict management. For some actors, may still be no.				No	No

3

Intervention

When Iraq invaded Kuwait in August 1990, it violated numerous international norms, including those against violating national sovereignty and the use of military force. In earlier centuries, such an act, along with the seizure of territory that accompanied it, might have been tolerated and even legitimated by other states in the international system. But in this instance, a coalition of military forces from multiple states (primarily from the United States, Saudi Arabia, the United Kingdom, and Egypt) intervened to drive Iraqi forces out of Kuwait and restore the Kuwaiti government to power.

It achieved this in little over a month, thereby ending the initial violence through military victory. The continuing security guarantees and placement of US and UK troops, as well as the establishment of no-fly zones, then provided the mechanisms to manage the conflict further, albeit without resolving the underlying sources of dispute.

Although common usage applies the term "intervention" to any third-party involvement in an ongoing conflict (that is, *any* conflict management approach covered in this book), we employ a narrower conception of the term. Intervention occurs when a third party introduces military forces into an existing war or a conflict with high levels of violence. Thus, verbal support or financial aid in support of a combatant does not constitute intervention, unless done in conjunction with military forces. Examples of intervention under this definition include Saudi Arabia's air cover and actions in the Yemeni civil war, the establishment of no-fly zones (e.g., over Kosovo), the delivery and protection of humanitarian aid in Somalia, and the North Atlantic Treaty Organization's (NATO) behavior in support of rebels in Libya.

It might seem paradoxical to begin the substantive review of conflict management approaches by focusing on intervention. If conflict management primarily seeks to reduce violence and save lives, how does the introduction of greater military force into a situation achieve that? In short, intervention promotes the values of conflict management. Two broad prototypes of intervention exist: traditional military and humanitarian. Each has its own form and logic, but both work toward conflict management, even if they increase violence in the short run or third parties have self-interested motivations for intervening. The goals involve limiting violence, alleviating human suffering, and incentivizing a permanent resolution to the issues under dispute.

Traditional Military Intervention

Traditional military intervention involves a foreign power sending its own troops to an ongoing conflict (for an overview, see Shirkey 2018). It is usually biased, in the sense that it is designed to favor one side or another in the dispute (see Linebarger and Enterline 2016). Most obvious would be intervention in favor of the extant government. The Russian and Iranian interventions in Syria, for example, supported the Assad government in the long civil war there. Similarly, American intervention in Afghanistan in recent years has directly aided the central government against the Taliban and other groups. Intervention, however, can alternatively support rebel groups against the government. An illustration is the support given by neighboring states to the African National Congress against the apartheid regime in South Africa during the 1970s and beyond. Finally, intervention is also possible, albeit less common, when the intervening state acts not to support a government or rebel group but to protect its own interests. This can be especially important for a state directly affected by the instability in a neighboring state and that intervenes to secure its border. Israel's air strikes against Iranian forces in Syria qualify as this type of action. So too would Turkish actions against Kurdish troops in Northern Iraq and Syria. In each instance, the intervening states were less interested in influencing the civil war per se than in weakening particular groups or states already fighting.

Scholars often evaluate the impact of interventions in terms of their ability to bring wars to an end, thereby shortening conflict duration (e.g., Regan 2000). Although third-party motivations may be wholly altruistic, this is not necessary or even likely the case. The intervening party does wish the war to end and the bloodshed to stop. Nevertheless, a ceasefire is not exclusively the preferred outcome. The proximate goal of an intervention is to change the balance of power or the conduct of a war such that conditions become more favorable to the side that the intervention supports. Intervening forces do result in more violence and death in the short term, but by changing the course of the war they hope to produce a more desirable long-term outcome. In one scenario, for example, intervention in favor of the government or the rebels could allow the favored actors to win the war. The alternative is likely a protracted civil war with neither side winning; this might produce a stalemate, but not necessarily a "hurting" one. Helping one side, in contrast, could produce a winner, shortening the conflict and thus saving lives in the long run. Such victories, in civil wars at least, appear more durable than other kinds of settlements (Toft 2009), so there might be additional long-term benefits as well. After two-and-a-half decades of war, for example, the Sri Lankan government defeated the Tamil rebels, and the outcome has endured for more than a decade at this writing. In instances like these, intervention

enhances negative peace (that is, ends the war), even if deleterious consequences might also accompany it (e.g., in terms of human rights and other
values).

Rather than try to produce a winner, intervention might instead attempt to
precipitate a negotiated settlement by *preventing* a disputant's victory. These
interventions, always on the weaker side, try to prevent the stronger side from
winning and, in effect, promote a hurting stalemate between the disputants.
A disputant previously winning a conflict, who now recognizes that victory is
unlikely and that costs will be ongoing, should be more willing to negotiate
an agreement rather than continue the war. NATO action against Serbs in the
Bosnian civil war had this effect. Although the Serbs were making progress
during the war, NATO bombing and Croatian and Bosnian offensives reversed
some Serbian gains and facilitated negotiations to end the conflict; the Dayton
Accords that ended the war are said to have been a result of that process
(Holbrooke 1999).

These various kinds of military intervention can be relatively small or
extremely large. The Russian soldiers sent to Syria, for example, numbered
only a few thousand by most estimates, but the air support they contributed
allowed the bombing of rebel targets and cities. In contrast, the United States
and United Kingdom intervention in Iraq beginning in 2003 involved over
200,000 personnel—primarily ground troops.

Three notable activities often accompany direct military intervention and further enhance a disputant's military position. First, third
parties might supply the disputant with arms. Advanced weaponry, such
as rocket-propelled grenades (RPGs) or artillery, can increase the battlefield
effectiveness of a combatant. Russia, for example, provides anti-aircraft
missiles to the Syrian government for this purpose. Second, third parties
can offer direct financial aid, which buys additional weapons, pays soldiers
and militia personnel, and allows either the recipient government or rebels
to provide services and goods to the local population without diverting
resources from the ongoing war effort. Spain, Italy, and other European
states offered such aid to rebel groups fighting the Gaddafi government in
Libya; the value of this aid lies largely in its fungibility. Finally, beyond
material aid, intervening states may offer political support. Official recognition is one form this support can take, bestowing legitimacy on the
disputant. For example, numerous states have recognized and even granted
diplomatic recognition to the Palestine Liberation Organization over
the years, which cements the PLO's position as an actor with which Israel
needs to negotiate. In addition, the government or rebels might benefit from
public statements, diplomatic pressure, critiques of opponents, and the
like, each of which furthers their causes or enhances their bargaining
positions.

Humanitarian Intervention

The term "humanitarian intervention" might appear to be an oxymoron, given that any use of military force will likely produce casualties in the target state. Nevertheless, such interventions have a different cost–benefit calculus than traditional military actions and spring from at least some different motivations (for a scholarly and political history, see Seybolt 2010). According to Adam Roberts' (1999) classic definition, humanitarian intervention is "coercive action by one or more states involving the use of armed force, in another state without the consent of its authorities, and with the purpose of preventing widespread suffering or death among its inhabitants." Although the target state's consent is not required, the intervention is not necessarily biased against the government. Rather, the intervention favors *civilians* (non-combatants). These might be government supporters, rebel allies, or those supporting neither side in the conflict; what they have in common is that they are experiencing hardship as a result of an ongoing war. Humanitarian intervention can therefore be labeled "impartial"; it neither inherently favors any combatant nor tries to change the balance of power between disputants (as military intervention does). Of course, one disputant may be more responsible for civilian suffering than the other(s), but the intervening force acts to mitigate or alleviate that suffering regardless of the perpetrators; indeed, sometimes, assigning specific blame for the hardship civilians encounter during war proves impossible.

Although humanitarian intervention might be impartial, it violates two longstanding and related state-based norms in world politics: sovereignty and non-intervention in domestic affairs (Weiss 2016). Sovereignty grants a state the exclusive right to exercise power within its borders. Similarly, non-intervention means that outside actors—other states or international organizations—cannot interfere with the internal affairs or sovereign power of another country. These two norms have been the hallmarks of international relations in the modern international system (post-1648). Nevertheless, the establishment of human rights standards and the placement of these in the international purview have loosened absolute notions of sovereignty and intervention. Humanitarian intervention represents one of several exceptions to these norms and therefore stands in contrast to most of the other conflict management approaches discussed in this book.

What types of situations should see humanitarian intervention? Any war will impose negative consequences on the civilian population. These include people fleeing their homes, either within the state (internally displaced persons) or across borders (refugees), as well as food and medical supply shortages. Nonetheless, humanitarian intervention is not expected or even likely in every war; a threshold of severe suffering must be crossed to precipitate the consideration of intervention options. Although there are no precise quantitative or qualitative standards, "normal" conflict consequences are insufficient to prompt intervention. Beyond this severity threshold, third parties usually need to also conclude that the government or other local actors lack the capacity or motivation to address or ameliorate the suffering, and therefore that civilians require third-party assistance. Relatedly, if a bad situation worsens, prospective intervention becomes more likely.

The above discussion might suggest that humanitarian intervention applies only to situations of immediate, material suffering (e.g., food, shelter, or medical care). This is not always the case. First, significant human rights abuses can prompt contemplation of humanitarian intervention. At the extreme, disputants who commit genocidal actions clearly cross the severity threshold for intervention noted above. Other human rights abuses, such as systematic rape, torture, political killings and the like, are other forms of war suffering that humanitarian intervention might be asked to quell. Furthermore, and especially in the case of genocide, *prospective* human rights abuses might be candidates for humanitarian intervention. That is, humanitarian intervention need not necessarily wait until such violations manifest, but could interfere before they occur or reach a severe level.

Humanitarian intervention works toward several outcomes, some of which depend on when the suffering occurs during a war. Preventive action— for example to avert the targeting of civilians in the Bosnian enclave of Srebrenica—seeks to ensure that suffering never takes place. Alternatively, intervention might halt suffering or stop it from worsening after a war begins; as an illustration, some evidence suggests that the intervention in Somalia lessened the intensity of the conflict there, at least for humanitarian purposes (Pedrosa de Sousa 2014). Through such actions, humanitarian forces restrain or deter disputants from carrying out actions that produce material suffering or human rights abuses. Beyond this, humanitarian intervention might ameliorate the deleterious consequences of war (e.g., by delivering medical aid), without affecting the conduct of the war.

Third parties recognize that any of these actions may worsen the situation and cause further suffering, especially if troops need to stop an actor from committing atrocities. Nevertheless, the logic of intervention rests on "consequentialism" (for a normative discussion, see Kennedy 2004), the idea that in the long run, the benefits (e.g., alleviation of suffering and death) will outweigh any costs the intervention causes.

Altruistic motivations are a defining feature of humanitarian intervention, but they are not necessarily the exclusive rationale for why third parties intervene. Third-party self-interests often inform intervention decisions. Neighboring states, for example, will want to prevent the spread of a conflict or its negative externalities (e.g., refugee flows). A broader set of third-party actors may also oppose a disputant's goals, even as the intervention itself remains impartial. NATO intervention in Kosovo, for example, not only protected Kosovar Albanians, but also essentially denied Serbian forces full control over that province (see Box 3.2). Thus, statements that interventions merely support humanitarian concerns can be misleading; they might mask other, or at least additional, motives the intervening parties possess. The US intervention in Grenada during the 1980s illustrates this well: although ostensibly undertaken to protect American medical students, its underlying goals had more to do with the Cuban troops and advisors in the country.

In contrast to traditional military interventions, humanitarian actions tend to be multilateral—or at least authorized by an international organization—rather than the exclusive act of one country. The exact form such interventions take will vary according to their purpose. Weiss (2016), for example, distinguishes between "compelling compliance" and "providing protection." The former involves more peacekeeping tasks that we discuss in Chapter 8. The latter includes a variety of activities that cordon off areas from conflict. "No-fly" zones prohibit a disputant's (usually a government's, given capabilities) helicopters and planes from entering certain airspace in order to conduct operations against civilians on the ground. NATO created such a space over Libya (see Box 3.1), and a similar plan was suggested early in the Syrian civil war, but was never realized. Likewise, protected zones on the ground ("safe havens") prevent disputants from attacking civilian targets—a task peacekeepers might also perform (see Chapter 8). Turkey's proposal to create a safe zone for refugees along the Syrian–Turkish border offers an illustration. Finally, safe corridors provide for the delivery of food and medical supplies to affected populations; they might entail either security protection for others (e.g., non-governmental organizations) or actually delivering and distributing the aid. US intervention in Somalia provided this service between the UN peacekeeping operations.

Although humanitarian interveners might use military force, and indeed are likely to, their rules of engagement typically fall between those of traditional peacekeepers (see Chapter 8), who only fight defensively, and those of traditional military forces, who use extensive, offensive force to achieve their goals. Ideally, the mere presence of a humanitarian force (whether patrolling no-fly zones or guarding aid delivery routes) sufficiently deters attacks, and no force is needed. In other cases, however, the operation might need to use force to repel actors who seek to harm the civilian population or disrupt aid deliveries. The French military intervention in Mali, for example, worked not only to defeat Islamist rebels, but also to protect civilians; this required the extensive use of military force.

Responsibility to Protect (R2P)

Ideas of humanitarian intervention have existed for many years, but were always conceptualized as one option for third parties; that is, along with other conflict management approaches, third parties could choose whether or not to intervene. As discussed below, there is considerable debate over the legality of such interventions, but nothing *requires* a state or organization to intervene. A shift in the discourse, and perhaps in the norms of humanitarian intervention, occurred with the "Responsibility to Protect" (or R2P) movement. The International Commission on Intervention and State Sovereignty (ICISS) was empaneled in 2001 to consider the conditions under which intervention would be justified to address gross human rights violations, as had occurred in Rwanda and Bosnia. Its report produced a new principle labeled R2P (ICISS 2001), which the UN General Assembly unanimously adopted in 2005 and again in 2009.

One of the foremost proponents of R2P, Alex Bellamy (2015), describes the three pillars or philosophical points that support it. First, states have a responsibility to protect their own populations from the most serious human rights abuses, including genocide, war crimes, and other crimes against humanity. Second, states have a duty to help one another ensure that they can achieve the first pillar. Were these first two pillars universally followed, no need for external intervention would arise; since they are not, intervention emerges from the third pillar: the international community has a responsibility to take timely and effective action to protect people when their state fails to do so. Note that this moves beyond a *right* to intervene to an *obligation* to do so. Unlike other forms of humanitarian intervention, the international community envisions R2P for only the most severe human rights abuses—beyond what might trigger standard humanitarian intervention. They also expect "just war" principles, including using the minimum force necessary and the action having a reasonable chance of success, to govern R2P interventions strictly.

R2P can be characterized as military action to stop atrocities, but this is perhaps too narrow. Weiss (2016) describes three "temporal phases" of R2P, revealing a much broader and deeper strategy of conflict management. The first phase prevents atrocities when possible; that is, states should address the root causes of conflict and work to ensure that the worst crimes never occur. This strategy does not wait for serious conflict to break out, but rather heads it off. The second phase kicks in when abuses do occur: sanctions and international pressure. Such actions are preferable to military intervention, provided they are effective; this preference results from the just war principle of "last resort," which argues that intervention should only be used when less coercive options are either unavailable or have failed. Finally, the third phase constitutes a "responsibility to rebuild," which aims for recovery, reconstruction, and reconciliation in the societies that experience the atrocities (i.e., major crimes). This conflict resolution strategy circles back to the first phase, removing the impetus for human rights abuses and therefore preventing their recurrence.

BOX 3.1 Intervention in the Libyan Civil War

Case: Intervention in the Libyan Civil War
Date of Conflict Management: 2011
Disputing Parties: Libyan government versus various rebel groups
Third Party: North Atlantic Treaty Organization (NATO)
Outcome: Failure

When the "Arab Spring" uprisings reached Libya, the protests turned into a civil war, with rebel forces quickly gaining control of parts of the country. Libya's leader, Muammar Gaddafi, responded with a counter-offensive comprised of massive military force, including air strikes against civilian targets in the rebel-held areas. Prospects for large-scale human rights abuses and widespread civilian deaths became evident from existing government action and rhetoric. Thus, the conditions for a humanitarian intervention were manifest.

The UN Security Council responded by passing Resolution 1970, which expressly referred to the Responsibility to Protect (R2P) and, consistent with that principle, initially called for a halt to the violence and a peaceful resolution to the conflict. The Libyan government ignored those calls, largely because it was poised to retake the city of Benghazi and (possibly) engage in the mass killing of rebels and civilians there. The Security Council therefore next passed Resolution 1973, the first time the UN had authorized the use of military force for humanitarian purposes without host-state consent.

An intervention led primarily by NATO, but ultimately including up to nineteen countries, followed. It established a no-fly zone over the country, followed by an arms embargo and the freezing of Libyan government officials' assets. Although the initial purpose might have been civilian protection in the form of R2P, the intervention soon resembled a military intervention to support rebel groups and regime change. Backed by Resolution 1973 that called for "all means necessary" (diplomatic words for offensive military force), allied forces transitioned from being a third party to the conflict to being a primary party in support of the rebel forces, carrying out extensive air strikes against government forces. Gaddafi was killed in October 2011, and soon thereafter fighting ended with a provisional government nominally replacing him, although it did not have control over large swathes of the country. The new government requested that NATO forces stay for an additional year, but the Security Council declined to extend its mandate. The operation therefore ended at the end of that month.

Many consider the Libyan intervention a failure in multiple dimensions. On the one hand, the feared mass killing and humanitarian disaster that prompted the intervention was avoided, in large part because of the NATO action. Nevertheless, the civil war dragged on for many more months, with significant casualties on both sides and a large number of internally displaced persons. Indeed, NATO air strikes were said to be responsible for a significant number of civilian deaths themselves. Thus, there exists some ambiguity about whether the operation achieved its humanitarian goals. From a longer-term perspective, the impact of the intervention appears much less successful. The original Security Council authorization did not envision regime change, yet the leading states in the coalition that implemented the mandate had anticipated that the intervention would produce such a change in the long run, and in particular establish a democratic government. Regime change did occur, but democracy did not follow. Indeed, the new central government is weak, and the country resembles a failed state more than a functioning, sovereign entity, regardless of its form. A second civil war has also occurred since, involving competing government factions as well as several smaller groups. Thus, civilians still suffer hardship and death years after the intervention that sought to protect them.

The Libyan operation was supposed to set a positive precedent for humanitarian intervention in future conflicts, but it has seemingly had the opposite effect. Security Council support for future operations, especially from China, Russia, and others, has withered. This resulted largely because the Libyan operation became a biased intervention that clearly favored one side and extended beyond its humanitarian purposes. Even those who were most supportive of the intervention have been disappointed with its aftermath. Currently, the willingness of the UN, and perhaps others, to repeat this exercise is in serious doubt, even as the R2P principle is widely accepted.

Legal Considerations for Intervention

Intervention raises international legal concerns that almost never arise with the other conflict management approaches covered in this book. Of these other approaches, many are conducted with the consent of the disputants and are consistent with state sovereignty rights (e.g., negotiation, mediation, or traditional peacekeeping). Others—legal processes such as arbitration and adjudication—are, by definition, consistent with and rely on international law to operate. Even sanctions are legal, provided that they do not violate existing agreements; indeed, sanctions fall within the purview of the individual state (which does not have to trade with anyone against its will) and are frequently authorized by international organizations like the UN Security Council (which would make them legal under international law). Intervention, however, is a different matter. It involves third parties using military force—long regulated by international law—against or within a state, often without the latter's consent. Thus, one must consider the legal parameters under which such intervention can occur. Legality might enhance the prospect of third parties intervening, whereas illegality might lessen, but not eliminate, it.

International law assumes that the use of military force should be kept to a minimum, giving preference to peaceful forms of conflict management and resolution instead; the UN Charter, specifically Article 2(4), reflects this orientation. Intervention in existing conflicts is therefore *prima facie* illegal unless the circumstances fall under one of the exceptions permitted by the law. Self-defense constitutes the most obvious exception. This extends to third-party intervention through the permission for collective self-defense granted under Article 51 of the UN Charter. Resting on this permission, alliances and less formal arrangements that permit states to aid other states under attack therefore constitute legally permissible interventions, as for example in the American and British intervention in support of Kuwait following the 1991 Iraqi invasion.

Provisions for self-defense were primarily designed to apply to state-state conflicts. Intervention in civil conflicts raises different legal concerns (see Shaw 2017 for a general discussion). International law permits intervention in civil wars when approved or requested by the government of the country affected. This is consistent with principles of sovereignty, in that states have control over activities within their borders. For example, although not immediately, the Afghan government permitted the presence of US and NATO troops there, granting the intervention legality. Of course, if an intervention relies on host-state permission, then the host state can also withdraw its permission, as occurred in Iraq when the lack of an agreement with the government caused US forces to leave the country in 2011.

It is somewhat less clear whether international law permits intervention on the side of rebel groups. For the most part, the assumption is that it does not. Groups fighting a state's government fall within its sovereign jurisdiction. If these groups attain "belligerent" status—which involves controlling a substantial portion of territory, observing the rules of war, and behaving in other ways as a state actor would—and are recognized as such by other states, then third parties are obligated to remain neutral. That is, aid to the government side becomes prohibited, as states should remain neutral in conflicts between entities of equal status under international law (i.e., states). Belligerent status, then, does not make an intervention to support rebel groups legal.

Beyond host-government consent, intervention is legal when authorized by an international organization endowed with such powers by its members. Most obviously, the UN Security Council can provide this authorization under Chapter VII of its Charter. In 2011, for example, the Security Council approved such an intervention in Libya, which NATO then implemented (see Box 3.1). This intervention allegedly sought to facilitate a ceasefire and prevent war crimes from being committed against civilians by the Gaddafi-led government. Similarly, in 1994, the UN authorized intervention in Haiti to restore the democratically elected government there. State actors carried out the interventions in both cases, but legal authority for the intervention derived from the UN.

Although humanitarian intervention receives much rhetorical support from many countries, its legality without the permission of the host state is not well established. In the *Nicaragua v. United States* case, the International Court of Justice (ICJ) suggested that humanitarian intervention to alleviate suffering can be legitimate, opening the door for a legal right to do so. Nevertheless, the court also reflected that this legitimacy should be tied to the UN Charter; this implies the need for authorization from the Security Council, consistent with the general management of threats to international peace and security. Furthermore, in the same case, the ICJ rejected the legality of intervention for the purpose of protecting human rights. This does not mean that states can do whatever they wish within their borders, but rather that the international community cannot use military force to impose external standards on a given state. Since the ICJ's decision in 1986, a normative shift in favor of humanitarianism has occurred, including the development of R2P. Yet despite unanimous approval of the principles of R2P by the UN General Assembly, it is not a part of international law in either treaty or customary practice as of this writing. Although humanitarian intervention might have laudable goals and might one day be recognized in international law, it presently lacks a strong legal foundation as an approach to conflict management (Joyner 2015).

Patterns of Intervention

To gain insight into the patterns of intervention, we will analyze data from Pickering and Kisangani (2009). These data cover all military interventions during the period 1947–2005 (see also Regan 2000; Sullivan and Koch 2009). Interpretation of these data requires two notes. First, each data point represents one intervener-target pairing. Thus, if an intervener deploys to multiple states (e.g., the United Nations Truce Supervision Organization [UNTSO], which deployed to Egypt, Israel, Jordan, Lebanon, and Syria in 1948), the data contain one observation for each state to which the intervener went (e.g., UNTSO-Egypt, UNTSO-Israel, etc.). In other words, although there are 1,111 intervener-target pairings in the data (i.e., "interventions"; see Table 3.1 below), there are not 1,111 *missions*; the number of missions will be much lower than this. As an illustration, forty-eight different third-party actors began to intervene in the first Gulf War in 1991 within a single mission (or 80% of the peak that occurs at 1990 in the left panel of Figure 3.1). The data therefore reflect *individual* third-party decisions to intervene, rather than the deployment of missions per se. Second, and as noted in the example above, these data contain numerous peacekeeping operations, particularly those conducted by the UN. We

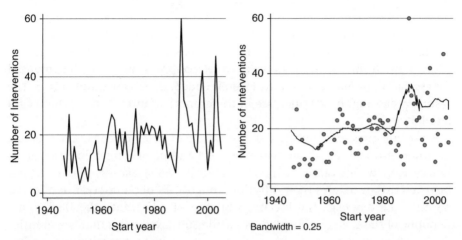

Figure 3.1 Interventions, 1947–2005
DATA SOURCE: Pickering and Kisangani (2009).

cover this specific conflict management approach separately in Chapter 8. Nonetheless, because peacekeeping operations feature in the data we use, they constitute a subset of the analysis presented throughout this chapter too.

Three questions about intervention typically arise. The first asks how common it is and whether its prevalence changes over time. Figure 3.1 supplies an answer. The first (left) panel charts the total number of interventions begun by year during the period. The Arab–Israeli conflict produced a flurry of interventions that started in the 1940s. This activity died off in the 1950s, with a low of three new interventions in 1952. After that, Middle Eastern conflicts combined with decolonization (e.g., in Tanzania, Uganda, Kenya, Laos, Vietnam) created a longer-lasting wave of intervention through the 1960s and 1970s. In this period, roughly fifteen to twenty new interventions occurred each year. Starting in 1990, however, new interventions begin at a higher average rate. In 1990, for example, the first Gulf War secured intervention from an unprecedented number of states acting in concert under United Nations auspices to expel Iraq from Kuwait. Somalia (1992), the Balkan Wars of the 1990s, Eritrea (1998), the Democratic Republic of the Congo (DRC), Papua New Guinea, and the second Gulf War (2003), among others, also attracted significant attention from third-party interveners.

The average number of interventions started per year remains relatively constant prior to 1990 and then shifts to a higher level. The second (right) panel of Figure 3.1 shows this trend. The dots represent the same data used in the first panel. To these, we add a moving average that reveals any trends over time. As the line demonstrates, the average number of interventions that occur annually sits between fifteen and twenty during the period 1945–60, hovers around twenty from 1960 to 1985, spikes at around thirty-five in 1990, and then settles into a new, stable rate of about thirty from the mid-1990s onward. These data suggest that the end of the Cold War created a structural break in intervention behavior. Studies of peacekeeping note a similar trend (Diehl and Balas 2014), and there are good reasons for it. The Cold War suppressed much intervention—in order to reduce proxy wars and the potential for escalation to major state war; when it ended, these constraints lifted. The result was a roughly 50% increase in the number of interventions that begin annually.

A second question concerns the duration of interventions. On average, an intervention lasts about two years. A handful of longer interventions, however, skew this value. In fact, the majority (65%) last less than one year, but even this overstates their duration; roughly 9% of all interventions occur on only one day (e.g., the Rwandan pursuit of rebels into the Democratic Republic of the Congo in April 2004), while 50% last for less than six months. In all, 95% of interventions end within ten years. Some interventions therefore constitute long-term commitments (e.g., the US involvement in Iraq beginning in 2003). Most, however, are short-term, whether because the action prompting the intervention ceased (e.g., pursuit of rebels), the intervener achieved its objectives (e.g., NATO's Operation Deny Flight, which created a no-fly zone over Bosnia from 1993 until the successful signing of the Dayton Peace Accords in 1995), or the intervener no longer wished to pay the costs associated with continued intervention (e.g., the United States' decision to leave Somalia in 1994).

Finally, one might ask where interventions take place. To answer this, Table 3.1 shows where interventions (both humanitarian and non-humanitarian) deploy by region. Although a common belief holds that the world ignores African conflicts, a significant number of interventions have been deployed there. Nonetheless, this belief gained traction in the 1990s. The US unilateral intervention in Somalia ended quickly, followed by the collapse of support for the UN peace operation in the country. When the Rwandan genocide then occurred in 1994, the US initially decided not to respond. The UN, in contrast, had an assistance mission on the ground as the genocide unfolded, but it was given neither the mandate nor the resources to halt the violence. The scale of atrocities committed in Rwanda, combined with global inaction, seemed to suggest that Western states would not intervene (even minimally) in the most severe African conflicts, even while their interventions in Bosnia and (later) Kosovo continued to escalate.

Is Africa ignored? Is Europe supported at the expense of Africa? Table 3.1 suggests negative answers to these questions. Of all non-humanitarian interventions during the period 1947–2005, 24.34% deployed to Sub-Saharan Africa. Only the Middle East and North Africa saw greater levels of non-humanitarian intervention (at 34.37%), and Africa experienced at least twice as many as any other region (i.e., no other region sees more than 12% of all non-humanitarian missions). Humanitarian interventions reveal a similar trend: nearly 30%

Table 3.1 Intervention by Region, 1947–2005

Target	Intervention		
	Non-Humanitarian	Humanitarian	Total
Americas	82 (9.79%)	20 (7.33%)	102 (9.18%)
West Europe	35 (4.18%)	1 (0.37%)	36 (3.24%)
East Europe	48 (5.73%)	34 (12.45%)	82 (7.38%)
Sub-Saharan Africa	204 (24.34%)	81 (29.67%)	285 (25.65%)
Middle East and North Africa	288 (34.37%)	81 (29.67%)	369 (33.21%)
Asia	100 (11.93%)	30 (10.99%)	130 (11.70%)
Pacific	81 (9.67%)	26 (9.52%)	107 (9.63%)
Total	838	273	1,111

NOTE: The Humanitarian column includes only those missions for which a humanitarian motive could be determined.

DATA SOURCE: Pickering and Kisangani (2009) for interventions; Correlates of War Project (2008) for regional divisions.

deployed to Sub-Saharan Africa, exactly on par with those occurring in the Middle East. Intervention within every other region falls significantly below these figures (for a similar finding with respect to peace operations, see Gilligan and Stedman 2003).

This discussion naturally suggests a second characteristic: intervention occurs less frequently in major states' spheres of influence. The regions that experience the fewest interventions include the Americas, Europe (West and East), Asia, and the Pacific. Some might argue that these regions experience less conflict, thereby demanding fewer interventions. For Western Europe, this may be true; indeed, states there experience few militarized interstate disputes (MIDs)—that is, cases in which one state threatens, displays, or uses force against another (Palmer et al. 2015)—and there has been little serious domestic conflict in the post-World War II period. A significant number of MIDs, however, occurred between states in the remaining regions during this time.

Given the presence of conflict in these regions, why do they see lower intervention rates? For the Americas, Asia, and the Pacific, the answer lies with the major states—the US and China—that direct behavior within these regions. The US has a longstanding policy that discourages other states' intervention in the Western Hemisphere (i.e., the Monroe Doctrine). It therefore not only intervenes more often than any other third party in the Americas, but also prevents other third parties from intervening there without its permission (e.g., UN intervention may occur with US consent in the UN Security Council). In a similar vein, China espouses a consistent preference for regional solutions to Asian conflicts and guards the principle of state sovereignty carefully. The Chinese also established and advocate for weaker regional organizations in

Asia, which then do not themselves engage in intervention, as opposed to the regional organizations in Africa or Europe. Although China does not exclude the United States entirely from the region (e.g., US interests in Taiwan, Japan, and Korea continue to create American incentives for involvement in Asia), it does restrict US autonomy there.

Agents of Intervention: States and International Organizations

Both states and international organizations intervene in international conflicts; nonetheless, intervention is primarily a state-based enterprise. States or coalitions of states conduct roughly 90% of all interventions, including 96% of non-humanitarian and 67% of humanitarian missions. Intergovernmental organizations (IGOs) conduct the interventions that states or state-based coalitions do not—roughly 10% of the total. Of this latter subset, 94% fall under UN auspices, with regional organizations picking up the balance (e.g., the African Union, the Economic Community of West African States, or the European Union).

These data align with theoretical expectations in two ways. On the one hand IGOs often defer or delegate intervention to states. Deference results largely from how IGOs operate. IGO intervention requires the organization to take action. This, in turn, demands that its members make a decision about what to do (e.g., pass a resolution). If members disagree on whether to intervene and the decision-making structure of the IGO permits these preferences to stalemate organizational action, then the IGO will be hamstrung. States then act where IGOs cannot.

In addition, states cede limited power to IGOs, affording them few military resources (if any) with which to intervene independently. Much of this results from concerns over state sovereignty and the power of IGOs over state members. US politicians regularly espouse this view, arguing that the placement of US forces under UN auspices violates US sovereignty. In 1995, for example, President Clinton asserted that he would not relinquish control of US forces to the UN; any US contribution to UN forces would be heavily conditioned; and, as the US contribution grew, the US would necessarily assert greater command over those forces. Thus, although some believe that the UN Charter envisions a standing military force under UN command (Article 47), this never occurred (Boutros-Ghali 1995). The European Union seemingly achieved such a standing force with its Battlegroups—multinational units of approximately 1,500 personnel capable of rapid deployment; yet even these are subject to voluntary contribution and member state consensus for deployment (Reykers 2017). In short, state leaders view military force as a critical currency in international relations, and they are reluctant to give that currency away.

When IGOs want to intervene but lack the military capabilities to do so, delegation becomes the next-best option. In this process, IGOs such as the UN first *authorize* an intervention. If they cannot subsequently shoulder the mission themselves, they then delegate its execution to a coalition of states (as in the first Gulf War) or a more capable organization (e.g., NATO enforcement of UN Security Council Resolution 1973 in Libya in 2011, see Box 3.1). The UN typically does this through a Security Council Resolution in which it "acts under Chapter VII of the Charter of the United Nations" and "authorizes Member States ... to take all necessary measures." This indirect phrasing to authorize the use of force highlights an additional characteristic of IGO delegation: it may be voluntary or not. For example, a coalition of states may assert its intention to enforce the organization's authorization, even if the organization does not directly delegate that responsibility to it (as in NATO's intervention in Kosovo; see Box 3.2). Organizations and their members therefore guard authorizing language closely (see, e.g., France's position in the build-up to the 2003 Iraq War), for it is the lynchpin in the intervention process and a desirable one. States seek such an authorization so their (desired) intervention accords with international law (as in US President Bush's attempt to secure UN support for the 2003 Iraq War).

A second way that the patterns noted at the outset of this section support theoretical expectations concerns the humanitarian/non-humanitarian divide. Third parties can intervene in conflicts for myriad reasons, including military (or strategic), economic, territorial, diplomatic, or ethnic considerations (see next section). Of these, humanitarian concerns offer the weakest motivation for state-based intervention. We might consequently expect states to undertake fewer humanitarian interventions and pass responsibility for these on to organizations instead. The data confirm this. Whereas states conduct almost all non-humanitarian interventions, they take responsibility for only two-thirds of all humanitarian interventions. Organizations carry the balance.

If organizations prove weaker than states and play a larger role in humanitarian interventions, this suggests that humanitarian interventions may be "weaker"—either in commitment or resources—than their counterparts. This, however, could be an inaccurate inference. States find organizational intervention appealing because it limits their own costs. Reputational, military, and economic costs for an organizational intervention fall not on a single state or a small group of states but on the larger membership. Moreover, organizations are more likely to be unbiased (that is, disinterested in a specific, substantive outcome) and therefore less susceptible to joining the conflict. This, too, carries consequences. Joining a conflict will likely prove more costly than not doing so; if so, organization-led interventions create the promise of an intervention whose costs will not escalate. These characteristics encourage states to support more (costly) interventions, if they are undertaken by organizations;

in other words, where it might otherwise not occur, cost-sharing makes intervention feasible. The trade-off is not between organizational humanitarian interventions and the state-based ones they replace, but between these organizational interventions and none at all.

Finally, although we have categorized states uniformly thus far, they are clearly not all equally active. As one might expect, major states prove more active than their minor state counterparts; nearly one in three interventions involves at least one of the United States (9% of all interventions), the United Kingdom (10%), France (6%), Russia (3%), and China (2%). Other active states include regional powers, such as South Africa (2%), Israel (4%), India (2%), and Pakistan (2%). These data suggest what scholars know and others infer: major global and regional powers possess broader interests than their counterparts, and these interests spark a greater number of interventions.

When Does Intervention Occur?

Any conflict management occurs when two factors intersect: demand and supply. The demand for conflict management depends on the existence of a conflict in which to intervene, the characteristics of the conflict and the disputants (e.g., major states often do not want third-party involvement and can prevent it), and the attitude of the disputants toward conflict management. Disputants can, for example, oppose (leading to intervention or sanctions; see NATO in Libya, Box 3.1), acquiesce to (e.g., a peace operation/intervention; see NATO in Kosovo, Box 3.2), or support (e.g., mediation) conflict management. The supply for conflict management stresses a different set of factors: the capabilities and motivations of third-party actors.

The theoretical distinction between the demand and supply of conflict management helps organize and focus our discussion of when intervention occurs. On the demand side, the critical question is: which disputants and conflicts are likely to need, desire, or oppose intervention? A couple of characteristics stand out. First, intervention *almost never* occurs in major states, e.g., the United States, the United Kingdom, Germany, France, Russia, China, and Japan. Pickering and Kisangani (2009) report that 3.51% of all interventions have deployed to a major state. Nevertheless, this figure is misleading. The vast majority of these interventions involved either the collapse of the British Empire (e.g., Yemen, 1954–65) or Chinese territorial and status issues (e.g., border disputes, Taiwan, and Korea). Thus, intervention into major states is rarer than the data suggest, and for good reason. Major state disputants prefer to manage their own disputes, eschewing intervention from outside actors. Moreover, their status and capabilities not only allow them to handle domestic concerns that arise, but also threaten to make intervention costly for those that might try it. The former precludes intervention, while the latter deters it.

Second, the conflicts most in need of intervention, particularly humanitarian intervention, will be those with high levels of violence that other, non-violent approaches fail to manage effectively (e.g., the NATO intervention in Kosovo, Box 3.2). Conflicts with greater casualties attract the attention of third parties, although they may postpone intervention if the casualty rate climbs steeply within a short period of time, because this places third-party forces at greater risk (Regan 2000; Corbetta and Dixon 2005). The issues underlying such conflicts typically drive this violence; when disputants consider the issues involved to be highly salient (e.g., territorial control or political inclusion), they struggle to negotiate successfully. Non-violent approaches then stall or fail, and the conflict persists. Thus, intervention occurs in the conflicts that are difficult to manage: those with a history of conflict management failure, valuable issues at stake, and high levels of violence. It will unfortunately also tend to occur later in a conflict, after non-violent approaches fail and the escalating violence has clarified the costs associated with *not* intervening.

On the supply side, the question becomes: which third parties are likely to intervene and what motivates them? The previous section partially answered this question (see also Linebarger and Enterline 2016; Shirkey 2018). States intervene more than intergovernmental organizations, particularly in non-humanitarian interventions. Nevertheless, as we have seen, not all states behave alike, and major states prove more active interveners than minor states. Major states possess not only the capabilities to intervene across a wider geographic area, but also the global interests that motivate intervention. To this, however, we can add that actors in closer proximity to a conflict are also more likely to intervene in it. The negative externalities of a conflict fall disproportionately on nearby states (e.g., rebel group activity in border regions or refugee flows). They therefore have an added incentive to manage the conflict. Indeed, as the first column of Table 3.2 shows, just over 60% of intervening third parties are land contiguous to (that is, share a border with) the state in which they intervene.

Table 3.2 contains a list of motivations captured by Pickering and Kisangani (2009). These include: (a) land contiguity (discussed above), (b) protection of an ethnic faction, (c) protection of economic resources, (d) strategic concerns, such as regional stability or ideology, (e) protection of diplomatic or military personnel or property, (f) territorial issues (e.g., acquiring, retaining, or recognizing another's territory), and (g) a desire to affect the policies of the target state. One or more of these factors can motivate each third-party intervention. Note, however, that the role of certain issues may be unknown or not applicable in specific cases. These cases therefore do not appear in Table 3.2, which explains why the column totals (i.e., "Yes" + "No") are both unequal across the issues and do not always add up to the 1,111 intervener-target pairing observations underlying the analysis.

Table 3.2 Motivations for Third-Party Intervention

	Land contiguous	Ethnic	Economic	Strategic	Diplomatic/military	Territorial	Affect policies of target
No	418	738	442	263	546	590	572
Yes	660	97	264	704	168	329	529
% Yes (out of Yes+No)	61.22%	11.62%	37.39%	72.80%	23.53%	35.80%	48.05%

Total   1,111 intervener-target pairings

DATA SOURCE: Pickering and Kisangani (2009).

Table 3.2 suggests that third parties are highly motivated by strategic considerations—more so than by any other factor. Ideological struggles (e.g., communist versus non-communist) or concerns over the possible destabilization of a region (e.g., North Africa or the Balkans; see Box 3.2) appear in nearly three-quarters of all interventions. After that, third parties seek most to affect the policy of the target state (48% of all interventions). Interveners often claim that they intend their actions to encourage disputants to abandon the use of violence in favor of a non-violent conflict management approach; these data suggest that the desire to see such policy shifts informs their actions. Economic and territorial issues follow next in prevalence (each found in approximately 35% of interventions). Trade agreements and investments generate prosperity and influence, whereas territorial issues are both high on the international agenda and are what most often lead to international conflict (Vasquez 2009). When conflict places these at significant risk, third parties will find intervention to be a wise policy. Finally, few interventions concern the protection of ethnic groups (12%) or military or diplomatic resources (23%). This may be surprising, given that many of the interventions that garner media attention involve conflicts in which disputants commit atrocities against ethnic groups. Nevertheless, ethnic concerns incentivize fewer interventions than do other factors.

In addition to these motivations, third parties may have a unique relationship with the disputing state that encourages their intervention (Aydin 2012). Allied states, for example, intertwine their security policy to varying levels; it therefore becomes important to manage an ally's conflict, either because it threatens to pull in external actors or because it might distract the alliance from its intended purpose (e.g., Greece and Turkey fighting within NATO, which perhaps weakens a unified NATO stance). Similarly, democratic states often support other democratic states, whether to protect democratic institutions or values. In interstate disputes, this may manifest as a biased intervention in favor of the democratic state; in intrastate disputes, in contrast, it likely encourages neutral intervention (that is, one that favors no single disputant). This discrepancy arises because intervention in a democracy's intrastate conflict will, by definition, involve multiple groups that (purportedly) adopt democratic values. Democratic interveners will want to support each of these democratic brethren.

When Does Intervention Promote Conflict Management?

For the purposes of this discussion, conflict management goals might be divided into two broad categories: settling the issues that drive violence and mitigating the violence itself. The former—although desirable because it promises to reduce the possibility of renewed or future conflict over the same

BOX 3.2 Intervention in Kosovo

Case: Intervention in Kosovo
Date of Conflict Management: 1999–present
Disputing Parties: Serbian government (former Yugoslavia) versus Kosovars
Third Party: North Atlantic Treaty Organization (NATO)
Outcome: Mixed

The Kosovo conflict occurred in the Former Republic of Yugoslavia (FRY), as Serbian leader Slobodan Milosevic attempted to consolidate power. In 1998, Serb forces tried to quell what they considered to be a domestic rebellion by organized, militarized Kosovar Albanians. Violence, atrocities, and refugee flows then started to rise significantly. In response, major states ushered a resolution through the United Nations Security Council, in which the UN did not take sides, encouraged dialogue between combatants, and instituted an arms embargo on the conflict zone. In the months that followed, the situation deteriorated further, and NATO threatened air strikes if the trend continued (Clinton 2004).

The United States and the United Kingdom mediated talks to find a solution to the conflict in February 1999. A proposed agreement emerged, but Milosevic rejected it in March. The Serbian government adopted the position that NATO members "attempted to impose a project of self-government, non-existent anywhere in the world, which encompasses elements of sovereignty and jurisdiction over and above those of federal units." No sovereign state, it claimed, could accept such terms. Serbia would continue handling what it deemed a domestic matter. Milosevic could not be persuaded to negotiate further.

NATO commenced its intervention, involving air strikes against Serbian targets, on 24 March 1999. The intervention had three goals: (a) to deter Serbia from violating the human rights of Kosovar Albanian civilians (i.e., to prevent ethnic cleansing), (b) to demonstrate resolve and encourage the cessation of the overall conflict, and (c) to damage Serbian military capabilities (Clinton 2004). The conflict—and therefore the NATO air strikes—continued until June 1999. As a condition for ending the bombing, NATO negotiated the deployment of an international peace force. The UN subsequently endorsed this idea and authorized member states to create it. NATO's Kosovo Force (KFOR) deployed on 11 June 1999 and remains on the ground as of this writing.

Whether the NATO intervention succeeded depends on how one measures success. Milosevic eventually conceded and turned from violence to negotiations, but only after three months of continued fighting. During this time, NATO bombing and disputant forces killed many and destroyed much.

Nonetheless, the conflict ended perhaps sooner than it otherwise might have. The intervention could therefore be deemed a success, especially to the extent that it prevented greater atrocities against Kosovar Albanian civilians.

On the other hand, the intervention left two notable failures in its wake. First, although the International Criminal Tribunal for the former Yugoslavia indicted Milosevic during the NATO intervention in May 1999, he was not arrested until two years later. NATO therefore cannot receive direct credit for bringing him to justice. Second, the conflict remains unresolved; almost twenty years after the initial intervention, NATO forces remain in Kosovo to facilitate a secure environment.

issues—remains difficult for intervention to achieve. Any settlement that emerges through force (e.g., war or intervention) will likely be unstable unless the settlement derives from one side achieving a decisive victory. This results from a "time-inconsistency" problem, in which the acceptability of a settlement changes for at least one disputant after the violence ends (Favretto 2009; see also Beardsley 2011). The costs of continued conflict to the disputants rise when an intervention begins; indeed, this is its intended purpose. As this happens, the disputants' preferences shift, and they begin to see the cessation of violence as preferable to continuing it. When these costs fall again (i.e., when the intervention ends), however, the disputant's preferences shift back. If a disputant can afford to fight, it may therefore start again, especially if it finds the issues involved to be particularly important.

Although a pessimistic assessment, the discussion above highlights how intervention can contribute to conflict management by reducing violence. Indeed, studies of the effectiveness of intervention typically label it "successful" if violence stops for a designated period of time (e.g., six months) after the intervention occurs (Regan 2000). Using this criterion, interventions succeed most when conducted by a major state in support of a government, as opposed to rebel forces, in an intrastate conflict. Success falters, on the other hand, in more intense conflicts, namely those with higher casualties (see Regan 2000).

These findings suggest a conundrum: the conflicts most in need of intervention will be those in which it is least likely to succeed. As casualties mount against a minority (i.e., non-government) group, the Responsibility to Protect norm should precipitate intervention. Intervening against a government in the face of high casualties, however, leads less often to a successful halting of violence. Moreover, some suggest that the best interventions never actually take place. They argue that the *threat* of intervention should be sufficient to foster an end to hostilities if the third party effectively demonstrates its resolve to intervene and the target of the intervention can be deterred from violence (Favretto 2009). The interventions that do occur, from this perspective, have already failed in some sense, and they are unlikely to succeed, at least easily. Finally, interventions that stop violence may prevent disputants from reaching the hurting stalemate that scholars and practitioners believe is necessary for successful non-violent conflict management (Zartman 2000). If true—and the hurting stalemate proves necessary—violence may stop during or immediately after the intervention, only to begin again later.

Conclusion

This chapter has considered how, despite the seeming paradox, military force might contribute to conflict management. Our discussion yielded a number of insights, including:

- Intervention takes two forms: military and humanitarian. In the former, a third party usually sends its forces into a conflict to tilt it toward a more desirable outcome—whether to produce a decisive victor or to create the hurting stalemate necessary for non-violent conflict management to occur.
- In humanitarian intervention, a third party deploys forces to alleviate civilian suffering. These interventions are "impartial," favoring no one disputant's substantive position over another's, but rather working to mitigate violence against civilians or supply them with aid (e.g., medicine, food, or shelter). Third parties commonly cordon off areas from conflict to achieve these goals (e.g., creating no-fly zones, safe havens, or secure corridors). Although humanitarian intervention appears altruistic, other self-interested motives may drive third-party behavior (e.g., mitigating conflict externalities or achieving a specific substantive outcome).
- The Responsibility to Protect (R2P) norm emerged in the 2000s. It argues that: (a) states must protect their populations from serious human rights abuses, (b) states should ensure that all other states can achieve this goal, and (c) if a state fails to protect its population, the international community has an obligation to intervene. Contemporary debates concerning humanitarian intervention often use the R2P language.
- Intervention raises international legal questions that do not arise with the other conflict management approaches we cover in the remainder of this book. In particular, international law restricts the ability of third parties to interfere with a state's domestic matters and generally proscribes the use of force. A few exceptions exist. Third parties may use force in a state: (a) in collective self-defense, (b) with the consent of that state, or (c) when authorized to do so by an international organization endowed with such powers by its members (e.g., the UN Security Council). Interventions on behalf of

governments will therefore be legal more often than those on behalf of rebels, and the R2P norm offers no strong legal foundation on which to intervene on behalf of civilians.

- The modal intervention deploys to either the Middle East or Sub-Saharan Africa and persists for less than a year. This contradicts the common arguments that interveners ignore Africa and that interventions typically constitute long-term commitments. Moreover, interventions have been 50% more likely to begin annually since the end of the Cold War than during it.

- Intervention is generally a state-based enterprise. States or coalitions of states conduct nearly all non-humanitarian and two-thirds of humanitarian interventions, with major states and regional powers being most active. Organizations, particularly the United Nations, then carry the balance. This general trend results from organizations—voluntarily or involuntarily—deferring or delegating much intervention to states. Although this implies a passive role for organizations, this is far from true in practice. Organizations not only authorize many state-based interventions (thereby aligning them with international legal norms), but also permit and coordinate interventions when they might not otherwise have occurred (e.g., in many humanitarian disasters).

- Interventions most often occur in non-major states that experience difficult conflicts (i.e., those where non-violent conflict management fails, disputants struggle to negotiate over highly valuable issues, and high levels of violence demand a third-party response). Although motivations for these interventions vary widely, the third parties most likely to intervene in a state in conflict are (a) those located adjacent to it, (b) those particularly worried about regional (in)stability or ideological struggles, (c) those seeking to change the state's policy, (d) those who share either security concerns (e.g., an alliance) or values (e.g., democracy) with the state concerned.

- Interventions rarely succeed at resolving the issues under dispute. Nonetheless, they can mitigate violence, especially if a major state intervenes in support of a government (as opposed to rebel groups). These efforts falter as casualties mount, however, suggesting that interventions are least likely to succeed in those cases where the Responsibility to Protect movement needs them most: conflicts in which a government commits widespread atrocities against a minority group.

4

Sanctions

Before the international community intervened militarily to expel Iraq from Kuwait (see Chapter 3), it first imposed significant economic sanctions on Iraq. These aimed, through increasing the costs of non-compliance, to force Iraq to accede to the United Nations demand that it withdraw from Kuwait. Among the sanctions imposed were a trade embargo that barred all trade between UN member states and Iraq—with the exception of a narrow group of humanitarian supplies—and a naval blockade to enforce the embargo.

The use of sanctions and military force in the wake of Iraq's invasion of Kuwait underscores the trade-offs between military intervention and sanctions. The deployment of military personnel to an ongoing conflict represents a major commitment by states and international organizations. It is also not without significant risk and expense, sometimes with no guarantee of success. To manage a conflict, states and organizations might therefore choose other coercive mechanisms, which supplement intervention or substitute for it. The imposition of sanctions seeks to achieve many of the same ends as intervention—often based on similar logic—but the tactic carries less risk and (frequently) cost. Yet, because sanctions rely on the imposition of economic costs to pressure an actor to undertake a desired action (or, in the case of Iraq's occupation of Kuwait, cease an unwanted action), it can sometimes be more difficult to impose enough costs from sanctions to force compliance with a demand.

Logic and Motivations for Sanctions

Sanctions are an inherently coercive conflict management strategy, whereby a third party (the sender) threatens to impose unacceptably high economic harm on a party (the target) unless the latter complies with the third party's demands (Drezner 2003; Morgan and Schwebach 1997). The third party typically achieves this by adopting at least one of two non-mutually-exclusive policies: (a) stopping the import or export of products or (b) restricting financial transactions from or to a target. These policies inflict economic harm, but they also foreclose policy options for belligerent targets (Hovi et al. 2011). An arms embargo, if effectively implemented, limits the ability of warring sides to continue their conflict and pushes them toward a negotiated settlement. The US arms embargo against South Sudan in 2018 provides an illustration, wherein the US tried to limit the belligerents' capacity to sustain the war. The US Ambassador to the United Nations, Nikki Haley, highlighted this intended goal: "This isn't punishment. Nor is it a meaningless gesture. It is something we can do to actually help the people of South Sudan—to slow the violence, slow the flow of arms and ammunition, and protect innocent lives" (Wroughton 2018).

As third parties deliberate about how to exert influence over an ongoing conflict, they must weigh both the effectiveness and the potential costs of any policy chosen. Third parties find sanctions attractive because they provide a means for imposing costs upon targets while also limiting the costs paid by themselves. Mediation, while a relatively low-cost strategy, limits the pressure that third parties can bring to bear to push disputants toward a settlement. Military intervention, in contrast, allows third parties a greater capacity to impose costs directly on belligerents, thereby making the continuation of conflict both more difficult and painful. Yet military intervention also brings substantial risks and costs for a third party. Thus, in terms of the balance between the ability to impose costs upon belligerents reluctant to end a conflict and third parties' desire to minimize their own costs, sanctions provide a middle-ground strategy. They offer a vehicle through which a third party (or a group of third parties) can punish warring sides in order to pressure them toward peace. At the same time, they are also substantially less costly to implement than a military intervention.

Sanctions are, however, not costless for third parties. In order for an economic or arms embargo to impose costs upon warring sides, there must be some trade connection to disrupt between the sanction sender and target. Otherwise, an embargo becomes a purely symbolic act and the target remains unaffected. When trade ties exist costs accumulate for the third party applying the sanctions. If, for example, a third party exports large amounts of agricultural products, consumer goods, or arms to a target, then the imposition of an embargo will cause a segment of the sender's export markets to dry up. These economic costs mount while the sanction remains in place, since the effect on trade continues.

Although sanctions can be used to pressure disputants toward peace, third parties also employ them for more self-interested reasons. Outside powers facing a conflict in which they perceive few viable policy options or are unwilling to employ higher-cost strategies, such as peacekeeping or military intervention, may turn to sanctions for the political benefits of appearing to do something to address the problem. Weiss (1999: 500) highlights the use of sanctions during humanitarian emergencies as an example of this sort of politically motivated, but ultimately ineffective, use of sanctions—what he refers to as "collective spinelessness." Sanctions also serve as a protectionist tool, closing off foreign producers' access to the sanction sender's market (Cox and Drury 2006). In such cases, sanctions ostensibly emerge to manage an ongoing conflict, but their implementation springs more directly from the sanctioning state trying to privilege its domestic producers and protect them from foreign imports.

As Table 4.1 shows, actors in the international system display a diverse set of motivations for both threatening and implementing sanctions. Although efforts to manage ongoing conflicts or shape the broader security environment underlie some sanction activity, many sanctions stem from more limited goals. During the 1945–2005 period, the largest share (nearly 50%) of sanction threats and impositions involved disputes over trade practices (at least in part). Another significant portion of sanctions activity (slightly more than 10%) during this period featured balance-of-power considerations, with sanctions threatened or imposed as a consequence of the target potentially or actually joining an alliance. A narrower subset of sanctions (about 8%) was driven by the sender's desire to improve the human rights practices within the target state.

Sanctions activity motivated by conflict management concerns might be captured by five categories within the Threat and Imposition of Economic Sanctions (TIES) v4.0 data set (Morgan et al. 2014), which covers 1,412 cases of sanction threats and impositions during the 1945–2005 period: (1) containing the military behavior of a target, (2) destabilizing the target's political regime, (3) resolving a territorial dispute, (4) ending the dissemination of weapons to other actors, or (5) ending a target state's support of non-state

Table 4.1 Frequency of Sanction Issues, 1945–2005

Issue Type	Frequency
Trade practices	704
Alliance choice	147
Human rights	110
Military behavior	102
Economic reform	56
Destabilize regime	54
Release of citizens, property, or material	53
Political influence	49
Environmental practices	47
Territorial dispute	45
Weapon dissemination	38
Strategic materials	28
Non-state actor support	25
Drug trafficking	18

DATA SOURCE: Morgan et al. (2014).

actors, such as rebel factions or terrorist groups. Each activity seeks to limit conflict between parties or address the root causes of the conflict. Based upon this conceptualization of sanctions as a conflict management tool, nearly 16% of all sanction threats and impositions during the period 1945–2005 were at least partially motivated by conflict management concerns. This use of sanctions, however, falls to 8% in the post-Cold War era, unlike other conflict management approaches (e.g., peacekeeping). This suggests that third parties rely on sanctions less for conflict management than for self-interested reasons in the post-Cold War world.

Sanctions take a wide variety of forms. Von Soest and Wahman (2015), for example, distinguish between comprehensive sanctions (aimed at broad segments of a target state's population) and targeted or "smart" sanctions (focused on the target's political elite). Comprehensive sanctions include embargoes—both commodity embargoes, cutting off some forms of trade but not others, and comprehensive embargoes, restricting trade between a sanction target and sender entirely. Commodity embargoes focus on specific products (e.g., the 1973 Organization of the Petroleum Exporting Countries' oil embargo against supporters of Israel, such as the US, the Netherlands, Portugal, and South Africa). More comprehensive sanctions, in contrast, preclude particular transactions altogether; they halt trade or impose broad-based financial restrictions, such as freezing a target state's assets, suspending loans, reducing or withdrawing foreign aid, or reducing financial activity between a sender and a target. The US decision to suspend military aid to Pakistan in 2018, amid US accusations of Pakistani support for the Taliban in Afghanistan, provides an example of these financial sanctions. Finally, third parties may also tailor targeted sanctions more finely, in an attempt to inflict economic pain upon only a subset of the target state's society. Examples of such sanctions include travel restrictions for members of the political elite, arms embargoes to alter the military's capabilities, or financial restrictions that limit regime supporters' access to their foreign-deposited wealth and undermine the ability of elites to access capital for investment. Regardless of what exact form sanctions take, they can bar the export of goods (or money) to a target, the importation of goods (or money) from the target, or both. The key is to maximize the economic pain felt by the recipient of the sanctions.

Table 4.2 offers greater detail about the particular form sanctions take. As the table shows, import restrictions – where the sender bars the import of specific products from a target state – are the most commonly used type of sanctions. Beyond closing off markets to a target, third parties also frequently threaten or apply cuts to foreign aid. More draconian forms of sanctions appear less frequently. Full embargoes, which ban all economic exchange between a sender and target, have only been applied in fifteen sanction cases from 1945 to 2005. Similarly, although partial embargoes—trade bans on both imports and exports in limited economic sectors—occur more often than full

Table 4.2 Frequency of Types of Sanctions
Threatened or Imposed, 1945–2005

Sanction Type	Frequency
Import restrictions	457
Suspend foreign aid	244
Other	152
Partial embargo	94
Suspend agreement	79
Export restrictions	63
Travel ban	33
Full embargo	27
Blockade	15
Asset freeze	12

DATA SOURCE: Morgan et al. (2014).

embargoes, they are still relatively rare. Finally, senders are substantially less likely to threaten or use sanctions that impose high costs on themselves. Restrictions on exports, for example, which impose costs on the export products of the sending state's companies, are much less commonly applied as sanctions than import restrictions, which can often benefit domestic producers. Indeed, import restrictions are more than seven times more frequently used than export restrictions, highlighting states' preference for minimizing the costs of sanctions to their own domestic industries.

The salience of the issues involved generally influences the type of sanctions imposed by senders. When these issues focus on security concerns, senders become more likely to apply harsher trade restrictions. We define security concerns as those involving military behavior, regime destabilization efforts, support of non-state actors within a target state, territorial disputes, and weapons distribution. When security issues are at stake, about 9% of sanctions cases threaten or impose a full embargo against the target state, while an additional 19% employ a partial embargo. Moreover, if security issues arise, senders are four times more likely to threaten or impose asset freezes and travel bans, which inflict pain directly on the target's elite. Each of these figures is significantly higher than the general averages noted above.

Types of Sanctions—Traditional vs "Smart"

At their core, sanctions seek to induce a change in the target's policy or behavior, whether that target is a government or a non-state actor (e.g., a rebel organization). To achieve this, they must impart sufficient costs to make non-compliance with the sender's demands more costly for the target than compliance. This logic suggests that those with the authority to make changes in policy or behavior necessarily pay the costs imposed by sanctions. But what if those who are most deeply impacted by the costs lack the ability to force policy change by their governments? This question has been the source of debate about the merits of traditional sanctions versus smart, or targeted, sanctions.

Traditional sanctions represent the broadest use of sanctions as a tool—a ban on economic relations with an actor. US sanctions against Fidel Castro's regime in Cuba and, in the aftermath of the first Gulf War, against Saddam Hussein's Iraq both serve as prominent examples. In each case, the US instituted comprehensive trade bans, barring virtually all imports and exports by American businesses to Cuba and Iraq. The multinational sanctions campaign against the South African apartheid regime offers a similar example, as it prohibited trade and financial links between the sanctioning states and South Africa. The sanction senders in these instances sought to impose economic pain upon broad swathes of the target state's economy, as a means of forcing compliance with their demands. With respect to Cuba, for example, the US expected that the economic costs imposed would undermine the Castro regime's ability to maintain the support of the Cuban people and, ultimately, produce a groundswell of opposition that would compel regime change. The anti-apartheid sanctions imposed on South Africa followed a similar logic: the international community expected the sanctions to underscore the international pariah status of the apartheid government and create pressure within the country for political change.

The fundamental assumption underlying traditional sanctions is that the economic pain inflicted upon the target's support base (e.g., the civilian population of a state) will translate into supporters pressuring their leaders for policy change as a means of ameliorating the effects of the sanctions (Tostensen and Bull 2002). This raises three important issues. First, much of the motivation for using economic sanctions over other instruments of power is that sanctions are not only lower in cost (to the sender) but also impose less human suffering (on the target) than alternative policy tools. Thus, although both military strikes and sanctions allow an outside power to impose costs on another state to force a change in their behavior, sanctions often seem more palatable because senders deem them less harmful to the civilian population of the target.

As noted above, however, traditional sanctions deliberately harm civilians in order to encourage policy change. They can therefore carry dire human costs (Giumelli 2015). They might, for example, dry up supplies of food and vital medicines (Weiss 1999); even if these supplies remain available, sanctions can cause their costs to skyrocket dramatically as black markets emerge for the provision of goods that sanctions make scarce. Moreover, by encouraging efforts to circumvent them, traditional sanctions foster smuggling and organized crime, which also tend to encourage corruption among government officials (Drezner 2015). Each of these effects makes life more difficult for the civilians in an affected state, with the gravest effects being heaped upon the most vulnerable segments of the population (Weiss 1999). The sanctions imposed on Sudan in 1993 for its sponsorship of terrorism, for example, impacted the Sudanese healthcare system's ability to adequately treat its population—despite exceptions for medicine and food—because the sanctions created barriers to the importation of medical supplies, the conduct of medical research, and the delivery of healthcare (Maxmen 2016).

A second issue concerns the extent to which the leaders that traditional sanctions aim to influence are able to use the sanctions as a source of power. Sanctions allow political leaders to scapegoat the imposer of sanctions and shift blame away from the regime for a wide range of economic and social problems facing the country, even those that are not a consequence of the sanctions themselves. Former Zimbabwean President Robert Mugabe, for example, blamed Western sanctions for a wide range of his country's problems—from its inability to pay government officials to its failing infrastructure. In addition, political elites have a wide variety of policy tools at their disposal that allow them to direct the costs of sanctions to particular segments of society (Pape 1997). If sanctions limit access to vital resources such as food, fuel, and medicine, governments might adopt policies to ensure that any remaining resources are directed toward the political elite and its supporters (Peksen 2009). Even more insidiously, political leaders can also use the resource scarcity produced by sanctions to harm societal groups that represent a threat to their political control. Rather than encouraging a change in behavior (or regime), then, traditional sanctions may actually strengthen the hand of precisely the leaders they are intended to influence. Venezuelan President Nicolas Maduro, for example, used the 2017 financial sanctions imposed by the United States against his government as the basis for attacks against regime opponents, including Julio Borges, the President of Venezuela's National Assembly, arguing that "you've got to be a big traitor to your country to ask for sanctions against Venezuela" and calling for the prosecution of Borges for treason (Sanchez and Goodman 2017).

The third issue involves the assumption that the costs imposed upon supporters at large will necessarily translate into a policy change within the targeted state. Sanctions sometimes produce grassroots pressure from citizens who favor policy change, but a government must be responsive to its citizenry in order for these demands to translate into such a change. In democracies, civilians who are unhappy with government policy may vote their leaders out of office. In non-democratic regimes, however, the barriers to the dissatisfied population removing political leaders are far higher. As a consequence, the mechanism that translates economic pain into the government's willingness to change its policy is much less likely to be effective in non-democratic regimes than democratic ones—an important challenge for the effectiveness of sanctions because states are often targeted in the first place due to their authoritarianism (Tostensen and Bull 2002). Moreover, even when governments feel the domestic pressure intended to produce policy change, they may respond with political repression rather than yield to the sender's demands. According to the logic underlying this argument, sanctions signal the potential weakness of leaders to their constituents; this, in turn, encourages opponents to take advantage of this perceived weakness to initiate protests against the regime (Carneiro and Apolinario 2016). In response to such protests, regimes turn toward repression, as a means to demonstrate their strength and maintain control over the populace.

For these reasons, both scholars and policymakers have sought better sanctioning mechanisms that jointly minimize the attendant costs paid by the population at large and maximize the pressure applied to political leaders. One approach to achieve the former is to allow humanitarian exceptions to the sanctions. This would permit the targeted state to receive goods such as medicine and food that are vital to the population. However, even if such exceptions are put in place, there is no guarantee that these goods will make their way to the population at large, rather than be hoarded by the regime and its supporters (see above). Humanitarian exceptions also increase the potential for smuggling, as smugglers use the transport of excepted goods as a means to hide non-excepted goods, thereby undermining the effectiveness of the sanctions campaign as a whole.

As an alternative to the creation of exceptions, senders can attempt to deliver the pain of sanctions more precisely to the decision-makers they want to influence. This is the logic of targeted, or smart, sanctions. Rather than impose broad restrictions, target sanctions instead focus on narrower sectors of a target state's economy, with an eye toward placing these costs as directly as possible on the target's political leaders and their supporters (Biersteker et al. 2013). The virtue of targeted sanctions is that they are seen as both more humanitarian and more effective against their targets; they maximize the costs imposed on leaders while minimizing the unintended, negative effects on the general populace (Drezner 2015). Examples of targeted sanctions include arms embargoes against warring sides, travel restrictions against leaders and their supporters, and financial sanctions such as the suspension of international loans, asset freezes, and the restriction of access to financial markets (Tostensen and Bull 2002). The targeted sanctions imposed against Iran's nuclear activities, for example, emphasized financial restrictions that effectively cut off all foreign bank transactions with Iranian banks and eliminated Iranian access to the markets for insuring its commercial ships (Drezner 2015). For the Iranian regime, which relies upon shipping to export much of its oil and depends upon foreign capital for investment in its energy production sector, these sanctions brought high costs, while minimizing the pain experienced by other sectors of the economy.

Not only can targeted sanctions increase effectiveness by maximizing the pressure applied to targeted leaders, they can also increase the willingness of senders to sustain the sanctions. Senders will be more likely to stick with sanctions over the long term when their negative effects on civilians are minimized and the costs to the senders themselves are reduced—goals that targeted sanctions help achieve (Drezner 2015). This is especially important to the effectiveness of multilateral sanctions. If parties to multilateral sanctions have economic incentives to defect from a sanctioning effort, cooperation among the various senders will be difficult to achieve, in terms of both keeping the sanctions in place and imposing enough costs on the target to force changes in policy. Thus, financial sanctions can be an especially attractive form of targeted sanctions as they simultaneously minimize the sender's costs while imposing economic costs on targets that are similar in magnitude to comprehensive sanctions (Drezner 2015).

Given the perceived benefits of targeted sanctions, it is not surprising that the international community has increasingly turned toward their use and away from comprehensive sanctions. Until the mid-1990s, most sanctions imposed by the UN were comprehensive rather than targeted (Giumelli 2015). Since 1994, the pattern has shifted dramatically such that all UN sanctions have been targeted, with the exception of the 2011 comprehensive sanctions imposed on Libya as punishment for government repression against regime opponents there (Carneiro and Apolinario 2016). Most UN targeted sanctions since the end of the Cold War have been aimed at either ending an ongoing conflict or maintaining an existing peace in the aftermath of conflict (e.g., in the Democratic Republic of the Congo in 2005), with governments being the primary target of sanctions in just less than half of cases, rebel groups the primary target in 25% of cases, and both parties targeted in 16% of cases (the remaining small fraction of sanctions are targeted at domestic constituencies) (Giumelli 2015). These sanctions usually involve bans on specific sectors, most typically arms embargoes, trade restrictions on a targeted state's economy (95% of cases), travel bans (75% of cases), and asset freezes (63% of cases) (Giumelli 2015).

United States and European Union sanctions against Russia following its invasion of Ukraine and occupation of Crimea in 2014 are consistent with this pattern. The US and EU imposed not only travel restrictions on members and supporters of the Putin regime but also sanctions targeted at leading Russian banking and energy firms. The US energy sanctions, for example, barred the export of goods, services, and technology used for energy exploration and production by five Russian energy companies (US Department of the Treasury 2014). Consistent with the logic of targeted sanctions, the EU noted that the sanctions were "not punitive, but designed to bring about a change in policy

or activity by the target country, entities or individuals. Measures are therefore always targeted at such policies or activities, the means to conduct them
and those responsible for them. At the same time, the EU makes every effort to
minimise adverse consequences for the civilian population or for legitimate
activities" (Council of the European Union 2014: 1).

Patterns in the Use of Sanctions Over Time

Both the threat and the imposition of sanctions have increased over time.
Weiss (1999) connects this trend to two general forces. First, the sovereignty
principle has weakened at the same time that states' conceptualization of
security has broadened. The change in attitude toward sovereignty–where
states and international organizations increasingly see governance and
human rights practices within individual states as issues of concern for the
wider international community, a pattern noted in the last chapter as responsible for an increase in humanitarian intervention–has also encouraged the
increased use of sanctions as a means of pressure for governance and human
rights reforms. Second, at the same time, sanctions are seen as a less costly
means of "doing something" about the deadliest conflicts in the international
system. This fits with the increased interconnectedness of the international
community. Whereas conflicts in places such as Syria or Sudan might have
received little attention from the international community in the past, the
media coverage of and the ability of the international community to see the
human suffering produced by these conflicts has grown. As a consequence,
policymakers feel greater pressure to respond with conflict management
efforts. The interconnectedness among states has also deepened trade ties
among them. These trade links not only provide enhanced leverage to international actors for sanctions over security, governance, and human rights issues,
they also increase the prevalence of trade disputes between states that also
encourage the use of sanctions to settle them.

Given that strategic motivations drive the use of sanctions, actors must
think carefully about both when and where to threaten and impose sanctions
in order to maximize the benefits to the sender. As evidence from the TIES
v4.0 sanction data set shows (Morgan et al. 2014), the states that are the most
frequent targets of sanctions in many respects mirror those that are the most
likely to impose sanctions on other states. The United States, for example, has
historically been the most frequent target of sanction threats and impositions
during the 1945–2005 period, accounting for about 7% of all sanction activity. Other leading targets of sanctions include Japan (about 6%), South Korea
(4%), China (3%), and Israel (slightly less than 3%). In addition, both Canada
and Mexico feature prominently as targets of sanctions. This is surprising,
given that neither state is a major power. This pattern points, however, to

the presence of webs of sanctions, collections of states that are mutually responsible for imposing sanctions upon one another. These webs are often rooted in trade disputes, rather than violent conflict, between the contending sides. Canada and Mexico, for example, account for nearly half of all sanction threats and impositions directed at the United States, with a large segment of the sanctions resulting from trade disputes over agricultural products. Symmetrically, nearly 70% of sanction activity directed at Canada and Mexico derives from the United States.

Figure 4.1 describes sanction activity during the 1945–2004 period. During the first decade after World War II, sanctions were threatened and used sparingly. Overall, there were fifty-eight threats and seventy-two impositions of sanctions during the 1945–1954 period. This pattern remained relatively stable over the next two decades. By the mid-1970s, however, both the threat and the use of sanctions began to gain momentum as a statecraft tool. By the 1995–2004 period, there were 365 threats and 265 impositions, comprising 35% and 32% of all post-World War II sanction threats and uses respectively.

Even as there has been a sharp increase in both the threat and the imposition of sanctions, the follow-through rate from sanction threats to actual imposition has varied considerably from decade to decade with little discernable pattern during the post-war period. The follow-through rate captures

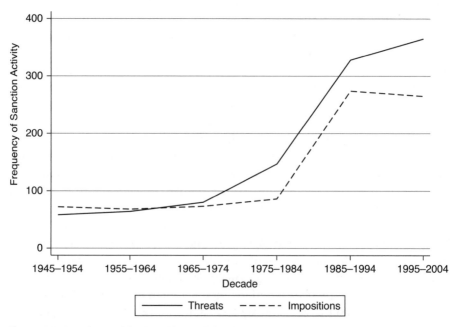

Figure 4.1 Sanction Activity Over Time, 1945–2004
DATA SOURCE: Morgan, Bapat, and Kobayashi (2014).

two dimensions in the connection between sanction threats and sanction impositions: (a) the extent to which the targets of sanction threats yield to sender demands at the threat stage, and (b) the degree to which sanction senders are sufficiently committed to follow through with sanctions when a target fails to yield to a threat. The likelihood of a target yielding at the threat stage is a function of the target's expectations of the costs of sanctions, if they are imposed, relative to the benefits of maintaining the status quo. Similarly, the likelihood of a sender following through and imposing sanctions, once a threat is resisted by the target, is shaped by the sender's own expectations regarding the costs of sanctions and the benefits yielded from imposing them. Importantly, while a decision by the target to yield to imposed sanctions is an important benefit of imposing sanctions for a sender, it is not the only potential benefit. Senders must also factor into their decision to impose sanctions the reputational benefits of doing so, both among their constituents as well as among other actors in the international community. Even if a sender does not expect sanctions to bring compliance, it may still choose to impose them if it believes that failure to follow through on its current threat may undermine its reputation in making future threats.

Agents of Sanctions—States and International Organizations

Just as sanctions take a variety of forms, they are also employed by a wide variety of actors. Sanctions can be imposed bilaterally or multilaterally, by individual states, ad hoc collections of states, or international organizations. US sanctions against the Cuban government, which imposed deep restrictions on imports, exports, and travel, provide an example of bilateral sanctions (i.e., those applied by one state against another). Other sanctions are more deeply institutionalized, with states using international organizations as a means by which to organize, coordinate, and sustain a sanctions regime against a target. The UN Security Council sanctions regime begun in 2006 to pressure Iran into abandoning its development of nuclear weapons offers an example of an institutionalized sanctions campaign. This regime imposed a variety of economic restrictions on Iran, including freezes on Iranian assets, the suspension of international banking activity, an arms embargo, and travel restrictions.

Although sanctions are most commonly directed at governments, they can also be applied to non-state actors. Third parties seeking to manage an ongoing civil war, for example, may choose to direct sanctions at a government, a rebel group, or both. Sanctions against the Assad regime in Syria, for example, supply an example of economic pressure levied at a government during a civil war. In contrast, US sanctions instituted against the Allied Democratic Forces (ADF) in the Democratic Republic of the Congo illustrate sanctions levied against a rebel group. These resulted from reports of the ADF systematically violating Congolese human rights, including those of children, during the civil war in 2014. Nonetheless, even in civil wars, sanctions more commonly target state governments. With the exception of arms embargoes and travel bans, this tendency is a consequence of the limited trade ties between rebels and the wider international community, which leave fewer economic levers through which to pressure rebels.

Although sanctions are a policy tool hypothetically available to a broad cross-section of states and international organizations, in practice they tend to be most commonly threatened and imposed by a disproportionately small subset of states. Major powers and resource-rich states, particularly oil states, are most likely to do so. The United States, in particular, is far and away the most active state that makes sanction threats and imposes sanctions. As the TIES sanction data set reflects (Morgan et al. 2014), American sanction threats constituted nearly 60% of all such threats during the 1945–2005 period. Similarly, the US accounted for slightly more than 50% of all impositions of sanctions during this same time frame. Other states frequently making sanction threats include Canada, the United Kingdom, France, Russia/Soviet Union, and India. In terms of imposing sanctions, Canada, Mexico, and India stand out—beyond the major states—as those most frequently using this approach.

States, however, do not exclusively use sanctions as an instrument of influence. The TIES data set shows that during the post-World War II era, nearly 30% of sanction threats and slightly more than 22% of sanction impositions came from intergovernmental organizations (IGOs). As with states, IGO sanction activity has increased over time. Among the 305 cases of IGO sanction threats during the 1945–2005 period, less than 25% occurred between 1945 and 1974. In contrast, about 58% of IGO sanction threats occurred from 1985 to 2005. IGO's imposition of sanctions follows a similar trajectory. Among the 187 cases of IGO sanction impositions during the same period, just 23% occurred from 1945 to 1974. These impositions ramped up considerably, however, beginning in the 1980s, with the period from 1985 to 1994 representing a high-water mark, accounting for more than 32% of all post-World War II IGO sanctions. Overall, about 63% of all sanctions imposed by IGOs occurred between 1985 and 2005. Nonetheless, despite this expansion, the share of sanctions imposed by IGOs has not changed substantially over time. From 1945 to 1974, IGOs imposed slightly more than 20% of all sanctions. This number remained relatively constant in the 1985 to 2005 period (22%). Thus, although states have grown more willing to use sanctions as a foreign policy tool, their desire to institutionalize those sanctions via IGOs has not changed.

Table 4.3 describes the top senders of sanctions by international organizations. The European Union (EU) and its predecessor, the European Economic

Table 4.3 Top Sanction Senders—International Organizations, 1945–2005

International Organization	Threats	% of Threats	Impositions	% of Impositions
European Union/EEC	155	44.8%	115	53.0%
United Nations	71	20.5%	41	18.9%
Organization of Arab Petroleum Exporting Countries	3	0.9%	9	4.1%
WTO	18	5.2%	8	3.7%
NATO	6	1.7%	8	3.7%
Arab League	24	6.9%	7	3.2%
IMF	2	0.6%	7	3.2%
Organization of American States	13	3.8%	4	1.8%
African Union/OAU	11	3.2%	4	1.8%
Intl Bank for Reconstruction & Development	2	0.6%	4	1.8%
IAEA	5	1.4%	3	1.4%
Commonwealth Secretariat	3	0.9%	3	1.4%
OECD	27	7.8%	2	0.9%
Organization of the Islamic Conference	1	0.3%	2	0.9%
OPEC	3	0.9%	0	0.0%
Non-Aligned Movement	2	0.6%	0	0.0%

DATA SOURCE: Morgan et al. (2014).

Community (EEC), have been the most active IGOs at both threatening and imposing sanctions. From 1945 to 2005, the EU/EEC accounted for more than half of all sanctions imposed by international organizations. The UN accounted for about 19% of all sanctions imposed by IGOs within this same period. The remaining IGOs largely fall into three groups: regional, global trade and finance, and security organizations. The African Union, the Organization of American States, and the Arab League, for example, are regional organizations that often use sanctions. Among global trade and finance organizations, both the World Trade Organization and the International Monetary Fund lead the imposition of sanctions; combined, they constitute roughly 7% of all sanctions imposed by IGOs. Finally, NATO stands out among security organizations, accounting for nearly 4% of all IGO-imposed sanctions during the post-World War II era.

BOX 4.1 Bosnian War

Case: Bosnian War
Date of Conflict Management: 1992–95
Disputing Parties: Bosnian Serbs, Muslims, Croats, and Serbia
Third Parties: United Nations, European Economic Community (EEC)/European Union, United Nations
Outcome: Success

The Bosnian War grew out of the broader breakup of Yugoslavia in 1991 and demonstrates how sanctions can push a warring side to negotiate and reach an agreement when effectively applied and enforced. Bosnia and Herzegovina is a multi-ethnic territory; Bosniaks comprise the largest portion of the population, but Serbs and Croats constitute significant minority populations. Following independence declarations by Slovenia and Croatia, Bosnia and Herzegovina held an independence referendum in March 1992. Bosniak and Bosnian-Croat support for independence was high, while Bosnian Serbs, most of whom boycotted the referendum, strongly opposed independence (Paris 2004).

The country moved inexorably toward war after the approval of the independence referendum. Once fighting began, a challenge to conflict management arose: Bosniaks refused to sign any agreement ceding territory that had been ethnically cleansed by Bosnian Serbs, and Bosnian Serbs saw few incentives to negotiate while they were succeeding on the battlefield (Paris 2004). These calculations eventually changed when the combined effects of economic sanctions, NATO air strikes, and Croatian and Bosniak military advances pressured the Bosnian Serbs to the bargaining table (Curran et al. 2004). In particular, the international community imposed a set of comprehensive sanctions on the Federal Republic of Yugoslavia (FYR) in May 1992. These included restrictions on trade, travel, financial transactions, and cultural exchanges with the FYR. Eventually, the sanctions expanded further to freezes on foreign assets held by the FYR elites. This focus on the FYR was deliberate. Serbia, the dominant of the two remaining constituent parts of the FYR, provided the core source of financial and military support for Bosnian Serb forces. As such, the sanctions sought to maximize pressure on the FYR to incentivize it to cut its support to the Bosnian Serbs. Eventually, however, the sanctions extended to Bosnian Serb-held territory within Bosnia itself.

Beyond the broad scope of the sanctions imposed, NATO and UN enforcement of the sanctions was unprecedented too. Beginning in 1992, NATO forces conducted interdiction efforts in the Adriatic Sea to prevent violations of the trade sanctions and arms embargo, while the UN established Sanctions Assistance Missions in the region to help monitor compliance with the sanctions resolutions (Andreas 2005). As a result, the sanctions inflicted significant economic harm on the FYR, with the Serbian economy contracting by 26% and 32% in 1992 and 1993 respectively (Andreas 2005).

Although the sanctions, as intended, produced considerable economic pressure on Serbia, they also carried unintended consequences. As with many other conflicts, outside actors instituted an arms embargo early in the Bosnian conflict (1991). The rationale for such embargoes is that disputants' ability to fight will diminish if their ability to acquire arms can be impeded. Yet this assumes that all parties will be equally affected by an arms embargo, which was not the case during the Bosnian War. Serb forces remained largely unaffected by the arms embargo, and Bosnian Serb forces—who already enjoyed a military advantage against Bosnian government forces—were able to rely on Serbian military support and arms left behind by the Yugoslav military (Andreas 2004). Moreover, because Bosnia is landlocked, making arms smuggling especially difficult, the embargo hit Bosnian government forces disproportionately hard, serving to enhance the military superiority of Bosnian Serb forces (Andreas 2004). Ironically, it required efforts to circumvent the arms embargo and channel arms to Bosniak forces to level the battlefield for Bosnian government forces and apply military pressure on Bosnian Serb forces (Sremac 1999).

Over time, NATO deepened its military involvement in the conflict (e.g., air strikes and attacks against Serbian air forces), which brought increasing military pressure to bear on Serbia and the Bosnian Serbs. This military intervention, coupled with the increasingly crippling economic effects of the sanctions imposed against the FYR and the Bosnian Serbs, pushed the Serbian side toward negotiations. Eventually, the economic and military pressure grew so great that the FYR turned on its Bosnian Serb allies, imposing sanctions on them for refusing to negotiate. This set in motion a chain of events that brought all of the parties to the bargaining table and ultimately yielded the Dayton Accords, which settled the conflict in December 1995. In the end, the Dayton agreement maintained Bosnia and Herzegovina as a sovereign state, but carved out significant levels of autonomy for the three major ethnic groups in the country. Highlighting the role of the sanctions in forcing this settlement, Rogers argues that "Without the sanctions it seems very unlikely that the Serb side would have considered the terms of the Dayton Accords, let alone accepted them" (1996: 425).

When and How Often are Sanctions Effective?

Given that many actors do not back down when sanctions are threatened or imposed, this raises a key question for sanctions as a policy tool: do they work? The success of sanctions can be evaluated by two criteria: (a) the degree to which they yield concessions from the target by imposing costs, and (b) the extent to which they force compliance with the sender's demands by closing off options for the target (Hovi et al. 2011). A trade embargo, for example, can succeed by imposing costs that hurt a government involved in a civil war and pressure it to enter into negotiations with a rebel group to end their conflict. By contrast, an arms embargo seeks to force warring sides to stop fighting by drying up their access to the tools of war-making, limiting their options on the battlefield.

The criteria by which to evaluate the success of sanctions may seem clear, but judging the effectiveness of sanctions is in practice decidedly more difficult, raising some important challenges for analysts. First, judging the effectiveness of a sanctions regime, as with other forms of conflict management, often requires the evaluation of a counterfactual: what would conditions look like if sanctions had *not* been used? Sanctions might be deemed at least partially successful, for example, if their imposition reduces the intensity or spread of violence, even if they do not end a conflict outright. Second, sanctions require time for their full effects to bite and pressure parties toward peace. This raises additional evaluation concerns. What, for example, is the appropriate time horizon for gauging the effectiveness of sanctions? Given the time required and the other conflict management activities likely to occur in the interim (e.g., negotiations; see Box 5.1), how might one disentangle the effects of sanctions on a conflict from the effects of other conflict management efforts? This is not easily done. An economic embargo may be used to pressure warring sides toward a mediated settlement. If mediation subsequently fails, it will be difficult to discern the extent to which the failure was a consequence of the conduct of the mediation effort, insufficient economic costs arising from sanctions, the intractability of the conflict itself, or some combination of all of these factors.

Finally, fairly exploring the effectiveness of sanctions also demands that we recognize how selection effects pervade the process by which sanctions are threatened and applied. In theory, when sanctions are first threatened, a target that fears the potential costs will back down before sanctions are even imposed (Drezner 2003). In a world of rational actors and perfect information—that is, where senders have full information about the commitment of targets, and the latter have full information about both the costs that they will experience from sanctions and the willingness of third parties to impose them—sanctions should only have to be threatened but never implemented. In short, senders will only threaten targets who will be responsive to the costs of sanctions, and these targets will adjust their behavior before the sender implements the sanctions (Lacy and Niou 2004). If true, then this logic suggests that the imposition of sanctions must result from *incomplete* information. With incomplete information, however, it becomes possible for senders to impose sanctions on highly resolved targets, those willing to bear the costs of sanctions without backing down. On the target side, incomplete information also creates a potential scenario where a target fails to respond to the threats of sanctions either because it (a) underestimates either the costs of the sanctions threatened or the willingness of the sender to implement them, or (b) expects that sanctions will be implemented regardless of how it responds (Hovi et al. 2011).

In practice, this logic complicates any assessment of the effectiveness of sanctions as a conflict management approach. If such an assessment rests solely on the effect of imposed sanctions, it will understate the true effectiveness rate. The most resolved targets (those not willing to change their behavior) disproportionately experience sanctions imposition. In other words, senders impose sanctions on targets less likely to change their behavior. Targets that do change their behavior do so when threatened with sanctions, but before the sender needs to impose them (Lacy and Niou 2004). Effectiveness therefore requires an examination of target behavior at both the threat and the imposition stages.

Nonetheless, there remains considerable disagreement about the overall success rate of sanctions as a policy tool. Hufbauer et al. (1990) supply perhaps the most positive outlook on the effectiveness of sanctions, suggesting that they are effective approximately 25% of the time. Estimates of the effectiveness of targeted sanctions are largely in line with this, being described as effective somewhere between 20% and 34% of the time (Wallensteen and Grusell 2012). Pape (1997) reaches a considerably more pessimistic conclusion: his estimated overall sanction success rate of 5% suggests that sanctions rarely provide punishments sufficient to force behavioral changes in targets—and that sanctions can often be circumvented. Similarly, Morgan and Schwebach (1997) conclude that sanctions have only a limited effect, even if the costs they impose upon the target exceed those associated with continuing the policy that the sender seeks to change.

One challenge in implementing successful sanctions concerns both the ability of targets to circumvent them as well as the tendency of sanctions to produce unintended effects that run counter to the goals of the sanction campaign. One factor that tends to reduce the effectiveness of sanctions is the tendency of firms from non-sanctioning countries to fill market gaps created by a sanctioning country (Lektzian and Biglaiser 2013). Even when sanctions are sufficiently costly to impact a target regime, they can still bring negative consequences for the goals of the sender. Sanctions can destabilize regimes, increasing the likelihood of leadership change by 28% while they are in place (Marinov 2005). To the extent that this leadership-instability effect encourages

transitions from autocracy to democracy, this is a form of success for sanction campaigns with a goal of pressuring for democratization (von Soest and
Wahman (2015). At the same time, however, this same political instability
typically brings with it more violence and a greater risk of regime repression
against the population—unintended consequences of sanctions (Peksen 2009).
In this sense, if the goal of sanctions is to encourage democracy, then even
when they are effective in achieving this goal they can still bring unintended
harm to the citizens of a target state. As a result, judging the effectiveness of
sanctions must reflect both the goals of the sanctions campaign (von Soest and
Wahman 2015) and the attendant costs, intended and unintended, that the
sanctions bring with them.

As Figure 4.2 shows, slightly more than 40% of all sanction threats result in
either complete or partial acquiescence to the sender's demands at the threat
stage. This overall concession rate, however, has varied considerably by decade
over the post-World War II period. Sanction threats during the 1945–54 and
1995–2004 periods showed the highest rates of complete acquiescence by
targets: 46% and 41% respectively. When partial compliance is included, the

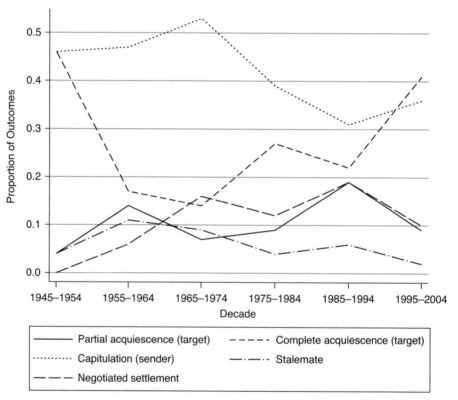

Figure 4.2 Sanction Threat Outcomes, 1945–2004
DATA SOURCE: Morgan et al. (2014).

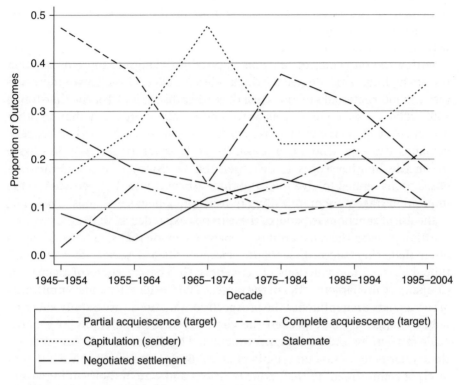

Figure 4.3 Sanction Imposition Outcomes, 1945–2004
DATA SOURCE: Morgan et al. (2014).

concession rate climbs to nearly 50% for both 1945–54 and 1995–2004. Other periods, however, reveal a substantially poorer target response to sanction threats. Both the 1955–64 and 1964–74 periods, for example, saw complete acquiescence rates drop substantially to 17% and 14% respectively. Sanction threats were least effective during the 1965–74 period, when nearly 54% of such threats resulted in the capitulation of the *sender* without imposing sanctions and without securing compliance from the target.

Once a sender imposes sanctions, the pattern of outcomes begins to shift. As Figure 4.3 shows, the most frequent outcome of sanction impositions during the 1945–54 and 1955–64 periods was complete acquiescence by the sanction targets. During 1945–54, 47% of sanction impositions resulted in complete acquiescence by the target. In the ensuing decades, the effect of imposed sanctions shifted considerably. For the 1975–84 and 1985–94 periods, the most common outcome of impositions was a negotiated settlement between the sender and the target. This shift in outcomes suggests that sanctions gave senders the most leverage early in the post-war era. Indeed, by 1995–2004, the outcomes of imposed sanctions indicate that they were becoming a less effective tool for pushing targets to yield or negotiate a settlement of the issues under dispute. Instead, the most common outcome of sanctions imposed from 1995 to 2004 was for the sender to capitulate without the target conceding.

Setting the outcomes of sanction impositions alongside those of sanction threats highlights the degree to which selection effects have grown more pervasive in international sanctions (see the earlier discussion). For the time frame 1995–2004, for example, targets were substantially more likely than in other decades to yield to sanction *threats* by giving in (at least partially) to the senders' demands. Once the sender *imposed* sanctions, however, targets were less likely to concede. In other words, those targets that were most sensitive to the costs of sanctions tended to give in at the threat stage. Those that persisted to the imposition stage were more willing to resist the sender's demands. Over time, as the use of sanctions expanded, these trends expanded as well.

Although even the most optimistic views conclude that sanctions fail more often than they succeed, scholars have identified a variety of conditions thought to facilitate sanctions' effectiveness. The characteristics of a sanctions campaign, the characteristics of the targets, and the identity and commitment of the senders each influence the prospects for sanctions successfully affecting policy change. With respect to the characteristics of sanctions in general, trade restrictions and bans on investment and lending tend to be less effective than other types of sanctions (Shin et al. 2016). Because targets have different levels of commitment to their issue positions and vary in their willingness to bear costs, sanctions that are designed to better fit these characteristics of the target are more likely to be successful. When sanctions are specifically tailored to most directly impact the base of support of a target, they are more likely to produce compliance with the demands of the sanction sender (Lektzian and Souva 2007). Sanctions that undermine the fighting capacity of warring sides, such as arms embargoes, tend to reduce the intensity of conflict but, paradoxically, also create short-run incentives for more fighting before the full effects of the sanctions are imposed (Hultman and Peksen 2017). Just as sanctions are more apt to prove effective the better they fit their target, so, too, are they more likely to fit the better they reflect the level of commitment of the sender. A key determinant of the success of a sanction effort is the balance between the costs incurrred by the sender and the costs imposed on the target. When sanctions maximize the costs imposed while minimizing the costs of their imposition, they are more likely to be effective because it is easier for senders to sustain the sanctions and more difficult for targets to resist their effects (Hufbauer et al. 1990; Morgan and Schwebach 1997).

The shift by the international community toward the use of targeted sanctions over comprehensive sanctions during the last two decades has made understanding the effectiveness of targeted sanctions all the more important. Despite the appeal of targeted sanctions, skeptics question both their effectiveness and the degree to which they actually reduce unintended harm upon the population of targeted states. For example, while recognizing the general effectiveness of financial sanctions, Drezner (2015) argues that other types of targeted sanctions tend to be unsuccessful because they do not impose sufficiently high costs on their targets. Even if targeted sanctions tend to be ineffective, however, some might argue that they are better than the alternatives available (i.e., comprehensive sanctions or military force) and better than doing nothing for those interested in ending an ongoing conflict. These assessments rely on the effect targeted sanctions have on the populations of targeted countries, and evidence increasingly calls into question whether these effects are benign. Biersteker et al. (2013), for example, find that targeted sanctions deepen authoritarianism (54% of cases) and increase corruption (70% of cases) in targeted states. Moreover, the research links targeted sanctions to increased humanitarian dangers as well (Drezner 2015; Carneiro and Apolinario 2016; Wallensteen and Grusell 2012). Some of this work suggests that targeted sanctions can worsen humanitarian conditions by undermining the capacity of governments, thereby encouraging the outbreak of violent domestic challenges that would otherwise be unlikely to occur (Drezner 2015). In response to this combination of government weakness and the emergence of domestic threats, regimes facing targeted sanctions become more likely to repress their populations, harming civilians in the process. Carneiro and Apolinario (2016), for example, find evidence consistent with this point; respect for physical integrity rights (i.e., protections against torture or killing) in states subject to targeted sanctions are 75% more likely to worsen than in non-targeted states. The questions raised about both the effectiveness and unintended consequences of targeted sanctions suggest that they are not an easy solution for all ongoing conflicts. Those seeking to apply pressure to stop a conflict must therefore weigh their use carefully.

Exploring the effectiveness of different forms of sanctions using the TIES v4.0 sanction data set (Morgan et al. 2014) underscores the distinctions in their effectiveness, at both the threat and the imposition stages. At the threat stage, asset freezes and threats to suspend aid show the greatest success rates for senders. Threats to freeze assets resulted in either the partial or full capitulation of the target at the threat stage. Similarly, targets capitulated in nearly 58% of cases in which threats to aid were made. Threats to impose a full embargo, by contrast, show a much poorer track record of targets giving in at the threat stage, only resulting in a capitulation in less than a third of cases. Threats of a full embargo, however, had the highest rate of negotiated settlements of all sanction types. Blockade threats performed the most poorly, with no threats resulting in acquiescence by the target and 40% of cases resulting in the capitulation by the sender of the sanction threat. A broad look at the performance of sanction threats suggests that those threats where the sender (a) enjoys the most leverage (i.e., has the greatest ability to impose costs) over the target and (b) faces the fewest costs if sanctions are imposed are most likely to see the target give in at the threat stage, highlighting the extent to which sanction threats with the highest credibility of implementation are the most likely to bring target compliance. Asset freezes and threats to suspend aid meet both of these criteria. By contrast, those threats that bring the highest costs and potential risks for the sanction sender, such as the threat of a blockade, are less likely to see concessions by the target. In short, the costs and risks of these threats serve to weaken expectations that the sanctions will ultimately be imposed if the target does not give in. As described above, however, these sanctions are also the most likely to actually be implemented, underscoring the way that incomplete information between targets and senders of sanctions shapes their actions.

The performance of different types of sanctions changes at the imposition stage. Full embargoes, for example, which had only limited effectiveness at the threat stage, are much more effective at the imposition stage, with more than half of all imposed full embargoes resulting in partial or full acquiescence by the target. Partial embargoes and export restrictions, which are even more finely targeted sanctions, perform even better, succeeding 67% and 50% of the time respectively. Sanctions where foreign aid cuts are actually imposed have among the poorest track records of success at the imposition stage, contrary to their solid performance at the threat stage. This highlights the selection effects that are present among sanctions. Because threats to cut aid are highly credible given their low cost to the sender, those targets that are most sensitive to the costs of aid cuts should back down at the threat stage. This, however, leaves only the most resolved targets at the imposition stage for aid cuts, actors that are substantially less likely to bow to the costs because they have already factored these into their decision to resist the sender's demands at the threat stage.

Just as military intervention can increase the effectiveness of sanctions by signaling the commitment of third parties to enforcing them, so too can the choice of who participates in the sanctions. Sanction targets may question the commitment of a sender, hoping that they can wait out the effects of the sanctions until the sender wavers and removes them. This, however, becomes more difficult for targets when sanctions are applied multilaterally. If organized by a broad collection of states—and particularly when institutionalized through an international organization—sanctions convey a deeper level of sender commitment, thereby increasing their effectiveness (Lektzian and Regan 2016). This yields two interrelated benefits. First, multilateral sanctions raise the costs imposed on a target: it can be costly to a target for one state to impose trade restrictions or implement an arms embargo against it, but these costs mount as additional states join in, reducing the availability of replacement suppliers of the sanctioned products. Second, the institutionalization of sanctions through an international organization helps solve commitment problems between senders. States create international organizations to increase transparency, foster reciprocity, and encourage the development of norms of behavior, each of which can improve the ability of sending states to cooperate and remain compliant with a sanctions regime (Drezner 2000). Both characteristics increase the ability of outside powers to impose costs on a target, which then raises the likelihood that the target will comply with the senders' demands.

The characteristics of targets also influence the likelihood that sanctions will be effective. Sanctions targeting states with high levels of regime opposition are more likely to be effective (Weiss 1999). To the extent that this opposition is mobilized to pressure the government, and the capacity of the regime to respond to domestic challenges is sapped by economic sanctions, the latter are more likely to produce policy change. More narrowly, however, sanctions directed at non-democracies are less likely to succeed because these regimes have the greatest capacity both to ignore any domestic political pressure produced by the sanctions and to shift the accompanying costs onto regime opponents (see the earlier discussion; Lektzian and Souva 2007).

When sanctions are directed at autocracies, the type of autocracy matters for the effectiveness of sanctions. Sanctions tend to have different effects on personalist authoritarian governments, such as North Korea's, which are marked by one-person rule and a hereditary transfer of power, than on non-personalist regimes, such as China, which tend to be based on military or party control of the government (see Geddes 1999 for a discussion of these regimes). Non-personalistic autocratic regimes are particularly resilient to sanctions because, in addition to their ability to ignore domestic political pressure, they also enjoy a greater capacity to increase repression and domestic resource extraction to compensate for the effects of sanctions (Krasner and Weinstein 2014). In general, non-personalist autocracies, because of their tendency to be military- or party-based, enjoy the combination of a greater coercive capacity that can be employed in the face of any potential rise in domestic pressure occurring from sanctions, and a tendency to be less reliant than personalist autocracies upon resources such as raw materials and foreign aid that are ready targets for sanctions (Krasner and Weinstein 2014).

The vulnerability of a target to specific types of economic pressure is also an important determinant of sanctions' effectiveness. For example, how dependent a sanctions target is on a single export product, as well as the extent to which it depends upon (a given) import(s), significantly alter the power of sanctions (Weiss 1999). During civil wars, governments are therefore typically more vulnerable to trade embargoes than are rebels. Nevertheless, some forms of trade sanctions prove highly effective at pressuring rebel groups. In civil conflicts like those in Angola and the Democratic Republic of the Congo, sanctions that stem the flow of diamonds have limited an important source of financial support to insurgents. More broadly, rebels often prove vulnerable to arms embargoes, which directly limit their capacity to sustain violence against the government.

Beyond the specific features of sanctions themselves and the characteristics of the parties they are directed against, the extent to which sanctions are integrated into other third-party conflict management approaches plays an important role in their effectiveness (see Chapter 9 for discussion of the integration of conflict management efforts). Letzkian and Regan (2016), for example, argue that sanctions are unlikely to reduce the duration of civil wars by themselves. Instead, they argue that sanctions help transition civil wars toward peace when coupled with military intervention. In this sense, these two conflict management approaches interact; military intervention enforces imposed sanctions and signals the sender's commitment to sustaining them over the long term until peace is established. Predicting the effectiveness of sanctions therefore requires a more holistic evaluation of their characteristics, how they are applied, and the conditions under which they are implemented.

Box 4.2 Syrian Civil War

Case: Syrian Civil War
Date of Conflict Management: 2011–present
Disputing Parties: Syrian government, Russia, Iran, Saudi Arabia, Turkey, ISIS, and various Syrian rebel groups
Third Parties: United Nations, European Union, Arab League, United States
Outcome: Failure

The Syrian civil war began in March 2011, when effects of the Arab Spring led to protests in the Syrian city of Daraa. As these protests expanded across Syria, the regime of President Bashar al-Assad sought to crush the unrest militarily. The protests grew increasingly violent as a result, leading to the outbreak of a full-fledged civil war.

The Syrian civil war has been exceptionally bloody, with estimates of at least 511,000 people killed as of 2018 (Specia 2018). Similar to the Bosnian context discussed earlier, third parties established a broad portfolio of sanctions intended to quell the violence and encourage negotiation: the UN, EU, and US imposed trade bans, oil embargoes, asset freezes, and travel restrictions. Nevertheless, unlike the Bosnian sanctions, the Syrian sanctions have failed to change the status quo demonstrably or force the Syrian government to either end violence against civilians or reach a settlement with the insurgents.

The failure of sanctions against Syria stems from three interrelated factors, each of which undermines the senders' leverage against the Syrian government. First, the sanctions lack broad compliance, providing the Syrian government with a variety of ways to circumvent them and acquire the resources needed to maintain both the regime and the war effort. Both Russia and Iran, for example, have provided significant economic support to the Assad regime. In addition, Syria's long borders with both Iraq and Lebanon, who voted against Arab League sanctions, favor smuggling, which undercuts the effectiveness of sanctions further (Muir 2011). Second, the level of third-party commitment to the sanctions is substantially lower than it was in the Bosnian case. The Syrian sanctions have yielded nothing analogous to the NATO interdiction effort or the UN Sanctions Assistance Missions that occurred in Bosnia. Instead, even states that had initially assisted in enforcing sanctions against the Syrian regime, such as Jordan, sought to re-open cross-border trade ties when the tide of the conflict swung toward the Assad regime (Lund 2017). Finally, anti-regime military intervention has also been very limited. Following the Assad government's chemical weapon attacks against Syrian civilians, the US conducted a limited cruise missile strike against a Syrian airfield in April 2017 and a further small, coordinated air strike with British and French forces in April 2018. These actions did nothing to tip the military balance on the ground or increase US resolve for intervening (Chamberlain 2017).

These three factors—the Assad regime's ability to circumvent the sanctions, the difficulty of enforcing them, and the failure of the international community to back them up militarily—each undermined the effectiveness of the sanctions. Rather than maximizing pressure against the Assad government and signaling the resolve of international actors to press for an agreement or to foster regime change, the sanctions instead created the appearance of an international community doing something about the conflict without actually accomplishing anything substantial.

Conclusion

This chapter has examined the use of sanctions as a conflict management strategy in the international system. As part of our overview of sanctions, we examined the logic behind their use, how they are applied, and the influences on their effectiveness:

- Sanctions are a coercive policy tool by which an actor seeks to pressure another actor to comply with a demand by imposing economic costs. Import restrictions, asset freezes, embargoes, and travel restrictions are commonly employed forms of sanctions.
- Sanctions are used by international actors both as a conflict management tool and as a policy instrument in pursuit of more self-interested goals. One

of the chief benefits of sanctions is that they often entail fewer costs for the actors using them than do other types of conflict management strategies.

- There are important differences between comprehensive sanctions and targeted (or "smart") sanctions. Comprehensive sanctions have historically been the most commonly used form of sanctions and are aimed at broad segments of a target state's population. Targeted sanctions have increased in use over the last two decades and focus their costs on the political elite of a target.

- Proponents of targeted sanctions argue that, relative to comprehensive sanctions, they minimize the costs imposed by sanctions on innocent civilians while maximizing the pressure applied to policymakers, thereby increasing their effectiveness.

- Overall, the success rate of sanctions has historically been poor, with even the most positive estimates of their effectiveness arguing that they fail more often than they succeed. The presence of selection effects in the decision to employ sanctions and the response of targets to threats of sanctions makes evaluating their success rate more difficult.

5

Negotiations

Despite their shared communist ideologies, ongoing territorial disputes soured relations between China and the Soviet Union. These disputes, along the Sino-Soviet frontier, boiled over into military clashes on several occasions after World War II. In 1969, for example, they became the flashpoint for the outbreak of a border conflict that lasted six months, produced hundreds of casualties, and failed to resolve the dispute definitively. The lack of a clearly delineated border therefore created a persistent, latent potential for renewed conflict, a possibility that neither side saw as desirable. As a result, when their relations warmed sufficiently, China and the Soviet Union began negotiations in 1987 to find a permanent settlement to their border dispute. After several years of talks, these negotiations produced the 1991 Sino-Soviet Border Agreement, a document that resolved a broad set (but not all) of the border disagreements between the two countries.

The previous chapters detailed conflict management approaches that use coercion to alter disputants' cost–benefit calculations, thereby encouraging them to refrain from undesirable behavior or stop fighting if engaged in an ongoing war. In this chapter, we shift our attention from such conflict management approaches toward negotiation, a self-help approach in which disputants attempt to identify mutually acceptable outcomes to settle the issues under dispute.

Negotiation refers to diplomatic interactions and direct talks between actors who disagree over one or more issues (that is, disputants). Unlike mediation, the subject of the next chapter, negotiations only involve the primary parties; third-party actors not directly involved in the conflict remain out of these talks. We normally think of negotiation as a process involving two actors sitting face to face across a table in a formal setting after violence has ended. Yet negotiation may involve more than two disputants (e.g., some or all disputants in a multi-actor conflict), may be conducted informally (e.g., through ambassadors or representatives as part of repeated discussions), and can occur at all phases of a conflict—before the outbreak of violence, as a mechanism to end violence, or after the end of fighting to set the terms for conflict management in the long run. The Lomé Peace Accord between the government of Sierra Leone and the rebel Revolutionary United Front, for example, occurred in the midst of the conflict, seeking to end the fighting and establish the terms of settlement between the two sides. In contrast, the 2014–17 Cyprus reunification talks unfolded many years after the end of active fighting.

Negotiations involve a three-stage process, incorporating the decisions to negotiate, to offer concessions, and to implement any agreement reached (Walter 2002). In the sections that follow, we detail the underlying rationale for negotiation as a conflict management tool, as well as when disputants are likely to choose to use it.

Logic of Negotiation

For parties in a dispute over an issue or range of issues, negotiation is best thought of as part of a broader bargaining process in which disputants exchange proposals and counter-proposals in an effort to resolve the issues in contention among them. Disputants also put pressure on one another, seeking to constrain each other's options and extract concessions. As this bargaining process plays out, parties gain information about one another, learning about the salience of the issues at hand to the other side, their commitment to their bargaining position, and the capabilities they are able to marshal in support of that position (Fearon 1995). In this respect, the prospect of violence is an inherent part of the negotiating process between disputing sides (Sisk 2008). To the extent that the parties either cannot or will not rely on diplomacy to settle the issues in dispute, they might instead employ violence as a tool to pressure the other side into accepting a settlement (Slantchev 2003). The core assumption of this argument is that parties can initially misunderstand the costs and benefits of war, with each side believing that they can gain a better result through conflict than through a negotiated settlement. This inability of parties to correctly estimate the costs and benefits of conflict is a consequence of the uncertainty that each side has about the military capabilities and commitment of the other side, with each side having an incentive to portray itself as both strong and highly committed to its demands as a means of improving its bargaining position.

During a war, violence provides a signaling process by which, as the two sides learn from their battles with one another, they ultimately reach a settlement as their expectations about the costs of fighting and the eventual outcome of the conflict converge (Maoz and Siverson 2008). Outcomes on the battlefield function to provide information to the belligerents about each other's relative strength and prospects for victory (Stanley and Sawyer 2009). Beyond its signaling function, violence also brings a concrete benefit by providing a means for the warring sides to seek an improvement in their own bargaining position while weakening the position of their adversary. During the Mozambique civil war, the Mozambican National Resistance

(RENAMO) employed precisely this type of strategy, using violence to weaken the government in the hopes of causing the regime to collapse or negotiate (Quinn 2007).

Civil conflicts pose a unique bargaining challenge that has important implications for negotiations. Similar to interstate conflicts, parties in civil conflicts are uncertain about each other's capabilities and commitment (Fearon 1995). This informational challenge is especially acute for governments, who typically have great uncertainty about whether a rebel group they are facing is weak or strong (on intra-group division, see Cunningham 2011). Moreover, because governments fear legitimizing rebels and emboldening other domestic groups with grievances to take up arms, regimes tend to resist negotiating with rebels. All else being equal, governments therefore prefer only to negotiate with those rebel groups capable of inflicting unacceptably high costs, but informational problems make it difficult for them to discern weak from strong rebel groups, especially early in a conflict (Walter 2009).

As a consequence, rebels use violence in order to signal their military capacity and their commitment to the cause (Fearon 2004). Biafra separatists in Nigeria, for example, hoped that their ability to mount an insurgent challenge to the government would attract attention and draw international pressure that would force the Nigerian government to negotiate with them (Rubenzer 2007). That this strategy was unsuccessful highlights the degree to which governments tend to resist talks with rebels. Nevertheless, civil war fighting brings instrumental benefits for governments by allowing them to both deter other groups from taking up arms and demonstrate to rebels that the costs of fighting will be unacceptably high for them. These characteristics of civil wars give rise to an essential problem for negotiated efforts to end them: whereas rebels tend to use violence to pressure the government to the negotiating table, governments see violence as a means to force rebels to surrender (Zartman 1995).

Although negotiation and violence are both bargaining tools used to resolve conflicts, negotiation brings with it several distinct advantages as a conflict resolution mechanism. First, when it is successful, negotiation is a more efficient conflict resolution tool. Both negotiation and violence provide vehicles by which contending sides can exchange information that can ultimately settle a dispute, but negotiation substantially reduces the costs of this exchange. Successful negotiations avoid the death and destruction that violence uses to communicate salience, convey commitment, and exert leverage.

Second, effective negotiations maximize long-term benefits while reducing negative externalities in the disputants' relationship. Conflict may allow one side to impose settlement terms upon another, but in doing so it typically has long-term negative consequences for the disputants' relationship. War often embitters conflicting parties, and this deepening level of hostility and mistrust tends to freeze communication linkages, making peaceful resolution of other disputed issues more difficult. Successful negotiations over a subset of disputed issues, by contrast, by helping to build trust and reduce hostility, can create a diplomatic momentum that brings positive spillover effects that improve the prospects for negotiated settlements over other disputed issues.

Third, by avoiding the anger and pain that conflict produces, successful negotiations also frame the future relationship between contending sides. War requires parties to mobilize both supporters and resources for the fight. As a result, parties tend to demonize one another, both in order to marginalize their opponents politically and to strengthen support for their war effort (Spector 2003). Demonizing propaganda in Rwanda, especially through radio broadcasts, played a significant role in mobilizing violence by Hutus against Tutsis during the conflict. Such demonization has long-term consequences, coloring the way in which disputants see one another and framing the way in which they evaluate future interactions. This, in turn, can short-circuit future efforts at peaceful conflict resolution and increase the likelihood of future conflict, along with the attendant costs.

Despite their advantages, negotiations also carry some characteristics that can complicate their effectiveness. The first is that they suffer "first-mover" problems (i.e., disincentives for one side to advocate negotiations), particularly among disputants who have already resorted to violence. Once fighting begins, even if the parties are willing to negotiate and find a settlement, each side may fear that showing such willingness may signal weakness to the other side. This creates a situation in which neither side will offer the first olive branch necessary for talks. A prior history of dialogue and successful negotiations between disputants can reduce this obstacle, as can the assistance of a third party willing to initiate talks and encourage disputants to the table (i.e., mediation, the subject of Chapter 6).

Just as forces between disputing groups limit their amenability toward negotiation, so too do forces within each group. While disputants fear appearing weak to their opponents, political leaders within the state also fear appearing weak to their constituents (Kaplow 2016). These constituents may view negotiating with an adversary, particularly one with whom a long, painful conflict has been fought, as a reward to the enemy or, even worse, as treason by the political leader offering talks. Such domestic opposition will likely be most pronounced in the longest and most deadly conflicts—that is, those in which demonization of the opponent has become entrenched. Enemy images can therefore not only undermine future relations between conflicting parties but also reduce the likelihood of negotiations in the near term. As a consequence of these political costs, leaders whose supporters potentially oppose negotiations may eschew them altogether, even when the costs of continued conflict are otherwise unacceptably high and the prospects for victory low. The reaction to the Northern Ireland peace process illustrates how internal opposition can alter conflict management. During the Good Friday talks, hardliners on both the Republican and Unionist sides not only opposed the talks, but also formed splinter groups and committed violent acts to undermine the peace process. The negotiations were therefore begun in secret—to gain significant ground and build momentum before the hardliners learned of their progress (Pruitt 2008).

Even if disputants overcome their fears of appearing weak to both their opponents and their supporters, negotiations still require that they overcome their fear that the opponent will cheat on any agreement reached. A key challenge for successful negotiations is not only that disputants will be willing to make sufficient concessions to achieve an agreement, but also that they will live by the terms of that agreement afterward; that is, there must be the credible commitment described in Chapter 2 before disputants can accept an agreement. An advantage of settlements achieved through war is that the terms imposed by the victor are largely self-policing; the victor can enforce these terms by eliminating the ability of its opponent to continue to fight and by retaining its own ability to employ further violence to reinforce the terms. Negotiations, by themselves, lack such a self-policing mechanism, raising the fear among disputants that the other side will ultimately renege on the terms of the settlement. A rebel group in a civil war, for example, may fear that a negotiated settlement that requires it to disarm and demobilize its forces may place its people in a catastrophic position if the government cheats on the agreement and attacks the rebels once disarmed (Walter 2002). These fears reduce the likelihood not only that negotiations will succeed, but also that they will occur in the first place (Fearon 1998). Consistent with this logic, Kirschner (2010) finds that civil wars last longer when disputants fear that the other side will cheat on a potential agreement's terms. By way of example, Kirschner points to the Timorese skepticism of the credibility of Indonesian government commitments to offer autonomy as a factor encouraging the continuation of the Timorese fight for independence. If it is true that disputants will be punished for cooperating, why agree to negotiate in the first place?

Negotiators can overcome credible-commitment problems by including fear-reducing or cost-increasing provisions in agreements. Such provisions might include introducing peacekeepers to monitor compliance or ensure the protection of disarmed groups; denying access to arms imports to make a return to conflict more difficult; or creating power-sharing arrangements so that (former) disputants have joint control over military and security forces. Each of these illustrative provisions makes cheating on an agreement's terms more difficult; in so doing, they lower the likelihood that disputants will take advantage of one another, thereby reassuring them and opening the space for a settlement to emerge (Mattes and Savun 2009). However, these provisions also complicate negotiations, creating chains of preconditions. A government, for example, might refuse to negotiate with a rebel group until the latter disarms; meanwhile, the rebel group refuses to disarm without negotiations that will secure its members' safety. These complexities mean that the provisions outlined here will be needed most in conflicts where disputants will be least willing to risk working toward them. The 2006 Comprehensive Peace Agreement that ended the civil war in Nepal is illustrative of the types of fear-reducing provisions that can be included in a power-sharing agreement to reduce worries about one warring party being exploited by the other. The agreement gave the Communist Party of Nepal (CPN-M), the key rebel group, important cabinet positions, which allowed them a say in the main issues over which the conflict was fought and positioned the CPN-M well for subsequent elections (Ottman and Vüllers 2015).

Context for Negotiation

Conflict characteristics carry strong implications for both the likelihood that negotiation will take place as well as the prospects for its success. Different types of conflicts bring different challenges for negotiations. For example, because they typically involve deeply salient issues among the warring sides, civil conflicts tend to be more resistant to diplomatic efforts to settle them than interstate disputes. During the post-World War II period, only about one-third of civil wars have been successfully negotiated (Bapat 2005). Whereas half of all interstate conflicts are settled through negotiation, two-thirds of intrastate conflicts end with either the destruction or capitulation of one side (Zartman 1995). This difference in negotiation amenability points toward some important distinctions between civil and interstate conflicts. Although both types can produce intense human suffering, large-scale destruction, and entrenched animosity between the two sides, civil war negotiations face the added challenge of legitimacy and more acute commitment problems. Civil conflicts are also more likely to involve a greater number of disputants, thereby raising the prospect that one or more them will seek to derail the peace process (see, e.g., the ongoing conflict in Syria).

   Even in the most severe interstate conflicts, the warring states typically recognize each other's legitimacy as valid political representatives of their country. Iran and Iraq, for example, fought a long, deadly conflict during the 1980s that killed hundreds of thousands on both sides, involved the use of chemical weapons by both countries, and reflected profound ideological differences between the two governments. Nonetheless, neither government questioned the rights of its counterpart as the legitimate representative of that country. This recognition of legitimacy is often absent in civil conflicts. Inherent in the concept of state sovereignty is that governments have exclusive authority over their territory and the people living there, and enjoy a monopoly on the legitimate use of force within that territory. Because rebels represent a direct challenge to the sovereignty of a state, governments threatened by a rebel challenge resist taking actions that they see as likely to impart legitimacy upon the rebels. This makes governments particularly hesitant to negotiate because, from their perspective, negotiations both convey legitimacy to the rebels and risk signaling the government's weakness (Greig and Regan 2008; Melin and Svensson 2009).

Beyond the type of conflict, the issues in contention also play an important role in shaping the occurrence and outcome of negotiations. The salience of the issues influences both the willingness of disputants to negotiate as well as their amenability to making the concessions necessary to produce a settlement. When parties care deeply about an issue, offering concessions can be seen as too costly. These costs might mirror the material value of a disputed issue, but they can also reflect the political costs associated with making concessions (see the discussion of domestic costs above). Territorial issues, for example, often carry important symbolic value. This places powerful domestic political constraints on a state's leaders, making negotiation and compromise over these issues more difficult. Consequently, interstate rivalries that are rooted in disputed territorial claims tend to be more long-lived (Dreyer 2012). The South China Sea disputes over the Spratly and Paracel Islands, for example, involve both a significant, tangible value connected to the natural resource wealth surrounding them, but also strong symbolic value. The latter is especially strong for China and Vietnam, both of whom invest important elements of national identity in control of the islands, complicating the political efforts to settle the issues through negotiation. China, for example, sees the Spratly Islands as an ancient part of Chinese territory, and views challenges to its control over them through the lens of what it sees as a history of both regional and Western imperialism against China (Jie 1994).

Even though the salience of territorial issues can make them resistant to negotiations generally, this resistance decreases as disputants view the issues as more divisible. The level of divisibility—that is, the ease with which the disputed good can be divided among the parties in a settlement—carries important implications for negotiations. Highly divisible issues permit disputants to distribute the disputed good in more ways. A dispute between two parties over the distribution of $100, for example, might be settled via any of a large number of potential divisions of the money between the contending sides. So long as the parties can identify a division that is mutually agreeable, a negotiated settlement is possible. In contrast, issues with low levels of divisibility are ones where either (a) the good in question can only be divided in a very small number of ways (e.g., a dispute involving $100, where the disputants only have currency in denominations of $50 or $20), or (b) the issue at stake is one in which the value of the disputed good is effectively more than the sum total of its parts, thereby preventing a negotiated agreement that distributes shares between the two sides (e.g., the Preah Vihear Temple, previously disputed by Cambodia and Thailand).

The divisibility of a disputed issue is, in many respects, a function of the disputants' perceptions. Territory can have an intrinsic value to disputants, which can be divisible; yet it can also have symbolic or strategic value, which is less readily divisible (Toft 2014). In November 2016, Belgium and the Netherlands successfully negotiated a territorial dispute along the River Meuse, with each side seeing the need to overcome the uncertainty created by the territorial dispute as more important than the preservation of any symbolic value of the territory itself. By contrast, the status of Jerusalem—because of its deep religious and symbolic value to both the Jewish and Muslim peoples—is seen by some on each side as a wholly indivisible, winner-take-all territorial issue, with control of the entirety of the city being the only satisfactory outcome. Similarly, possession of the Golan Heights between Israel and Syria, while carrying little intrinsic or symbolic value, has enormous strategic value to Israel. Holding this land prevents Syria from being able to shell Israel from there, making it difficult for Israel to conceive of an acceptable division that meets its security needs. In contrast, territory disputed for its natural resource wealth can be more readily divided between the contending sides (e.g., oil reserves or water, which can be distributed between disputants).

The presence of divisible issues does not necessarily mean that negotiations over them will occur, or that, if they do, the talks will produce agreement. Disputed territories with significant power resources (e.g., oil) that carry major consequences for the future balance of power between disputants can make it difficult for them to commit to agreements to divide those resources (Rider and Owsiak 2015). Despite these commitment problems, the issues under dispute, and the way in which disputants perceive and value them, constitute an important part of the context that shapes the potential for negotiation.

Examining militarized interstate disputes (MIDs; see Palmer et al. 2015) reveals the different frequencies with which disputants negotiated settlements in territorial disputes as opposed to those over other issues. MIDs are "united historical cases of conflict in which the threat, display or use of military force short of war by one member state is explicitly directed towards the government, official representatives, official forces, property, or territory of another state" (Jones et al. 1996: 163). As Figure 5.1 shows, during the 1816–2010 period just over 34% of all MIDs ended with a negotiated settlement (note that the MID data includes both settlements produced by negotiations and mediation in its operationalization of negotiated settlements). The MIDs with territorial issues at stake, however, showed a higher propensity toward negotiated settlement, with nearly 47% ending with such a settlement. This pattern holds even for the most intense MIDs. For MIDs that involved displays of military force, uses of military force, or war, slightly less than 34% of the non-territorial MIDs ended in a negotiated settlement, while nearly 46% of the territory-based MIDs did so. Thus, even among the toughest cases—that is, those in which military force is used or war occurs—nearly 45% of territorial disputes end through negotiations; in contrast, only about one-third of non-territorial disputes end with a negotiated settlement (see also Ghosn 2010). The 2000 maritime dispute between Honduras and Nicaragua is an example of the way in which negotiations can be effective in dialing down tensions among parties, even after they have escalated to the use of force against one another. In February 2000, Nicaraguan and Honduran forces exchanged fire on several occasions over their disputed maritime boundary in the Gulf of Fonseca, with the seizure of fishing vessels in the region by security forces deepening tensions between the two sides. Ultimately, however, they backed away from further escalation and reached a negotiated settlement over their maritime boundary in May 2000 (see the MID case narratives described by Palmer et al. 2015).

The status of the relationship between parties and their past history together are also important components of the negotiating context. Disputants learn from their past conflict management efforts and use this to inform their approach to managing current issues (Wiegand and Powell 2011). A history of successful negotiations is likely to encourage the subsequent use of negotiation when similar issues arise in the future. This reinforcing effect seems particularly likely in cases where successful negotiations have been an ongoing part of the relationship between disputants. As an illustration, rival states with a history of negotiations and cooperative relations more

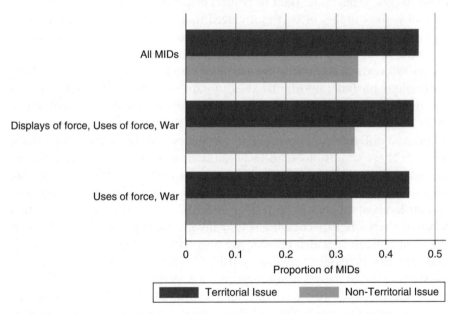

Figure 5.1 Proportion of Militarized Interstate Disputes Ending in Negotiated Settlement, 1816–2010
DATA SOURCE: Palmer et al. (2015).

often choose negotiation over violence to address their territorial disputes, and these negotiations tend to be more successful (Brochmann and Hensel 2011). The long history of negotiated settlements between the US and Canada is a reflection of this reinforcing effect. Importantly, once neighboring states reach a settlement over border issues, for example, they are less likely to engage in militarized disputes over *other* issues as well, making their overall relations more peaceful (Owsiak 2012).

The internal political context within disputing groups sets the foundation for negotiations as well. Because long-running conflict tends both to deepen the hostility between parties and to harden their negotiating positions, the political strength of the leadership within conflicting sides carries important repercussions for negotiations. Leaders with low levels of constituent support are unlikely to have the political strength to push for negotiations over contentious issues, and even if they do, their opponent is less likely to interpret these overtures as credible. From the opponent's perspective, the political weakness of the other side's leader raises doubts about that leader's ability to deliver on any agreement that the talks might produce, causing it to question whether negotiations are worthwhile in the first place. In this respect, the presence of a leader with sufficient political authority to both negotiate *and* deliver on an agreement is an important prerequisite for negotiations. Chiozza and Choi (2003), for example, find that leaders with long tenures in office—that is, those most likely to have the support base to draw on for peace efforts—are more likely to seek to negotiate their territorial disputes.

Finally, the number of parties involved in a dispute constitutes an important part of the context that influences negotiations. In some contexts, the presence of multiple parties can theoretically facilitate negotiated agreements by creating the ability for parties to trade off across issues—offering concessions on less important issues to gain on more important ones. For this to occur, though, there must be multiple issues at stake (or a willingness by at least some of the parties to offer side payments to encourage agreement), and differences in how salient the parties find the various issues under dispute. These conditions tend to be difficult to meet in the interstate and intrastate disputes most at risk of leading to violent conflict. Within such disputes, the contending sides often contest a narrower range of issues with similar levels of salience to both sides, making issue trade-offs harder to find. Scholars therefore expect conflicts that involve multiple warring sides to be the most difficult in which to achieve a negotiated settlement; as the number of disputants increases, it becomes harder to locate agreement terms that are satisfactory for all parties (Cunningham 2006; Walter 2009).

The specter of additional parties can also produce this effect. Governments will negotiate less often with rebels seeking independence as the number of other potential secessionist groups in the country increases, since they fear setting a precedent (Walter 2006). Moreover, opportunities for spoiling, both during negotiations and beyond, also increase as more parties join the dispute. The potential for spoiling behavior in civil conflicts is exacerbated by the fact that many groups who challenge a government are less cohesive than they initially appear. As Pearlman and Cunningham (2012) note, even among ethnic groups—that is, groups whose members would appear to have the strongest ties to one another—there is often significant disagreement about organizational structure and what strategy to pursue, which facilitates the emergence of splinter groups. As this intra-group division increases, so too does the complexity of negotiations, for they increase the commitment and informational problems between governments and rebels that negotiations must overcome (Cunningham 2013). Even when governments do overcome such problems and successfully offer concessions, this can, ironically, encourage the most extremist elements within an insurgent group to become more violent (see, e.g., the behavior of the Irish Republican Army at the start of the peace process in the 1990s; see also Bueno de Mesquita 2005).

When and Why Do Parties Come to the Negotiating Table?

If both negotiation and violence are mechanisms by which actors bargain with one another to settle their disputed issues, what conditions encourage parties to shift from violence to negotiation? The key factor is the disputants' mutual recognition that (a) the costs of conflict are unacceptably high, and (b) the probability that violence will produce a favorable alternative to the status quo is low. Once this mutually hurting stalemate emerges, then in order for parties to decide to negotiate—the first stage in Walter's (2002) three-stage negotiation process—actors must recognize that negotiations offer them a better path to achieve what they want. The shift required for these multiple recognitions is not an easy one to make. As discussed above, violence tends to entrench itself, hardening the bargaining positions of the contending sides, freezing communications between them, encouraging their hostile images of one another, and deepening the level of mutual mistrust. Each of these conditions inhibits the disputants' ability and willingness to get to the negotiating table, a challenge that is further exacerbated by their fears of appearing weak to one another or to their respective constituents.

The emergence of a mutually hurting stalemate facilitates an environment in which disputants become willing to overcome their fears of appearing weak and move toward negotiations in order to avoid continuing to pay the high costs of conflict. Although such a stalemate can provide a powerful motivating force for peace efforts, its emergence is insufficient to get negotiations off the ground. Instead, as noted above, conflicting parties must also perceive that negotiations provide a potential path toward a settlement of the contested issues, a "way out" from the costs and pain produced by the conflict

(Zartman 2000). The combination of the emergence of a mutually hurting stalemate and the perception that a way out exists creates an environment in which a conflict is "ripe" for negotiation or other peaceful resolution. In this sense, a disputant's willingness to negotiate or settle a conflict is shaped by how it evaluates the prospects for victory and what it expects achieving that victory will cost; as this evaluation grows more unfavorable, the utility of negotiation and settlement increases (Mason et al. 1999; Regan 2002). During the first Chadian civil war, for example, after nearly fifteen years of bloody fighting, both the government and the FROLINAT rebels recognized that neither side could defeat the other (Cunningham 2007); as a result, the two sides negotiated with one another. Similarly, the economic, political, and other costs experienced by Israel and Egypt during a long series of conflicts ultimately pushed them to the negotiating table, where they created and signed the Camp David Accords in 1978 (Greig 2001).

Just because parties in conflict experience significant conflict costs, however, does not necessarily mean that they will perceive the presence of a mutually hurting stalemate, or, therefore, that they will alter their strategies toward one another and shift away from conflict. Ironically, although the costs of fighting accumulate and the ability of disputants to estimate their prospects for victory sharpens the longer a conflict continues, impediments to recognizing opportunities for negotiation also mount over time. The bargaining characterization regards violence as a means by which parties can impose costs upon one another in order to pressure for their preferred settlement terms; yet as a conflict persists, the motivations for violence often shift in ways that undermine the prospects for negotiations. The costs of conflict, for example, can themselves encourage belligerents to eschew negotiations and continue fighting in an attempt to recoup the sunk costs from past fighting, effectively encouraging them to throw good money after bad (Mitchell 2000). Political considerations can contribute to this tendency as well. Leaders who pursue a conflict-based strategy may see a pivot toward negotiations as a repudiation of their past policies, a step that risks the potential weakening of their political power (Watkins and Lundberg 1998). Finally, over time, warring sides also see violence as a means of punishing their opponent, allowing them to exact vengeance for previous harms committed by the adversary (Zartman 2000). Not only does this sentiment push against the use of diplomacy, but the mistrust it brings with it further undermines the ability of disputants to identify the presence of conditions favorable for negotiations (Aggestam and Jönsson 1997).

The barriers to recognizing opportunities for negotiation and the emergence of a mutually hurting stalemate can be overcome, given the right combination of circumstances. The occurrence of shocks, either within (e.g., a change in leadership) or outside of (e.g., a structural break, like the end of the Cold War) the disputants' relationship, can encourage parties to rethink the strategies by which they engage one another (Zartman 2000). The emergence of another, more pressing threat might constitute one such shock, encouraging parties previously resistant to negotiation to reconsider their stance. For example, because of its hardline stance toward Israel as well as the political threat it represented to the Palestine Liberation Organization (PLO), Hamas represented a more pressing threat to both Israel and the PLO than the latter two were to each other, incentivizing them to improve their own relations (Pruitt 1997). This joint motivation ultimately yielded the talks between Israel and the PLO that produced the Oslo Accords. Along similar lines, the rising Chinese security challenge to both the United States and Vietnam in the Asia-Pacific region encouraged these former adversaries to deepen their relations; thus, in 2016, the United States lifted its decades-old arms embargo against Vietnam. Consistent with this logic, Nilsson (2010) finds that weaker rebel groups are better able to obtain concessions from governments who face multiple internal threats; given limited resources, governments settle some disputes to concentrate their resources on others.

A shock need not be a political event. Any unusual event might prompt parties to reevaluate the way in which they view one another, opening up space for negotiations. The post-earthquake diplomacy between Greece and Turkey offers an illustration. In August 1999, a massive earthquake struck Turkey, causing enormous destruction in several of its largest cities and killing tens of thousands of people. Greece, Turkey's historical adversary with whom it had a series of disputed issues, was the first country to respond with offers of assistance. In September 1999, a large earthquake then struck Greece, devastating significant portions of Athens. In response, Turkey mobilized assistance to Greece in a way that was similar to Greece's response to it the previous month. Both natural disasters provided an external shock that caused these historical rivals to reevaluate their adversarial relationship and made them more amenable toward bilateral negotiations.

The emergence of a new leader can also bring about a realignment that encourages negotiation. New leaders often enter office less invested in the status quo; they are therefore more willing to break with past conflictual strategies and positions, thereby increasing the possibility that negotiations will occur and succeed (Mitchell 2000; Stedman 1991). The evidence in support of this expectation is mixed, with important distinctions in the effects of leadership change on the occurrence and outcome of negotiations. Ghosn (2010), for example, finds that the emergence of a new leader in an interstate dispute does not increase the likelihood that negotiations will occur, but does improve the prospects that the negotiations that do occur will produce an agreement. The differences in the effects of leadership change relative to the stage of negotiations (e.g., getting to the table versus getting an agreement) underscore the distinct impediments at each stage. Although the willingness both to negotiate and to offer concessions comes with political costs, the costs associated with the concessions are higher. Parties can walk away from negotiations and return to the battlefield, or adopt inflexible bargaining positions at the negotiating table, with fewer political costs. Negotiated agreements, in contrast, not only necessitate concession-making—which conveys information about issue salience, commitment, and, relatedly, perceptions of weakness— but through these overt actions also inflict more significant political costs on leaders.

Leadership changes also impact the negotiation process in civil wars, where the issues at stake are highly salient and resistant to settlement. In civil wars, leadership changes impact both stages of negotiations: encouraging talks and facilitating agreements (Ryckman and Braithwaite 2017). New leaders (in government, or organized rebel groups) are better positioned to recognize the desirability of a negotiated settlement and less wedded personally to the continuation of the conflict, making negotiation more likely (Stanley and Sawyer 2009). Nevertheless, the source of the leadership change matters for these effects. Leadership changes that occur in a government involved in a civil war foster negotiations and settlements by injecting a willingness to reevaluate existing strategy and minimizing the uncertainty the other side experiences with respect to that leadership change (Ryckman and Braithwaite 2017). External leadership changes, in contrast, provide the opportunity for new thinking, but also carry increased uncertainty, which clouds the prospects for negotiation. The emergence of a Labour government in the United Kingdom, which brought a different approach to the Northern Ireland peace process following the 1997 elections, was an important contributing element to the eventual achievement of the Good Friday Agreement that settled the conflict.

Thus far, we have assumed that negotiations occur when disputants believe that talks are a better alternative to violence. Underlying this assumption is the belief that disputants want to settle the conflict (via negotiation). This need not be true. Disputants can use negotiations not to improve their relationship or settle disputed issues, but to enhance their ability to fight instead. These "devious" motivations include buying time to better position themselves for conflict; providing their forces with respite, reinforcements, or other support; improving their standing in the court of public opinion (both domestically and internationally); and bolstering the legitimacy of their bargaining positions (Urlacher 2011; Richmond 1998). Whatever the exact motivation, the choice to negotiate in these cases reflects an insincere act by the party (or parties)—one in which they feign an interest in peaceful conflict management. Diplomacy offers an attractive cover for this behavior precisely because the international community favors it and because it creates the temporary pause in fighting needed to pursue devious motivations. The Syrian government, for example, has been accused of using negotiations as an effort to divert attention away from its large-scale attacks on civilians rather than as a means to reach a settlement to end the civil war.

The possibility that an adversary might have such ulterior motives, rather than a genuine interest in settlement, further exacerbates the challenge of getting disputants to the negotiation table. In civil wars, a government often fears that failed negotiations will weaken its negotiating position in future talks, by revealing information about the issues over which it is prepared to offer concessions (Kaplow 2016). The possibility that opponents may hold a devious motivation for engaging in negotiation deepens this fear. It suggests that negotiations will *definitely* fail in some cases, namely those in which parties are negotiating in "bad faith." Such fears will be particularly acute in the most long-running, intense conflicts, where mistrust and a history of violence raise the disputants' suspicions about one another's intentions. Unfortunately, these conflicts are simultaneously those most in need of diplomatic solutions and those most resistant to negotiations in the first place.

When Do Parties Reach a Settlement?

Getting to the negotiating table is an important challenge for disputing parties, but reaching an agreement to manage the conflict, the second stage in the negotiation process (Walter 2002), is even more difficult. Beginning negotiations comes with significant costs for disputants, but actually making the concessions needed to produce a settlement comes with even steeper costs. Not only must the terms of settlement satisfy the interests of the parties at the negotiating table, they must also be ones that leaders can sell to their constituents. In addition, parties must also consider whether the other side will stick to the terms of the agreement. The role that expectations of future compliance and constituent political support play in getting an agreement should not be underestimated.

A useful framework pitches negotiations as a "two-level game," with the negotiations between the disputing groups representing one level and those between each group's leaders and their respective constituents comprising the second (Putnam 1988). In this framework, the leaders bargain with one another at the table on behalf of the disputing groups, and their constituents serve as a ratifying body. Thus, in order for an agreement to occur, leaders must agree to a settlement and each domestic ratifying body must approve of the agreement's terms. The ratifying body can be a formal institution (e.g., a legislature or cabinet of ministers) or an informal collection of elites. In the United States, the Senate is the ratifying body for treaties signed by the President, requiring two-thirds of senators to give "advice and consent" before it enters into force. Although highly autocratic regimes may lack a formal institutional body that approves of agreements—or where, if such a body exists, it serves as little more than a rubber stamp—this does not mean that domestic politics do not factor into autocratic leaders' international negotiations. Even though an autocratic leader may not have to worry about achieving a legislative super-majority vote to approve a treaty, the leader must still consider the wishes of his or her "selectorate" when negotiating an agreement. The selectorate is the group that provides the leader with the support they need to stay in power (Bueno de Mesquita et al. 2003). In a democracy, the selectorate is large, consisting of the segment of the population eligible to vote and effect a change in political leadership. In an autocracy, the selectorate is much smaller, enabling the leadership to offer private benefits to supporters in order to maintain their support in a way that is not possible in a democracy with its much larger selectorate (Bueno de Mesquita et al. 2003). In an autocratic regime, this selectorate may consist of influential actors, critical political bodies (e.g., the Soviet Union's Politburo) or members of the military (as in Pakistan, historically). In each case, if an autocratic leader proceeds with an agreement against the wishes of key elements of the regime's support, that leader risks removal from office.

Regardless of the form a ratifying body takes, its presence influences not only the potential for agreement but also the form any settlement will take. The range of potential agreements that prove both satisfactory to a negotiator at the bargaining table and acceptable to the negotiator's ratifying body is that negotiator's "win-set" (Putnam 1988). The influence of a domestic ratifying body therefore decisively impacts the size of its respective negotiator's win-set, offering one constraint on the range of acceptable agreement terms. When the win-sets of the negotiating disputants overlap, a potential for agreement exists. Whether an agreement actually occurs will be conditioned by the level of trust among the negotiating parties, the degree to which they are able to communicate with one another effectively, and how each views the issues at stake and the desirability of an agreement. In this logic, trust is a vital prerequisite for successful negotiations; parties must expect that their offers of cooperation will be reciprocated by the other side (Rathbun 2012). Parties with high levels of mutual distrust will be less likely to recognize indicators of cooperation from their negotiating partner, making agreement more difficult to reach (Larson 1997).

Expansive win-sets, encompassing a broader range of acceptable agreements, are desirable from the standpoint of achieving a settlement; larger win-sets offer more opportunities for win-sets to overlap. As Putnam (1988) demonstrates, however, a narrow win-set can be advantageous for a negotiator; if fewer agreements are acceptable to me, you will need to accept the terms I prefer or risk losing the settlement altogether. So long as the constraining win-set is not so limited that it prevents any overlap—that is, that there remain no agreements that are jointly acceptable to all sides—this strategy works. Mindful of this, some negotiators try to bluff a smaller win-set, which reduces the likelihood that negotiations will succeed.

Domestic politics shape the potential for settlements in a second way as well. Before reaching an agreement, negotiators consider the likelihood that the other side will implement (or comply with) any agreement reached over the long term. Although some leadership changes can encourage negotiations and agreement, potential future leadership changes can also undermine compliance with an agreement. US behavior illustrates this possibility. President Obama signed the Joint Comprehensive Plan of Action with Iran in 2015. This agreement restricted the growth of Iran's nuclear program in exchange for sanctions relief from the international community. In 2018, however, President Trump announced his intention to withdraw the US from the agreement, arguing that it was a "horrible, one-sided deal" that favored Iran.

As US actions demonstrate, even if a disputant believes that its counterpart is negotiating in good faith and fully intends to comply in the future, it must still worry about the possibility that a leadership change will alter the prospects for compliance. This worry is a consequence of "time-inconsistency" effects. Actors' assessments of the costs and benefits of agreement versus conflict can change over time, and this introduces instability. As Beardsley (2008) points out, not only can these time-inconsistency effects influence the likelihood of agreement, they also can alter the terms of a settlement. If a disputant believes that an opposing leader is more likely to comply with an agreement than an alternative opposing leader (i.e., a replacement), the disputant may give more favorable agreement terms to the current opposing leadership. Granting more concessions to the current leadership, if it helps that leader remain in office, increases the chances of the opponent's long-term compliance with that agreement. To illustrate this idea, imagine Obama negotiating the Iranian deal discussed above while still eligible for re-election in 2012. If Iranian leaders expected Obama to comply with the agreement more than Mitt Romney (the Republican candidate) would, they might offer Obama greater concessions. This would allow Obama to present a more favorable agreement to the American people, hand him a foreign policy win during an election, and therefore increase the chances that he would remain in office. If Iran's offer of concessions helped re-elect Obama, Iran would maximize the implementation of the agreement too, since Obama was more committed to implementation than Romney was (hypothetically here).

Pitfalls in the Implementation Stage

Although fears that an opponent will cheat on an agreement influence both the occurrence and the outcome of negotiations, they do not disappear after the signing of an agreement. Throughout the implementation stage, the third stage in the negotiation process (Walter 2002), disputants still remain concerned that their opponent will cheat. This concern intensifies as the costs

Box 5.1 Negotiation Success and Failure in the Colombian Civil War

Case: Colombian Civil War
Dates of Conflict Management: 1991–92; 1999–2002; 2012–16
Disputing Parties: Government of Colombia and Revolutionary Armed Forces of Colombia (FARC)
Third Party: None
Outcome: Long-running, repeated failure, followed by success

The Colombian civil war illustrates how the structural characteristics of a conflict, coupled with the actions of the warring sides, can create significant impediments to a negotiated settlement. These impediments caused the repeated failure of negotiations between the Colombian government and FARC over three decades, contributing to the loss of thousands of Colombian lives. The most significant efforts at a negotiated settlement occurred during three distinct periods over the course of the conflict: the 1991 talks in Tlaxaca, Mexico and Caracas, Venezuela; the El Caguan talks, which occurred from 1999 to 2002; and the Havana Peace Process that extended from 2012 to 2016. The Havana talks ultimately produced a settlement between the two sides, but only after four years of negotiation. Even then, Colombian voters initially rejected the agreement. The Tlaxaca/Caracas talks and the El Caguan negotiations both resulted in failure.

One impediment to a negotiated settlement in this case was the sheer complexity of the conflict. First, the issues under dispute were multi-dimensional, covering extensive demands by FARC for political, judicial, and economic reforms by the Colombian government (Segura and Mechoulan 2017). Second, the conflict was never exclusively a bilateral one. Beyond the FARC insurgency, the Colombian government faced rebel challenges from other groups, including the National Liberation Army (ELN), the Popular Liberation Army (EPL), and 19th of April Movement (M-19) (Kreutz 2007). Although these groups all opposed the Colombian government, they each had different political objectives and often competed with one another for resources and support. FARC and the ELN, for example, periodically coordinated their operations, but also fought one another in 2006 over territory near Colombia's border with Venezuela. These divisions added considerable complexity to diplomatic efforts to end the civil war. The Colombian government, too, did not present a unified front. Throughout the 1980s and 1990s, right-wing paramilitary groups grew and began targeting left-wing politicians, including those linked to FARC, underscoring the presence of disagreements on the pro-government side about how best to fight the insurgency (Dario 2014). Furthermore, because FARC financed many of its activities through drug trafficking, Colombian drug cartels had a stake in the conflict's continuance as well (Dario 2014).

The deep mistrust between the two sides further alienated them from one another and made reaching a negotiated settlement significantly more difficult. Each side feared that the other was likely to cheat on any agreement reached. This fear deepened when neither proved capable of controlling the various actors on its own side and, therefore, preventing the recurrence of violence once an agreement was in place (Segura and Mechoulan 2017). Given this mindset, the Colombian government and FARC repeatedly took advantage of negotiated ceasefires, not as an opportunity to lay the groundwork for a peace settlement but rather to enhance their ability to fight one another. During the El Caguan talks, for example, FARC benefitted from government demobilization in the region and increased its own deployment of forces there, while the government undertook a broad effort to reorganize its military, thereby increasing its fighting effectiveness (Dario 2014).

The Colombian civil war highlights how the emergence of a mutually hurting stalemate can facilitate negotiations. An uptick in violence preceded both the El Caguan talks (1991) and the Havana peace process (2012), increasing the intensity and pain of conflict before the disputants turned to negotiations. Beginning in the late 1990s, as FARC shifted its focus away from limited, isolated attacks to major strikes directed at Colombian military bases, the government showed a greater willingness to negotiate (Nasi 2009). The battlefield successes of FARC, however, diminished its own willingness to negotiate (Segura and Mechoulan 2017). After the collapse of peace efforts in 2002, the government adopted a more aggressive counterinsurgency strategy, with support from the United States. As the level of violence between the two sides grew more intense and the effects of the conflict on the Colombian people deepened, a hurting stalemate ultimately developed that was deep enough to overcome the previous impediments to a settlement. In 2016, Colombian President Enrique Santos stated unequivocally that the conflict had reached the point of a "mutually hurting stalemate," in which "a military defeat of the FARC-EP would take a very long time, if it was possible at all" (Segura and Mechoulan 2017: 9). These conditions created an environment favorable to the peace settlement reached between the two sides in August 2016.

This agreement, however, did not mark the final settlement to the conflict. In October 2016, Colombian voters narrowly rejected the peace deal in a referendum. Opponents of the deal argued that the settlement gave terms that were too favorable to FARC and called for further negotiations to produce a new agreement. Ultimately, the sides reached a revised peace agreement, which was subsequently ratified by the Colombian congress, rather than through a new referendum, in November 2016.

associated with cheating grow for the side that remains compliant. Disputants therefore seek mechanisms to reduce these concerns.

One prominent mechanism employs either observable indicators of compliance or monitoring programs. For agreement terms that are readily apparent, such as military withdrawals from a border area, observation may prove sufficient. If a state promised to remove its forces from a geographic area, did it do so? For less apparent terms, such as the demobilization of militia groups or the dismantling of a clandestine weapons program, disputants may include monitoring provisions to facilitate an agreement's implementation. The 1994 Agreed Framework between the United States and North Korea, for example, included provisions to monitor and inspect North Korea's efforts to dismantle its nuclear program and close the three nuclear reactors covered by the agreement (see Box 5.2). Less apparent terms such as these increase the chances of a disputant cheating on an agreement without getting caught. How does the US *know* North Korea dismantled its program? Monitoring provisions work to alleviate fears of cheating, build trust between disputants, and reassure everyone that the agreement is being implemented. Nonetheless, this is not a panacea. Even with monitoring provisions, US skepticism toward North Korea's compliance with the 1994 Framework continued, and the Framework collapsed in 2003.

Beyond taking steps to increase transparency, disputants can also design agreement provisions to encourage compliance and reduce fears of cheating. These provisions can be categorized into two groups: fear-reducing and cost-increasing provisions (Mattes and Savun 2009). Fear-reducing provisions include third-party guarantees and power-sharing agreements. The deployment of a peacekeeping force that separates warring sides inhibits the disputants' ability to renew fighting. The peacekeeping force can observe and report on aggressive actions, and ensures that a power shift (e.g., demobilization) does not allow the stronger side to attack the weaker one. UNOCI, the United Nations peacekeeping mission deployed to Côte d'Ivoire in 2004 following the civil war between the government and the rebel New Forces, served to separate the two sides, reducing the risk of renewed conflict. Similarly, a power-sharing agreement after a civil war gives each disputing party a stake in government, as well as levers of political and (often) police control, each of which reduces the chances of one party reneging on the agreement. In contrast to these, cost-increasing provisions make a return to conflict less desirable for the belligerents. Efforts to dry up external support for belligerents fall into this category. If successful, they increase the costs associated with abandoning the agreement and returning to fighting, thereby enhancing implementation of the agreement.

The Peace Accords Matrix data set traces the provisions contained within thirty-four comprehensive civil war peace agreements from 1989 to 2012, along with these provisions' implementation (Joshi et al. 2015). Figure 5.2 uses

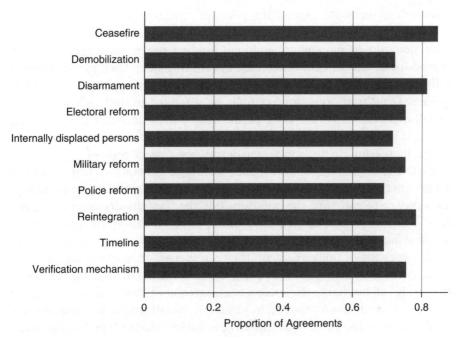

Figure 5.2 Most Common Civil War Peace Agreement Provisions
Data Source: Joshi et al. (2015).

these data to identify the ten provisions most commonly included in civil war peace agreements. Agreement provisions focus heavily on both cost-increasing and fear-reducing provisions, mechanisms that inhibit a return to conflict and increase transparency between the disputing parties. Not surprisingly, ceasefires, which are foundational for the establishment of a more durable peace, are the most commonly included provisions. With respect to cost-increasing provisions, disarmament provisions are included in about 81% of all peace agreements, and reintegration measures, which seek to reintroduce fighters back into civil society, are included 78% of the time. Coupled with demobilization provisions, which are included in 72% of agreements, these terms reduce the ability of warring sides to return to conflict. Verification agreement terms—fear-reducing provisions which include monitoring measures by outside actors such as the United Nations, or domestic monitoring mechanisms—are included in more than 75% of all civil war agreements. Trust-building measures such as electoral, military, and police reforms are also commonly included provisions in civil war peace agreements.

Implementation concerns not only color the relationship between the disputants but also offer third-party spoilers opportunities to scuttle an agreement. Parties excluded from the talks that produce an agreement, or participate in the negotiations but find the agreement terms to be unacceptable, can use violence in order to destabilize the signatories and undermine the peace process (Nilsson 2008). During the troubles in Northern Ireland, opponents of a settlement used threats of continued violence to exacerbate fears on the other side that an agreement would not produce peace, undermining efforts to produce an agreement between the negotiating sides. Even parties without a direct stake in the issues over which a conflict is being fought can act as spoilers. Drug traffickers, for example, have tended to find civil wars to be friendly environments for drug production, with significant illicit activity during the civil conflicts in Colombia, Syria, and Afghanistan, among many others, increasing their incentives to destabilize a peace process.

Key to the success of spoilers is their ability to generate mistrust between the groups that support an agreement (Kydd and Walter 2002). Spoiler groups use violence to convince the opposing side that compliance with the agreement will not protect them from conflict costs; to the extent that spoilers can convince the other side that renewed conflict is likely to be better than implementation of the agreement, they can succeed in undermining a settlement. Because spoilers can cause peace agreements to fail, dealing with them effectively can be vital to the success of an agreement. Parties to an agreement can employ strategies focused on inducement, socialization, coercion, or some combination of the three to mitigate the negative effects of spoilers (Stedman 1997). Key to the effect of spoilers on agreement implementation is the level of trust among the parties. When the signatories to an agreement have high levels of trust that the other side will keep to the terms of an agreement, they are better able to weather the threat that spoiler violence poses to the long-term viability of the settlement (Lounsbery and Cook 2011).

BOX 5.2 US–North Korea Agreement and Implementation

Case: US–North Korea Agreed Framework
Date of Conflict Management: 1994
Disputing Parties: United States and North Korea
Third Party: None
Negotiation Outcome: Initial success, followed by failure during implementation

The 1994 Agreed Framework was a negotiated agreement between the United States and North Korea that headed off a military confrontation by restricting North Korea's ability to develop nuclear weapons. The crisis that led to the Agreed Framework began in 1993, when North Korea—a signatory of the Treaty on the Non-Proliferation of Nuclear Weapons (NPT)—was suspected of developing a clandestine nuclear weapons program and refused to comply with requests by the International Atomic Energy Agency (IAEA) to inspect various facilities. Deepening the crisis, North Korea announced its intention to withdraw from the NPT. In response, the United States considered military action against North Korea, believing the prospect of a nuclear North Korea to be a direct threat to US allies, a force for instability in the Asia-Pacific region, and a threat to the long-term viability of the NPT.

US and North Korean negotiations resulted in the October 1994 Agreed Framework. This agreement offered material incentives to North Korea in exchange for its promises to freeze its nuclear activities and permit outside inspections of its program. In particular, the US not only offered North Korea the construction of two light-water nuclear reactors, which could not be repurposed for weapons development, but also supplied food and energy aid to the regime, along with the long-term incentive of normalized relations with the US. North Korea agreed to shutter its two reactors.

Negotiations initially succeeded, producing an agreement and preventing militarized conflict. Nevertheless, the agreement eventually collapsed in 2003, and the reframing of the US–North Korean relationship that the agreement promised never occurred. These were not the only failures, however. North Korea never fully closed its nuclear reactors and failed to comply fully with the inspection protocols proposed in the agreement (Jackson 2016). On the American side, the US failed to deliver fully on its pledge to provide the light-water nuclear reactors and, repeatedly over the course of the agreement's life, instituted new sanctions against North Korea.

The ultimate failure of the Agreed Framework points to the powerful role that mistrust and commitment problems pose for the implementation of agreements. In many respects, this raises the question of why the US and North Korea negotiated in the first place. Before the agreement, high levels of mistrust and suspicion existed between the two sides, tendencies that continued after the agreement was reached. From the US perspective, North Korea persisted in banned nuclear activities despite the agreement, with intelligence reports suggesting that it had constructed an underground plutonium processing facility (Jackson 2016). North Korea also continued to develop and test ballistic missile technology during this period, heightening US fears of a surreptitious nuclear breakout.

US behavior also increased mistrust in a way that undermined agreement implementation. Despite signing the agreement, the US continued to maintain its view of North Korea as a threat. Rather than seeing the agreement as the first step in the improvement and eventual normalization of relations, it instead interpreted the agreement as a "suboptimal but acceptable exigency to address a North Korean nuclear threat that it believed would otherwise grow" (Jackson 2016: 248). The lack of political consensus on North Korean policy within the US government further reinforced this view, with much of Congress skeptical of the agreement itself, the likelihood of North Korean compliance, and the desirability of improved relations with North Korea.

The levels of transparency on both sides also served to undermine the long-term success of the Agreed Framework, albeit in different ways. The opaqueness of the North Korean regime made it difficult not only to observe its compliance with the agreement, but also, more importantly, to identify its long-term intentions. This lack of information, in turn, fed American fears about future North Korean behavior (e.g., the likelihood of non-compliance with the Agreed Framework) and encouraged calls for regime change in North Korea, particularly from hawks in Congress. Ironically, the transparent US political system allowed the interpretation of North Korea as a continued threat and the calls for regime change to play out publicly, no doubt deepening North Korean fears and mistrust of US intentions as well (Jackson 2016).

This combination of mistrust and the fear of cheating ultimately led to the undoing of the Agreed Framework. In January 2002, President George W. Bush labeled North Korea part of the "Axis of Evil." Relations proceeded to deteriorate further over the next several years as the US accused North Korea of conducting a secret uranium enrichment program and North Korea withdrew from the NPT (2003). In October 2006, North Korea conducted its first nuclear test.

Conclusion

In this chapter, we have examined the role that negotiations play as a conflict resolution tool. As part of this discussion, we highlighted several important features of negotiation and its use in managing conflicts:

- Rather than being distinct from conflict, negotiation is best thought of alongside violence as an instrument of bargaining. In this view, parties in conflict use violence to impose costs upon one another to communicate both their capabilities and their commitment to the issues at stake in order to force the other side to acquiesce to their demands. Negotiations play a similar role, allowing the parties to exchange information with one another in order to arrive at a settlement. The chief benefit of negotiations is that they increase the efficiency of this information exchange process by avoiding the death and destruction that violence produces. Negotiations can lack the means of enforcement that military victories provide, unless such means are built into an agreement.
- The context in which a dispute occurs has a powerful bearing on the prospects for negotiation. The types of issues in dispute and the way in which parties see them influence the extent to which disputants see those issues as amenable to negotiated settlement. At the same time, the number of parties involved in a dispute, as well as the past relationship between those parties,

also influences the likelihood that negotiations will be fruitful. Disputants with high levels of hostility toward one another and with deep levels of mistrust are likely to find a negotiated settlement more difficult to achieve than parties with a past history of negotiation and compromise.

- Once parties resort to violence, the way in which the conflict evolves can create openings for negotiations. The emergence of a mutually hurting stalemate can encourage negotiations when they are seen as a "way out" by which disputants can end the pain of conflict.
- Credible-commitment problems, which cause parties to question whether their opponent will follow through with any agreement, create challenges at each stage of negotiations. Commitment problems reduce the incentives for disputants to join negotiations, make them less likely to reach agreements when they do negotiate, and create implementation problems after agreements are reached.
- The successful implementation of agreements is a function of the degree to which the parties to an agreement are able to mitigate the effects of commitment problems. Spoilers seek to take advantage of commitment problems by using violence to undermine the willingness of the other side to remain compliant with an agreement. Disputants can improve the chances for successful agreement implementation by including agreement provisions that reduce the incentives for parties to return to conflict and minimize the fears that each side has of the other violating the agreement.

6

Mediation

The Burundian civil war (1993–2005) produced hundreds of thousands of casualties. As the violence unfolded, numerous mediators attempted to help the disputants manage the conflict—their efforts stymied by the underlying, deep-rooted ethnic division between the Hutus and Tutsis. These mediators—including Julius Nyerere, Nelson Mandela, and Jacob Zuma—each brought a distinct approach, style, and set of relationships to the table. They also each exerted significant political pressure on the disputing parties. Despite these efforts, the conflict continued to grind on. Various parties refused to join the mediators' efforts, and, mediation being a voluntary process, this significantly undermined the mediators' effectiveness. Eventually, though, the combination of pressure and repeated mediation produced a settlement to the conflict and an end to the war in 2005, one that would have been difficult to envision without mediator assistance.

The previous chapter considered negotiation as a conflict management approach—a diplomatic process in which only the protagonists in a conflict participate. In this chapter, we examine a variation on that arrangement. This variant introduces a third-party mediator into the negotiations. As we note in the next section, this involves more than simply adding another seat at the negotiating table. A mediator can fulfill multiple functions, from facilitating communication and adding its own interests to the negotiations, to proposing solutions and incentivizing settlement. The logic, process, and strategy of mediation therefore differ from negotiations between disputants alone.

Differences with Negotiation

Mediation is an important third-party diplomatic tool used to manage both interstate and intrastate conflicts. Yet it is commonly misunderstood. Many interpret mediation as a variant of negotiations. In many respects, the similarities between the two approaches encourage this view. Both mediation and negotiation are voluntary diplomatic processes through which disputants seek to manage contentious issues between them, either to prevent violence, stop ongoing conflict, or resolve the issues underlying the dispute. Moreover, both processes are voluntary; disputants consent to use them and therefore

reserve the right to end the process at any time and reject any potential agreement that emerges from it.

The scope of what constitutes mediation is broad. It encompasses activities as diverse as good offices, in which a mediator largely makes logistical
arrangements for talks (e.g., providing a forum), and directive mediation, in
which the mediator exercises significant control over the communication
between disputants, proposes settlement options, and exerts leverage to foster
an agreement (Bercovitch et al. 1991). The good-offices end of the spectrum
lends itself to viewing mediation as an extension of negotiation, since the
third party plays a limited role. Kressel and Pruitt (1989), for example, discuss
mediation as a conflict management effort that brings the help of a third party
to the diplomatic process. Similarly, Zartman and Touval (1996) directly connect mediation to negotiation, arguing that mediation is effectively a subset
of negotiation that brings third-party assistance to the search for a settlement.

Simply describing mediation as a variant of negotiation, however, misses the
ways in which the addition of a third party significantly alters the bargaining
process. First, a mediator can act as a service provider to disputants (e.g., facilitating talks). Second, a mediator can play an important informational role;
this might involve fact-checking, supplying independent analysis, or serving
as a go-between among the contending sides (e.g., helping disputants reframe
issues and positions). In this role, a mediator helps disputants overcome some
of the bargaining challenges present in negotiations. The involvement of a
go-between, for example, allows disputants to engage in talks without fearing
that doing so will signal weakness to the other side, as when a government
worries about speaking directly with a rebel group. Third, mediators can
introduce resources (e.g., aid) that encourage disputants to negotiate and,
once this begins, can use both carrots and sticks to incentivize an agreement.
Finally, mediators can make it easier for disputants to sell to their own constituencies both the idea of talks with an adversary and any agreement that
flows from the effort. In effect, the mediator assumes some responsibility for
unpopular components of the conflict management process.

The addition of a mediator to the bargaining process has a "catalytic" effect
on the relationship between disputants, appreciably changing the dynamics of the interactions between them (Meyer 1960). Disputants, particularly
those whose disputes have escalated to violence, not only find it difficult to
engage one another diplomatically, but also frequently frame their relationship in winner-take-all terms. An effective mediator helps the parties reframe
their interactions and, therefore, their relationship with one another. This
subsequently allows disputants to identify areas of potential agreement or
recognize the variation in importance they give to the issues under dispute,
thereby allowing them to trade off across those issues to reach a settlement.
Moreover, a mediator can use its understanding of the situation, its information about the conflict and the disputants, and its relationship with both

parties, to identify potential settlement options that the parties themselves may be unable to find without assistance (Ott 1972; Zartman 2008).

Whatever role they play, mediators alter how disputants bargain in a way that is difficult within negotiations, particularly those rooted in the most intense and entrenched conflicts. Mediation is therefore best conceptualized as a conflict management process distinct from negotiation, wherein an outside actor intervenes diplomatically in order to assist the disputing parties, altering both their perceptions of one another and how they interact (Bercovitch 2002).

The Logic of Mediation

Mediation preserves the flexibility of disputants, since it is a voluntary process. Indeed, disputants can reject an overture to mediation if they regard talks as undesirable, or can withdraw from a potential agreement if they disapprove of its provisions. This likens mediation to negotiation, but mediation also brings benefits that negotiations lack. It can, for example, help disputants resolve the informational and commitment problems they experience, cause them to reevaluate the costs and benefits of potential agreements, and provide a face-saving mechanism that allows them to better sell an agreement to their constituents.

Information problems constitute a key barrier to diplomatic settlements. These arise because disputants get better agreement terms if they can convince their opponents that they are militarily stronger or so committed to achieving their preferred settlement terms that they will pay higher costs to secure those terms (see Chapter 5). Less capable or less resolved actors recognize this, however, prompting them to act *as if* they had larger capabilities and greater resolve than they do. Disputants then, in effect, play a poker game, in which each side has incentives to outbid the other and, where necessary, to bluff in order to achieve their goals.

This dynamic creates a problem that bilateral negotiations cannot easily surmount. It will be difficult for the disputants to discern whether they face a capable, highly committed adversary or one that will likely back down if challenged, especially if a deeply entrenched dispute has eroded trust between them. Such a problem is common in interstate wars, but compounds further in civil wars (Regan et al. 2009). A government facing an internal military challenge often perceives the rebels as weaker than it, because rebels lack legitimacy and access to state resources; the rebels, in turn, view the government as weak, since it cannot maintain a monopoly on the use of force. Both sides must therefore oversell their capabilities and resolve. The difficulty does not stop there, however. Governments generally prefer to avoid talks with rebels where possible; doing so legitimizes the rebels and incentivizes potential challenges from other groups (Melin and Svensson 2009). These same governments may nevertheless negotiate with the strongest, most highly resolved rebel groups, that is, those capable of imposing high costs on it (Walter 2009). Nevertheless, governments struggle to separate the strong and resolved groups from the weak and bluffing; each type has incentives to use violence to convince the government of its strength. Furthermore, each is exaggerating its capabilities and resolve.

A mediator can help disputants overcome this informational problem. It can, for example, supply a credible assessment of each side's capabilities and resolve, thereby allowing disputants to better understand where potential settlements might be found. Disputants can conceivably share this information with each other in the absence of a third party, but in practice this is difficult. Not only do they have incentives to misrepresent this information (see above), but parties who deeply mistrust each other also fear that sharing this information honestly may communicate weakness, undermine their bargaining position, and invite exploitation. A trusted third party, however, can be well positioned to understand the incentives and constraints that each side faces and communicate the required information in a way that allows disputants to transcend the concerns noted here (see, e.g., the Vatican's mediation of the United States–Cuba relationship, Box 6.1; see also Kydd 2003; Svensson 2007; Regan et al. 2009). The trustworthiness of the mediator therefore becomes key (Savun 2008; Svensson 2009; Crescenzi et al. 2011); it allows the mediator to engage in honest discussions with disputants and to gather and convey reliable information that each disputant finds credible. This trustworthiness, or credibility, derives from a myriad of sources, including cultural or moral standing (e.g., the Vatican), a historical relationship with the disputants (e.g., colonial), shared membership in international institutions (e.g., joint European Union membership), or the mediator's political institutions and power (e.g., alliance commitments or similar regime types; see Savun 2008; Svensson 2009; Crescenzi et al. 2011).

Lack of information, however, does not always present the main obstacle to settlement. In some cases, a settlement will fundamentally shift the relative power between disputants. When this might occur, the weakening disputant worries that the strengthening disputant will use its newfound power to exploit it. The lack of trust ensures that the stronger disputant cannot credibly promise to do otherwise. Thus, a credible-commitment problem arises. Government–rebel relations after civil war illustrate this problem well (Walter 2002). Rebels must disarm as part of a settlement process—the government needs this to restore its monopoly on the use of force. Yet if rebels lay down their weapons and the government does not, rebels worry that the government will renege on the agreement, alter the agreement's terms, and (perhaps) harm them.

A mediator can overcome this obstacle by being a guarantor to a mediated agreement (Quinn et al. 2006; Walter 2002). In this role, a mediator monitors compliance with the agreement. In particular, the mediator gathers and shares intelligence about the actions of the disputants during the agreement's implementation phase, deploys observer (i.e., peacekeeping) forces, or threatens sanctions to raise the costs of defecting from the agreement (see, e.g., the third-party actions in the Peru–Ecuador dispute, Box 6.2), and generally ensures that the disputant made stronger by the agreement does not exploit the weaker. Such actions undercut fears that disputants will cheat on the agreement. This strategy works so long as the mediator remains engaged and willing to assist the disputants after they sign the agreement.

As with information problems, a biased third party is better positioned to guarantee an agreement. It seems counterintuitive to seek a biased mediator, one with close(r) ties to the disputants and an interest in the issues being contested. Nonetheless, biased mediators often prove more effective than unbiased ones because they possess the incentives to continue managing a conflict over the long term (Svensson 2007; Gent and Shannon 2011; Kydd 2003, 2006). US mediation of the Egyptian–Israeli dispute offers a good example of how bias toward a particular disputant improves mediator effectiveness, as opposed to detracting from it as conventional wisdom holds. Because of its support for Israel, the disputants viewed the US as a third party with significant long-term interests in their relationship and, therefore, one that could be trusted both to provide credible information to Israel about Egypt and to reduce Egyptian concerns that Israel might not fully implement a peace agreement. Through such interests, biased mediators are more likely to succeed at producing mediated peace agreements; disputants trust not only their information, but also their willingness to enforce any agreement reached (Favretto 2009).

Beyond helping overcome information and commitment problems, mediators can also use leverage to encourage talks or to foster agreements that would otherwise be impossible among the disputants themselves. A mediator might, for example, offer incentives that make unacceptable negotiations or agreements more palatable (Touval and Zartman 1985). The US offered such rewards (notably, foreign aid to both Israel and Egypt) during the bargaining that led to the Camp David Accords in 1978; these rewards encouraged agreement. In contrast, powerful mediators might instead brandish sticks that threaten punishment if disputants do not come to the table or reach a mediated agreement (Lake and Rothchild 1996). The sanctions imposed on Yugoslavia during the Bosnian War illustrate this well, providing as they did an important motivating force behind the Dayton Accord (see Box 4.1). These carrots and sticks alter the cost–benefit analysis of disputants to facilitate talks that would otherwise not occur or agreements that would be difficult to achieve through bilateral negotiation alone.

Finally, mediators may help disputants to secure the approval of their constituents for an agreement. Conflicting parties fear appearing weak and irresolute not only toward one another but also toward their supporters. This is especially true when the disputants have already experienced a long history of intense conflict. Under these circumstances, a mediator can encourage peace by providing domestic political cover for an agreement (Beardsley 2010). Rather than interpreting an agreement as giving in to the demands of an adversary, a position that may be politically untenable among a disputant's constituents, a disputant justifies an agreement in terms of the necessity (or the desirability) of yielding to the third party and the incentives it offers. A major power mediator that can offer significant amounts of investment and foreign aid if disputants reach a mediated agreement therefore makes it easier for those disputants to sell the agreement to their people—not as concessions to an enemy, but as a means of extracting benefits from the mediator.

Patterns of Mediation

To explore patterns in the use and effectiveness of mediation, we rely on two data sets that provide the most up-to-date information available on mediation activities. Data from the International Conflict Management (ICM) data set tracks interstate mediation (Bercovitch 2004), providing detailed information on the characteristics, parties, providers, and outcomes of interstate mediation efforts. The Civil Wars Mediation (CWM) data set supplies information on mediation in civil conflict, providing information akin to that of the ICM data (DeRouen et al. 2011).

Given mediation's voluntary, flexible character, it is not surprising that it ranks among the most commonly used conflict management approaches for dealing with both interstate and civil conflicts. As Figure 6.1 shows, mediation has been frequently applied to both types of conflict during the post-World War II period. The frequency with which it has been used, however, has changed over time. The 1990s represent a high-water mark in mediation's application; this reflects both demand- and supply-side forces. On the demand side, an increased outbreak of civil conflicts followed the end of the Cold War. This stimulated an increased need for and reliance on mediation as a relatively low-cost conflict management approach. On the supply side, improved relations among the major powers after the Cold War ended not only enabled those powers to engage in more cooperative conflict management, but also empowered regional and international organizations to offer more mediation as well.

When mediation occurs, either the disputants or a third party must initiate it. Because it is voluntary, who initiates the mediation tells us something, albeit imperfectly, about how motivated the disputants are to reach a settlement. If

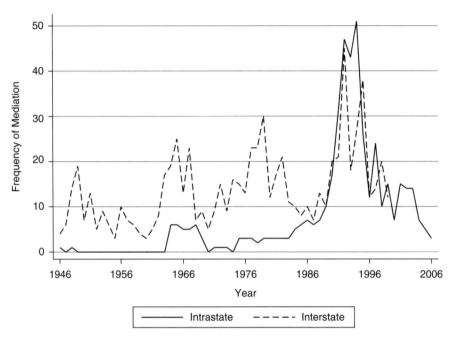

Figure 6.1 Frequency of Mediation by Conflict Type, 1946–2006
NOTE: Interstate mediation data only available through 1999
DATA SOURCES: Bercovitch (2004); DeRouen et al. (2011).

both parties jointly initiate mediation, then this signals that they recognize the desirability of mediation, at least in the short term. A hurting stalemate, for example, may cause those exhausted by conflict or unwilling to continue paying its costs to seek either a temporary reprieve or, ideally, a long-term settlement. Calling for mediation achieves this. Such calls can therefore indicate that a disputant believes promising conditions for reaching a settlement exist. This need not be the case, and disputant motivation to join mediation does not guarantee its success. Bargaining obstacles may still impede an agreement. Disputants might also consider mediation merely as an opportunity to improve their position on the battlefield or to gain positive reputational benefits (for their willingness to accept diplomatic talks), without having any intention of reaching an agreement.

If only one disputant initiates mediation, the situation gets murkier. The initiator may be signaling a desire to enter mediation, but this leaves the non-initiating side's intentions unclear. On the one hand, non-initiators motivated by reciprocity may see the initiator's actions as an overture from which to build; this could increase the non-initiator's amenability to both mediation and making concessions. On the other hand, the non-initiator could regard the initiation of mediation as a signal of weakness to be exploited, that is, as a sign that the initiator believes it might be losing; interpreting the signal like this might encourage the non-initiator to bargain harder if mediation occurs or, even worse, to redouble their efforts on the battlefield.

Mediation efforts initiated by a third party provide much less information about the disputants' motivation for settlement. Third parties must often initiate the mediation process for one of several reasons: the disputants cannot themselves recognize that favorable conditions for a mediated agreement exist; they fear signaling weakness; or they do not desire mediation. Under the first two scenarios, disputants *might* be motivated to pursue a mediated settlement, but under the last, they definitely are not. When third parties initiate mediation it is therefore more difficult to determine whether disputants participate in it because they have a genuine interest in pursuing a settlement, want to curry favor with the third party, are merely responding to third-party rewards and punishments, or hold some other, more devious motive (Richmond 1998).

Examining the differences in who initiates mediation in interstate and civil conflicts points to some important ways in which mediation across the two types of conflict varies. As Figure 6.2 demonstrates, among both types, the vast majority of mediation efforts are initiated by third parties themselves. Mediation efforts initiated by both disputants are the rarest form of mediation in both interstate and intrastate conflicts, no doubt as a consequence of the

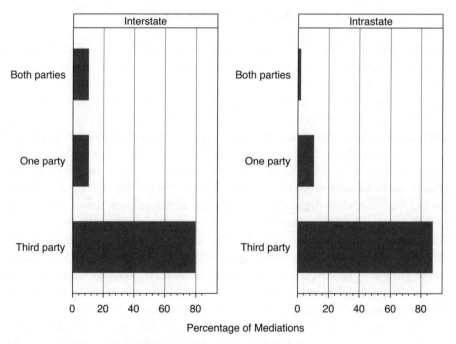

Figure 6.2 Initiators of Mediation by Conflict Type, 1946–2006
NOTE: Interstate mediation data only available through 1999
DATA SOURCES: Bercovitch (2004); DeRouen et al. (2011).

rarity of disputants each having sufficient information and confidence in the response of the other side for both sides to initiate mediation. When mediation is not initiated by a third party in interstate conflicts, it is more apt to be initiated by one side rather than both of the disputants.

The different patterns of mediation initiation in civil wars speak to some of the unique challenges faced in diplomatic efforts to manage intrastate conflicts. As we noted earlier, civil conflicts involve legitimacy issues (e.g., whether to recognize rebels as a negotiating power) and more severe information problems (e.g., higher incentives to misrepresent capabilities and resolve). These complicate disputants' willingness to launch mediation efforts. That third parties initiate even more mediation efforts in civil war contexts than they do in interstate conflicts, and that disputant parties initiate so few intrastate mediations, suggests that third parties play an important role in helping civil war parties overcome these barriers to diplomacy. It also underscores the importance of the supply of mediators in civil wars. Conflicts in which third parties have few interests, or that the international community deems too intractable to manage, may be significantly less likely to see *any* mediation, since the initiative hinges on a third party. This creates a risk that many of the civil conflicts most in need of mediation will not receive it.

Agents of Mediation

A wide array of actors in the international system mediate international conflicts, including private individuals (e.g., former US President Jimmy Carter), non-governmental organizations (most notably those with religious affiliations; e.g., the Quaker mediation in Sri Lanka, Nigeria, and India–Pakistan), state leaders (e.g., the Norwegian government), and representatives of intergovernmental organizations (e.g., the United Nations Secretary-General). Figure 6.3 shows the breakdown of mediation by actor type in both interstate and civil conflicts. Among civil conflicts, states dominate the provision of mediation efforts, accounting for nearly half of all such efforts during the 1946–2006 period. International organizations play an active role in these disputes as well; for example, dissuading rebels from escalating conflict (Tir and Karreth 2018), and creating relationships that reduce the likelihood of conflict generally (e.g., when two actors share membership in the same IGO; see Bakaki 2018). They also, however, serve as conflict mediators: global IGOs lead roughly 26% of all civil conflict mediation efforts, while regional organizations (e.g., the African Union or the Organization of American States) carry an additional 17%.

Unlike states and IGOs, non-governmental organizations (NGOs) rarely mediate civil conflicts, appearing in about 4% of mediation efforts. Given the major obstacles to getting civil war belligerents to the bargaining table, this is not surprising. NGOs possess fewer resources than governments and international

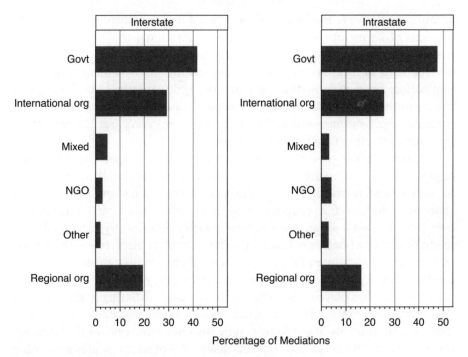

Figure 6.3 Mediation Providers by Conflict Type, 1946–2006
NOTE: Interstate mediation data only available through 1999
DATA SOURCES: Bercovitch (2004); DeRouen et al. (2011).

organizations that they can use as leverage to incentivize mediation. This may explain why the NGOs involved in civil war mediation are often religion-based. These NGOs bring a moral standing, a perceived lack of bias, a trustworthiness, and a commitment to conflict management and prevention that disputants will regard as valuable (Bercovitch and Kadayifci-Orellana 2009).

As with civil conflicts, governments most frequently mediate interstate conflicts; they conducted just over 40% of all mediation efforts within interstate disputes during the period 1946–99. International organizations provided about 30%, and regional organizations about 21%, of interstate conflict cases. The Organization of American States (OAS), for example, has mediated territorial disputes between Belize and Guatemala and Honduras and Nicaragua, among others. Diplomatic efforts to manage disputes constitute a core mission of regional organizations, since ensuring regional stability is one of their essential goals. Indeed, Chapter V of the OAS Charter calls for the peaceful settlement of disputes among member states and, when this cannot be achieved through negotiations, requests that member states employ other peaceful means to settle disputes. Similarly, the African Union Charter specifically calls for the peaceful settlement of disputes among members through "negotiation, mediation, conciliation or arbitration." In this respect, regional organizations seek to mediate conflicts when doing so coincides with both the interests of its members and the broader reputational role of the organization itself (Zartman 2002). Many intergovernmental organizations regard the development of a reputation for effective conflict management as a strong motivation for mediating disputes (Zartman 2008). Finally, a combination of private individuals—for example, former government leaders or heads of international organizations—and national organizations carry out the remaining mediation efforts within interstate disputes.

The above data suggest that governments (i.e., state leaders), international organizations, and regional organizations provide the bulk of mediation to both interstate and intrastate conflicts. As Figures 6.4 and 6.5 show, the share of mediation efforts conducted by these various third parties has shifted over time. Regional organizations, for example, significantly expanded their mediation role in both civil and interstate conflicts after 1990. The period 1991–95 alone accounted for nearly 35% of all civil conflict mediation efforts conducted by regional organizations during the post-World War II period. The African Union has played a particularly active role, mediating a wide range of civil conflicts including those in Chad and Burundi. Regional organizations increased their involvement in interstate disputes after 1990 as well. Indeed, the eight-year 1992–99 period contains nearly 40% of all regional organization mediation efforts across the entire 1946–99 period. This suggests that the footprint of regional organization diplomacy expanded dramatically during the last decade of the twentieth century.

States and international organizations also increased their mediation efforts after 1990. Within civil conflicts, for example, mediation by international organizations peaked during the early 1990s, after which it waned (see Figure 6.4). State-led mediation shows a similar trend, although states increased the relative share of conflicts they mediated over this period. Finally, the scope of civil war mediators also broadened; private individuals and national organizations adopted increasingly active portfolios as civil war mediators during this same period. Similar trends, albeit with more variation, appear within interstate conflicts (see Figure 6.5). A wave of mediation occurred in the early 1990s, and states once again mediated more (interstate) disputes than other actor types. Nevertheless, international organizations constantly mediated across the 1946–99 period; they may also have ceded some opportunities to regional organizations after the Cold War ended.

Just as who mediates a conflict affects the initiation and outcome of mediation, so too does the reputation of a third-party mediator. When deciding whether to accept mediation from a particular third party, disputants must weigh the benefits that the mediator brings. The third party's reputation comprises part of this calculation, since it conveys information to the disputants about how effective the third party will likely be and, just as important, what motivates its involvement (Tinsley et al. 2002). Ideally, a third party will

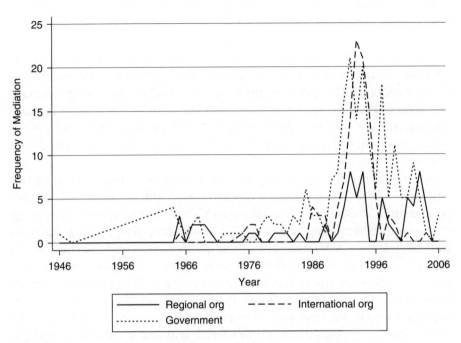

Figure 6.4 Frequency of Intrastate Mediation by Third Party, 1946–2006
DATA SOURCE: DeRouen et al. (2011).

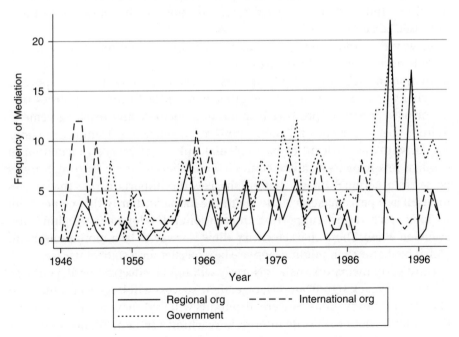

Figure 6.5 Frequency of Interstate Mediation by Third Party, 1946–1999
DATA SOURCE: Bercovitch (2004).

primarily be concerned about the long-term interests of the disputants and therefore mediate to produce a long-term improvement in their relationship. This, however, is not the only driver behind a third party's desire to mediate a conflict. Third parties sometimes prioritize their own interests over those of the disputants; thus, they might stabilize a conflict just enough to maintain access to critical resources or prevent the outbreak of a wider regional conflict, but not take the steps needed to settle the conflict entirely. Along similar lines, they may pursue a mediated agreement simply to further their own reputation.

To evaluate the desirability of a mediator, disputants must review numerous factors. First, they consider the mediator's track record, its previous performance in other conflicts (Maoz and Terris 2006). Second, they weigh the value of their relationship with the mediator (Pruitt 2002; Zartman 2002). Rejecting a mediation offer from an important trade partner or ally may imperil those relationships; these potential costs grant third parties leverage, increasing the chances of their offers of mediation being accepted. Importantly, these costs need not be tangible. The religious authority of the Catholic Church, for example, often empowers it to mediate conflicts, and those with strong connections to the Church will find it difficult to reject its mediation efforts. As a result, Guatemalan Cardinal Quezada helped mediate a 1996 settlement of the long-running Guatemalan civil war, while papal mediation staved off conflict during the Beagle Channel dispute between Argentina and Chile and thawed relations between the United States and Cuba (see Box 6.1).

Norway illustrates the pure role of mediator reputation well, as it is a notable outlier among third parties. On the one hand, it frequently provides mediation in high-profile conflicts, such as the Israel–Palestinian dispute or the civil war in Sri Lanka. On the other hand, it lacks the capabilities that major powers have to pressure disputants to mediate and reach agreement. Neither does it use cultural connections as currency; for example, religious ties (as with the Vatican) or past colonial links (e.g., France's mediation of conflicts involving its former colonies in Sub-Saharan Africa). Instead, Norway possesses a national image that emphasizes the important role that it sees for itself as a peacemaker, coupled with the moral authority that comes from its long track record supporting international development (Hoglund and Svensson 2009). These characteristics allow Norway to be a more prominent, global mediator than might otherwise be expected for a state of its size.

Third-party mediators such as Norway will not be effective for all conflicts. Because they lack significant leverage, their success will largely be a function of disputant motivations. Sincere disputants will find these weaker third parties helpful. Those with little interest in reaching a settlement, however, may also accept their efforts, precisely because they know the mediator cannot push them into a settlement (Beardsley 2009).

One way for third parties to maximize the resources available for mediation—both tangible and intangible—is to expand the number of mediators involved in the mediation effort. Weaker actors such as Norway possess few resources with which to influence the process (Greig and Diehl 2012). Multiparty mediation efforts overcome this limitation (Crocker et al. 2001), drawing together a group of third-party mediators, who then pool resources in either a coordinated, coalition-led mediation effort (see, e.g., the Ecuador–Peru dispute, Box 6.2) or a series of disconnected, sequential mediations conducted by different third parties (Böhmelt 2012; see also Chapter 9). These multiparty mediations also balance any mediator bias, giving disputants more confidence in the mediation effort (Böhmelt 2012). If a skeptical disputant believes a potential mediator to be too closely connected to its adversary, for example, the introduction of an additional mediator with closer links to the skeptic may alleviate any concerns and secure the skeptic's participation in the mediation process.

Despite these advantages, multiparty mediation also has drawbacks. Conflicting parties can take advantage of multiparty mediation by "forum shopping," seeking multiple mediators in an effort to find the one most sympathetic to their interests (Crocker et al. 2001). This is not inherently bad, but carries the danger that mediation never gets off the ground. A forum shopper will prefer the third party most aligned with its interests; if both disputants do this, they will likely disagree about the identity of the most suitable mediator. An additional problem emerges on the third-party side. Any coordinated conflict management effort requires effective communication between third parties and with the disputants. If third parties cannot achieve this (e.g., if they provide inconsistent information to disputants), they risk creating more informational problems than they solve (Greig and Diehl 2012). These informational problems, in turn, increase the likelihood that mediation will fail and run the risk of souring disputants on the utility of diplomacy to settle their contested issues.

When Does Mediation Occur?

In order for mediation to occur, a third party must be willing to mediate, and the disputants must be willing to participate. This confluence often occurs when at least one of four broad characteristics is present. First, as noted in the previous section, a third party's power (Zartman 1997) and reputation (Greig and Regan 2008; Melin and Svensson 2009) affect mediation occurrences and outcomes. Mediators who can offer significant benefits (or impose significant costs) incentivize coming to the table and reaching agreement (or disincentivize not doing so). Similarly, those with a strong reputation for effectively mediating disputes can use this track record to encourage disputants to accept their help (e.g., Norway or the United Nations). Once involved in a specific conflict, a third party then develops a relationship with the disputants, which fosters the acceptance of that third party's future mediation offers (Kelman 1996).

Second, third parties with interests in the disputants or the conflict have incentives to mediate. These interests take two general forms: relational and contextual. The relational interests capture ties to the disputants, which affect the occurrence of mediation in multiple ways. Greig and Regan (2008), for example, observe that the willingness of a third party to offer mediation in civil wars is closely connected to the depth of the historical connections between the third party and the disputants. Shared ethnic ties, for example, encourage the acceptance of mediation offers. In contrast, disputants are less likely to accept offers of mediation from their former colonizers (Melin and Svensson 2009). This reflects both the asymmetric power dynamic that former colonizers bring to a mediation process and the political costs to disputants of allowing those colonizers to manage their disputes.

The contextual side focuses on the conflict itself. A third party highly concerned that a conflict will destroy a critical resource (e.g., oil) may mediate to protect that resource. Similarly, a conflict that threatens to spill over and draw in neighboring states may prompt mediation offers from those neighboring states or other third parties concerned about regional stability, whether states or organizations. This explains why major states (with vast, global interests, e.g., the United States), regional powers and regional organizations (with high regional stability concerns; e.g., South Africa or the African Union), and global organizations (e.g., the United Nations) feature prominently as serial mediators.

The pool of available mediators constitutes a third characteristic that significantly conditions the likelihood of mediation. Crescenzi et al. (2011), for example, find that the systemic growth of democracy and organization density (i.e., the number of shared IGO memberships among disputants) promote mediation because these factors increase the supply of mediators. This supply also depends, however, on the characteristics of potential third parties (e.g., whether the mediator has a relationship with the disputants; see above) and the characteristics of the conflict itself (see below). In intractable conflicts, for example, third parties may consider mediation too difficult to try, while disputants lack the trust to participate in mediation together. This would reduce mediation attempts.

Finally, once violence occurs, its evolution influences mediation. Scholars generally identify two distinct windows during which disputants are most amenable to mediation offers. The first window occurs when the level of conflict is low (Bercovitch et al. 1991). At this time, communication lines remain largely open between disputants, and the level of hostility and bitterness between them remains relatively low. Accepting mediation therefore involves little tangible change in disputant behavior because they have not yet experienced significant conflict costs. As the conflict grows in intensity and duration, however, it becomes more difficult for disputants to accept mediation. At this point, Maoz and Terris (2006) argue, disputants perform a cost–benefit analysis to decide whether to accept mediation, comparing their prospects for victory on the battlefield against the expected pay-offs from mediation. As the probability of victory falls, mediation gains in attractiveness. This harkens back to the hurting stalemate logic. Disputants look for alternatives to war as conflict costs rise, thereby increasing their amenability to mediation offers (Zartman 2000; Regan and Stam 2000; Greig 2005). A disputant should therefore increasingly accept offers of mediation as a stronger opponent confronts it (Clayton 2013).

The hurting stalemate logic unpacks further how disputants consider events on the battlefield, which alter their strategic environment and, therefore, their cost–benefit assessment of mediation. Greig (2015), for example, finds that the locations and movement of battles between rebel and government forces shapes the likelihood of mediation in civil wars in three ways. First, as rebels fight closer to the country's major cities, they impose greater costs on the regime; these in turn increase the government's willingness to accept mediation. Second, as the fighting moves toward the country's capital city, mediation becomes more likely; in such cases, governments see a rapidly approaching threat to the regime and try to head it off. Finally, when fighting occurs *near* the country's capital, the likelihood of mediation falls. Rebels see themselves as poised on the brink of victory, and they therefore eschew mediation. Moreover, governments might consider mediation undesirable under such conditions, concluding that they lack sufficient bargaining power and therefore preferring to fight on in the hope of improving their bargaining position.

BOX 6.1 Mediation Success in US–Cuban Relations

Case: Cuba–United States
Date of Conflict Management: 2014
Disputants: Cuba and the United States
Third Party: The Vatican

Outcome: Near-term success, uncertain future

The United States initially recognized the government of Fidel Castro after it overthrew the Batista regime in Cuba in 1959. Nonetheless, US–Cuban relations quickly deteriorated; over the next eighteen months, the US significantly reduced its economic ties to Cuba and scaled back its diplomatic links. Relations soured further as Cuba drifted closer to the Soviet Union. The US instituted a trade embargo against Cuba in late 1960, broke diplomatic relations with it in early 1961, and sponsored Cuban exiles who attempted to overthrow the Castro regime that same year (the Bay of Pigs Invasion). In response, Cuba allowed the Soviet Union to deploy nuclear weapons to the island, a move that the US perceived as an existential threat and which sparked the Cuban Missile Crisis of 1962. Over the next several decades, the relationship between the two countries remained fraught. The US considered Cuba to be an exporter of communism, a supporter of insurgents that destabilized pro-American governments in the region, and a state sponsor of terrorism. It also accused Cuba of gross human rights violations at home and criticized the regime for persecuting political opponents. Cuba similarly vilified the US, accusing it of interfering in Cuban affairs and promoting the suffering of the Cuban people through its embargo.

The long history of US–Cuban animosity impeded any potential change in their relationship. The entrenched hostility fostered a great deal of mistrust, and the lack of formal diplomatic relations effectively froze communications. Furthermore, internal politics within both countries made rapprochement difficult. Within the US, there was strong, cross-party opposition to the Castro regime. Hardliners in Cuba also opposed any improvement in relations. Cumulatively, these forces locked in the hostile status quo and undermined any efforts to change it.

The Vatican mediation effort, led by Pope Francis, highlights how a mediator can facilitate a change in relations between hostile actors. The Vatican itself lacks traditional power to use as leverage in support of a settlement. Nonetheless, its efforts demonstrate how the moral standing of a third party, the level of trust disputants have in the mediator, and the ability of the latter to facilitate communications can still make a decisive difference in conflict management.

The Vatican's mediation formally began in March 2014 when Pope Francis dispatched letters to the presidents of both Cuba and the US. These letters encouraged the two sides to "resolve their humanitarian questions" and "initiate a new phase in relations" (Yardley and Pianigiani 2014). They gained traction because they built upon Pope John Paul II's and Pope Benedict's prior diplomatic visits to Cuba, during which the Vatican had established a strong working relationship and foundation of trust with Cuba. Indeed, this relationship developed such that the Cuban government came to see the Vatican as its natural ally against the US embargo (Squires 2014). Both disputants also viewed the Vatican as trustworthy because of its successful track record as an effective, even-handed mediator in managing conflicts within the Western Hemisphere and beyond. Finally, the Vatican proved a suitable third party for both sides not only because Pope Francis had close ties to the region himself, but also because his secretary of state, Cardinal Pietro Parolin, had significant experience as a diplomat in the region and personal connections to a leading Cuban figure, the Archbishop of Havana (Yardley and Pianigiani 2014).

In response to the overture from the Vatican, the US and Cuba requested mediation; indeed, one US official argued that Pope Francis's letter "gave us greater impetus and momentum for us to move forward" (Chandler 2014). The Vatican therefore provided good offices between Cuba and the US during a series of meetings in Canada and at the Vatican. Vatican representatives limited their role to facilitating dialogue between the two sides, rather than crafting solutions or pressing for an agreement. This was precisely what the two sides needed.

In December 2014, the US and Cuba announced the framework for an agreement that would restore diplomatic relations and end the US embargo against Cuba. In the following months, the US removed Cuba from its list of state sponsors of terror and eased travel restrictions; both sides also released prisoners. Nonetheless, despite these positive advances, political leadership changes raise questions about the agreement's future. Following the election of President Donald Trump, the US instituted new restrictions on American travel to Cuba, and Trump has suggested that the US may revisit the desirability of further improvement in US–Cuban relations.

When and How Often is Mediation Effective?

To assess mediation's effectiveness, one first must ask: what do mediation success and failure look like? This question is difficult to answer because no single definition of mediation success exists. Scholars nonetheless focus on three broad indicators. The first searches for a cessation of violence. How long a pause constitutes success? Some ceasefires last only a few hours (see, e.g., the Burkina Faso "Christmas War," Box 9.1), whereas others persist for days, years, or even decades (on the latter, see the ceasefire in the Cypriot civil war or the Korean War armistice). At what point should the mediation be credited with succeeding?

A second indicator—whether mediation produced an agreement—avoids this dilemma, but raises others. Agreements take three broad forms: ceasefires, partial settlements (e.g., confidence-building measures like prisoner exchanges), and full settlements (resolving all the contested issues). Ceasefires stop violence, perhaps temporarily, but fail to address the issues underlying the dispute. The latter two settlements, in contrast, try to resolve the contested issues, either partially or comprehensively, and may therefore be better candidates for defining mediation success. Nevertheless, what if the settlement does not hold? If it collapses after two weeks, did mediation fail? What if it disintegrates after two months or two years? More generally, how long must a settlement hold for mediation to be credited with success? The answer to such questions may be context-dependent

(Bercovitch 2002). A settlement that lasts two months could be a significant achievement within an intractable conflict, perhaps even portending future, more durable pacts. In other conflicts, however, such a settlement may be labeled a failure.

The third indicator is more difficult to observe: whether mediation changes the disputants' relationship. Mediation fosters communication, builds rapport and trust among participants and with the mediator, familiarizes disputants with the conflict management process, and humanizes adversaries. Disputants therefore gain valuable information about one another's interests and possible areas of agreement. These outcomes may not immediately translate into a settlement; nonetheless, they lay the groundwork upon which future efforts can build (Kochan and Jick 2011).

Of the above indicators, the second involves the least subjective judgment. Did mediation produce an agreement, and if so, what form did it take? Using this metric, Figure 6.6 indicates that mediation fails more often than it succeeds. Over half of all mediation efforts in interstate disputes are unsuccessful. More optimistically, this also means that more than 40% of mediations in such conflicts produce some sort of an agreement. Note, however, that full settlements are rare; only about 6% of mediations in interstate disputes produce them.

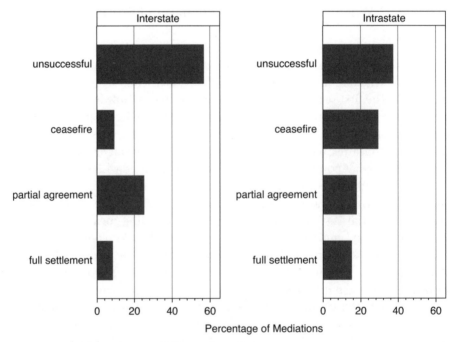

Figure 6.6 Mediation Outcomes by Type of Conflict, 1946–2006
NOTE: Interstate mediation data only available through 1999
DATA SOURCES: Bercovitch (2004); DeRouen et al. (2011).

Similar patterns emerge within intrastate conflicts. More than 37% of mediation efforts in these conflicts fail to achieve a ceasefire or settlement. An additional 33% produce either a partial agreement or a full settlement, but the latter remain uncommon, occurring in only 15% of cases. The greater propensity of mediation to produce full settlements in civil conflicts compared to interstate conflicts results from the situations in which the governments involved accept mediation. A government experiencing a civil war will often reject mediation because it wants to avoid legitimizing (other) rebel challengers. It accepts mediation only when the rebel group poses a significant threat to it, meaning that the governments that accept mediation are motivated to settle before the rebel position strengthens further.

Another distinction in mediation outcomes across interstate and civil conflicts is the prevalence of ceasefires. Only 5% of efforts to mediate an interstate dispute yield a ceasefire, while about 29% of efforts in civil wars do so. This sharp disparity likely reflects differences in the belligerents' relationship and the motivations of third parties. The civil war cases involve mediation efforts during ongoing fighting. As a result, these conflicts are "hot." Mediators will want to achieve a ceasefire in these conflicts, expecting that it will lay the groundwork for further efforts to settle the issues under dispute. In contrast, mediation in interstate disputes often addresses highly salient issues (e.g., territory) when active fighting is not occurring. Here, the mediators will focus more on obtaining a settlement of the issues, rather than a ceasefire.

Ideally, a mediated agreement not only settles contentious issues but also allows disputants to shift their relationship in a less adversarial, more cooperative direction. The 1994 peace treaty between Israel and Jordan, for example, set the stage for them to cooperate over water allocation, a vital issue to both states. Mediation succeeds in such cases because it changes the behavior of disputants toward one another. Importantly, agreements alone do not guarantee these behavioral changes. A Russian-brokered ceasefire between the Syrian government and rebel forces in Eastern Ghouta in March 2018, for example, lasted only a few hours; it is hard to argue that this agreement resulted in any tangible change in the disputants' relationship. Conversely, mediation can produce behavioral changes without necessarily settling the contested issues. The Cypriot civil war illustrates this type of frozen conflict. Despite recurring mediation efforts over decades, no peace settlement has resolved the Greek–Turkish Cypriot dispute, and the island remains divided. Nevertheless, active violence there remains largely absent. Mediation success is therefore contextual, depending on the conflict and the time horizon within which it is judged.

The challenges of distinguishing mediation success from failure have impeded consensus about the conditions under which mediation is most effective. In general, scholars connect the effectiveness of mediation to the characteristics of the mediator, the mediator's relationship with the disputants, the disputants' relationship with one another, and forces that affect the disputants' strategic calculus. None of these factors is deterministic, and much about mediation outcomes remains in the hands of the disputants and the mediator. Even when they take place under the most opportune conditions, poorly conducted mediations can still fail.

The factors influencing mediation success can be organized into categories similar to those that facilitate the initiation of mediation. First, the power and reputation of the third party affect mediation outcomes. More powerful third parties can marshal resources for leverage against disputants (Bercovitch and Gartner 2006; Crocker et al. 1999); these resources supply carrots to entice agreement or sticks to punish non-agreement. Major powers, for example, might use the threat of military intervention or economic sanctions to pressure disputants into an agreement (Smith and Stam 2003; see also Chapters 3 and 4). Similarly, a third party can exploit its reputation as leverage to foster agreement (e.g., the moral authority of the United Nations Secretary-General or the Vatican). This reputational leverage implicitly threatens to make disputants look bad to their key constituents if they walk away from the mediator without agreement.

A second set of factors stresses third-party interests and the relationship between the third party and the disputants. Mediator success increases when the mediator (a) possesses an interest in the disputants and their conflict, and (b) develops a good working relationship and establishes trust with the disputants (Zubek et al. 1992). These characteristics may derive from pre-established connections with the disputants (e.g., as alliance partners or in regional cooperation) or from a mediator's track record of success (as in the case of Norway). Regardless of the exact source, however, they increase the trustworthiness of the mediator, which then affects the prospects for reaching a mediated agreement (Maoz and Terris 2006). If information presents an obstacle to agreement, for example, then this trust proves vital; it allows a disputant to believe the mediator will accurately convey its interests to its counterpart, assess the latter's intentions, and reveal any third-party interests. Moreover, even power-based mediation strategies rely upon trust. For a third party to push disputants into an agreement, the disputants need to believe that the third party will make good on promises of rewards or threats of punishment. When a third party promises to guarantee an agreement (thus addressing the commitment problem), disputants similarly must trust that the third party will indeed enforce the agreement.

Both neutral and biased third parties can develop trust with disputants. Nonetheless, biased third parties may face some resistance; in particular, the disputant with whom the mediator lacks a close relationship may be hesitant to permit their involvement. Fears arise that the bias will unfairly advantage the counterpart or fail to account for the non-favored disputant's interests. Despite such drawbacks, however, biased mediators significantly benefit the bargaining process and facilitate mediation's success. A biased mediator, by virtue of its preference for a specific disputant, is often well positioned to extract concessions from the disputant they support. This favored disputant sees the mediator as safeguarding its long-term interests, and as unlikely to encourage it to make unwise concessions (Kydd 2003; Savun 2008; Svensson 2009). The bias also gives the mediator a stake in the conflict, thereby increasing its willingness to support the implementation of a mediated agreement (Kydd 2003, 2006).

The third set of factors focuses on the conflict context. Diplomatic settlements grow more appealing as disputants believe they are less likely to be victorious militarily. Consistent with this, the likelihood of reaching a mediated agreement increases as disputants approach rough equality in military power; under such conditions, an outright victory proves difficult, if not impossible (Touval 1982; Bercovitch 1989; Zartman 1981). As noted earlier, however, information barriers can interfere with disputants' ability to recognize when this equality has been reached. Fighting reveals the information that yields this recognition, and if the costs of conflict rise high enough, then a hurting stalemate sets in. The latter not only encourages disputants to accept mediation, but also increases the likelihood that mediation will produce an agreement (Greig 2001, 2015). Disputants facing such conditions understand that mediation, rather than violence, offers the best promise of managing and settling their conflict.

Finally, other contextual circumstances magnify the effects of a hurting stalemate. Political leadership changes, for example, can introduce new negotiators who are more open to considering and pursuing diplomatic solutions (Greig 2001). Similarly, when its broader threat environment changes, a disputant may need to adjust its conflict management strategy (Hopmann 1996; Kriesberg 1992). China, for example, settled its territorial issues with several neighboring states in the 1960s in order to refocus its resources and attention on internal challenges to the government's authority (Fravel 2008).

These various conditions highlight the importance of timing in mediation outcomes (Regan and Stam 2000; Zartman 2000). The notion of "ripeness" offers one lens through which to view this factor (see Chapter 2), suggesting that a concatenation of forces converge and favor diplomatic agreements (Zartman 2000; Pruitt 1997; Greig 2001; Walch 2016). General negotiation theory often invokes the ripeness concept; yet, unlike in bilateral negotiations (see Chapter 5), mediation permits a third party to *create* ripeness. By using its resources as leverage, for example, a mediator can alter disputants' perceptions about whether a mutually hurting stalemate exists, or can hasten its arrival. Mediators can also convey the information that an adversary believes a hurting stalemate exists, something that disputants fear doing themselves since this may signal weakness and invite exploitation. Yet mediators must also avoid overplaying their hand. If they manipulate a situation to induce a settlement, but the incentives offered are insufficient to change the disputants' behavior toward one another, then the agreement reached may not prove durable (Beardsley 2008).

BOX 6.2 Mediation Success and Failure in the Peru–Ecuador Dispute

Case: Peru–Ecuador Border Dispute
Dates of Conflict Management: 1941–42; 1981; 1995; 1996–98
Disputing Parties: Peru and Ecuador
Third Parties: Argentina, Brazil, Chile, and the United States
Outcome: Long-running, repeated failure, followed by success

The dispute between Peru and Ecuador stemmed from contradictory territorial claims dating back to borders drawn during the Spanish colonial era, with both countries basing their claims on different colonial-era delimitations. The intensity and intractability of this dispute is surprising given that the territory in question is difficult to access and has few natural resources (Simmons 1999). Nonetheless, Peru and Ecuador engaged in a series of militarized conflicts and wars over the disputed territory (e.g., in 1829, 1859, 1941, and 1995). They also attempted on thirteen occasions to resolve the matter (Cui 2014). However, because the conflict was embedded in a deep sense of national identity for both disputants, compromise proved difficult and violence likely. Attitude shifts within the two states ultimately set the stage for a permanent settlement of the dispute in 1998.

The Peru–Ecuador case illustrates both the way in which mediated settlements may be short-lived and the vital role that mediators can play in crafting a long-term settlement. Following a four-month conflict in 1941, the disputing states signed the 1942 Rio Protocol. This document was noteworthy not only because it sought to establish specific boundaries between the two countries, but also because four guarantors backed it: Argentina, Brazil, Chile, and the United States. Under the terms of the Protocol, the guarantors would assist with the agreement's implementation and help resolve any additional, related disputes that might arise. Although it initially seemed a clear case of mediation success, the settlement quickly unwound. A 1946 aerial survey charted a much more extensive watershed of the Cenepa River than had been known about in 1942. Ecuador then disavowed the Protocol and its terms, arguing both that the new survey demonstrably changed the conditions under which it was signed and that it had been imposed under duress as a result of the 1941 conflict (Cui 2014). This argument sought not only to alter the territorial status quo, but also to eliminate the role of the four guarantors by declaring the treaty null and void.

Despite a series of skirmishes, the guarantors held the Protocol's terms in place until 1995, when Ecuador and Peru fought the Cenepa War—a thirty-four-day confrontation that cost roughly $500 million and 1,500 fatalities (Palmer 2001). These costs motivated the disputants and third parties to find a permanent settlement to the dispute. The hurting stalemate had been building for some time. During the 1970s and 1980s, for example, military spending accounted for 17% of Ecuador's national budget and 30% of Peru's fiscal spending (Cui 2014). In addition to these monetary costs, opportunity costs arose as well. The need to divert resources to the military exacerbated the high levels of inflation, the significant foreign debt, and the soaring poverty within each state during this time. As the Cenepa War demonstrated, the Peru–Ecuador relationship undermined the broader goals of regional integration and economic development held by other actors (Simmons 1999). The latter incentivized third parties to renew their efforts to settle the conflict.

Argentina, Brazil, Chile, and the United States ultimately took a series of steps to foster the October 1998 agreement that settled the dispute. First, they pushed Peru and Ecuador to clarify the issues under dispute, something that had, surprisingly, not been done previously (Cui 2014). Second, they established the Military Observer Mission Ecuador–Peru (MOMEP), a 100-strong peacekeeper monitoring mission with personnel from all four guarantors. This monitoring force proved vital for the establishment of a long-term settlement because it significantly enhanced transparency and separated the combatants from one another; the border configuration and the disputants' past interactions necessitated this move (Simmons 1999). Finally, the guarantors employed a technical commission of border specialists to help develop precise settlement terms and offer the disputants a valuable face-saving device to deflect responsibility for unpopular terms (Palmer 2001). Thus, the eventual mediated settlement between Peru and Ecuador resulted from a concatenation of pressures: pushing the contending sides toward a settlement and encouraging trust and transparency between them. These actions illustrate the constructive role that effective mediators can play.

Conclusion

This chapter has examined the role that mediation plays in managing interstate and intrastate conflicts. As part of this discussion, we highlighted several important features of mediation and its use in managing conflicts:

- Mediation differs substantially from negotiation, although the two share key similarities. Both are voluntary diplomatic efforts that give disputants control over the conflict management process and outcome. The addition of a mediator changes how the disputants bargain. Mediators can help disputants convey information more credibly, guarantee agreements to assuage fears about their implementation, and take some responsibility for unpopular actions (e.g., concessions) to overcome disputants' domestic opposition. They also, however, introduce their own interests and motives into the process.

- Mediation encompasses a broad range of third-party diplomatic activities: from good offices (arranging and facilitating talks between disputants) to directive mediation (exercising strict control over the process by controlling communication, proposing settlement terms, and using rewards and punishments to incentivize getting to the table or to an agreement). The exact activities the mediator performs will depend on the mediator, the disputants, and the conflict.
- Either a third party or one or more disputants must initiate the mediation process. Third parties initiate 36% of mediations in interstate disputes and 88% of mediations in intrastate disputes. This discrepancy likely results from how the information problem affects disputants differently across these two types of conflict.
- A wide range of third parties serve as mediators. Whether in interstate or intrastate disputes, these mediators are largely state leaders (e.g., the Norwegian government: 45–50% of mediations), international organizations (e.g., the United Nations: 25–30%), and regional organizations (e.g., the African Union: 15–20%). Advantages accompany each mediator type. Powerful third parties can leverage resources to induce agreements through rewards or punishments; less powerful third parties can rely upon their relationship with the disputants (e.g., an ally) or their moral standing (e.g., the Vatican) to enhance the prospects for agreement.
- Defining mediation success is no easy task. Common indicators include whether the mediation stops violence (and for how long), produces an agreement, or changes the disputants' relationship. Scholars frequently rely on the second indicator—whether agreements occur as a result of mediation—because it is less subjective. Based on this indicator, over 50% of interstate conflict mediations and 35% of intrastate mediations prove unsuccessful. In both conflict types, a full settlement of all contested issues occurs less than 15% of the time.
- Mediation occurs and succeeds when a number of characteristics are present, including: (a) a powerful mediator (e.g., a major power or one with a reputation for successful conflict management); (b) a mediator with an interest in the conflict (e.g., preventing conflict spillover) or the disputants (e.g., a pre-existing relationship); and (c) a hurting stalemate (or ripeness). Importantly, third parties can foster the perception of a hurting stalemate by punishing disputants who refuse to negotiate or reach agreement; if the costs of continued conflict rise sufficiently, disputants will abandon violence and search for a diplomatic approach through which to settle their issues.

7

Legal Approaches

Five years after gaining its independence, Eritrea engaged in armed conflict with neighboring Ethiopia over the proper placement of their mutual border. When hostilities ceased in 2000, the disputing states established a Boundary Commission to arbitrate the issues that had caused the conflict—that is, to delimit and demarcate the border—as well as decide damage claims resulting from the armed conflict. To achieve this, the disputants asked the neutral, five-member Commission to gather evidence (e.g., from the United Nations Cartographer), receive their written and oral arguments, deliberate, and decide how to resolve any outstanding disagreements. They also agreed, at the outset, to consider the Commission's decision final and binding. The Commission began its work in earnest, mapping the boundary, completing demarcation, and hearing all injury and damage claims by 2009. As a result of these efforts, relations between Ethiopia and Eritrea slowly thawed. In 2018, diplomatic and trade relations resumed, and people started crossing through the newly (re)opened border posts.

Such legal approaches to international conflict management—arbitration and adjudication, in which a third party hears evidence through a formalized, legal process and issues a binding ruling that decides disputed issues with finality—seem a modern innovation, designed to handle the disputes that inevitably arise as globalization increases interdependence among states. There is some truth in this perception. The number of international courts, for example, exploded from the 1980s onward (see Figure 7.1). These courts also address an expanding litany of issues (e.g., the environment, trade, human rights, and territorial disagreements) and create an ever more complex, interrelated web of legal bodies (e.g., in Europe). Nevertheless, the use of legal approaches was well publicized before 1980. States first formalized arbitration, for example, in 1899, and established the first permanent international court, the Permanent Court of International Justice, in 1922. Prior to this, Latin American states had used arbitration to determine where to place their mutual borders (e.g., the 1883–91 Spanish arbitration of the Colombia and Venezuela dispute; see Ireland 1938), and international tribunals had worked to suppress the slave trade in Africa during the 1800s (Bethell 1966). Ancient Greece also not only relied upon a form of interstate arbitration to manage its disputes in the second century BC, but likely passed it on as a conflict management tool to the Romans (Matthaei 1908). Legal approaches therefore have a rich historical tradition as well as an expanding role in international politics.

Our focus throughout this chapter will largely be on interstate as opposed to civil conflict. This results from the general inapplicability of international law to the civil war context (see also Chapter 3). Those challenging a government for the authority of the state have no standing before many international legal bodies. Rebel groups, for example, are not permitted to bring cases before the International Court of Justice or some regional courts such as the Court of Justice of the Andean Community. Individual group members can bring cases alleging human rights violations to numerous international courts (e.g., the European Court of Human Rights or the Court of Justice of the Economic Community of West African States); these courts will not, however, resolve general concerns about who should govern a state and how (e.g., how much autonomy to grant a region). In addition, international law interprets a dispute *within* a given state as falling under that state's purview. There is therefore no legal basis on which an international legal body can intervene in domestic matters. An exception occurs for cases of grave humanitarian concern, but even then the legal foundation for such actions remains weak and the legal body will lack the capabilities to halt the violence (Joyner 2015). Legal approaches therefore almost exclusively handle interstate disputes.

Differences with Negotiation and Mediation

Although states' use of legal approaches has expanded over time, they are still employed less frequently than many of their common alternatives (e.g., negotiation or mediation). Three interrelated factors explain these trends. First, legal approaches are *binding*. This constitutes the primary characteristic that distinguishes legal approaches from negotiation and mediation. The latter two are consensual, non-binding strategies. If a disputing state dislikes how the mediation process unfolds or the solutions being proposed, it can walk away, even if a final, negotiated agreement exists and merely awaits its signature. The same holds true for negotiations. Legal approaches, however, remove this autonomy. At the time a state submits its dispute to a legal body, it agrees to allow a third party to consider its dispute (most often through a pre-established procedure) and provide a resolution (within certain constraints; see discussion below), and to abide by the third party's "award" or decision (we will use the term "award," rather than ruling, throughout the chapter because both arbiters and courts issue awards, whereas only courts typically issue rulings). These promises render legal approaches "binding" on disputants, who are—in theory—committed (or bound) to implement the third party's award, even if they do not like its terms.

Legal approaches therefore offer a key advantage over their alternatives: they can virtually guarantee a solution will be reached. Because control of both the conflict management process and its outcome depend on the third party, rather than the disputants, legal approaches, *once started*, proceed whether disputants accept or protest the third party's involvement as it deliberates. The "once started" caveat serves an important purpose. In order for a legal approach to begin, states must permit it to do so. This can occur through a special agreement dealing with a particular issue (that is, a *compromis*) or a standing treaty's terms, which refer disagreements concerning the treaty's content to a judicial body (e.g., the United Nations Convention on the Law of the Sea [UNCLOS], which refers maritime disputes to specified judicial actors like the International Tribunal for the Law of the Sea). It also occurs if states grant a judicial body standing permission to exercise jurisdiction over specified dispute(s) (e.g., the International Court of Justice [ICJ]).

As an illustration of this last point, the United Kingdom's 2017 declaration permits the ICJ to hear interstate disputes arising after 1 January 1987, but not *all* disputes. The UK specifies that the ICJ may not hear disputes between the UK and commonwealth countries, those involving nuclear disarmament or weapons, or those subject to other noted restrictions. Similarly, Ireland's 2011 declaration excludes its dispute with the United Kingdom over Northern Ireland from the ICJ's jurisdiction, while Equatorial Guinea's 2017 declaration allows the ICJ to hear "all disputes relating to the privileges and immunities of States, senior State officials and State property." As these examples demonstrate, international courts and arbiters do not automatically possess the jurisdiction to manage interstate disputes, and states frequently restrict their capacity to do so.

Given such restrictions, states will frequently *protest* as legal approaches unfold, arguing that the third party lacks the jurisdiction to decide its case. These protests do not exist in negotiation and mediation processes, as any complaining disputant can simply end the process at its discretion. They are, however, a necessary part of any legal approach, domestic or international. As with individuals in domestic society, states submit to a legal process because they want (or need) a resolution to their dispute, but are unable to reach it on their own. It is therefore unlikely that a mutually preferable and mutually ideal solution exists. This, in turn, suggests that one or more disputants will not wholeheartedly support the outcome a legal process might produce. Were these dissatisfied actors to abandon the process altogether, legal approaches would lose their binding element and collapse into a mediation-like approach instead. Somewhat dissatisfied actors, along with their protests, therefore derive from the key characteristic associated with legal approaches—their binding character.

The second characteristic that distinguishes legal approaches from negotiation and mediation concerns the actors involved and how they behave.
Negotiations lack a third-party conflict manager. Mediations incorporate a
third party, but do so in an entirely ad hoc and informal way. Disputants can
select any mediator they choose, including state actors (e.g., the President
of South Africa), representatives of international organizations (e.g., the
United Nations Secretary-General), religious leaders (e.g., the Pope), or private
individuals (e.g., former US President Jimmy Carter). The functions these
mediators serve then vary across and within disputes, ranging from a facilitative model, in which the mediator simply betters communication between
disputants, to a directive model, in which the mediator proposes settlement
terms, pressures the disputants to settle, or alters the rewards and punishments associated with settlement and non-settlement. The purpose is not
necessarily to find an *unbiased* third party (i.e., one that has no preference
regarding the substantive outcome of the mediation), but rather one that can
facilitate settlement.

Legal approaches to conflict management negate each of the mediation
characteristics noted here. First, disputants wishing to avail themselves of
a legal approach must generally select among a limited set of third-party
conflict managers. An exception might be made for arbitration because states
can technically permit any third party to arbitrate their disputes; yet, in
practice, the pool of arbiters is much more constrained. This results from the
confluence of two factors: the specialized legal knowledge needed to decide
a case involving a given, disputed issue, as well as the statutory authority
to do so. International courts typically possess these traits, and disputants
seeking legal approaches (e.g., adjudication) therefore often need a standing court to which they can apply for assistance. This, in turn, presupposes
the existence of standing courts, which become the first limitation on the
set of third parties that might oversee legal approaches. Nevertheless, disputants do not typically have access to the full universe of international
courts for any given dispute; each court does not have jurisdiction to hear all
issues. The World Trade Organization (WTO) Dispute Settlement Mechanism,
for example, hears trade disputes arising under the WTO Agreement; the
International Tribunal for the Law of the Sea hears cases that result from
diverging interpretations of the UNCLOS; and the International Criminal
Court (ICC) investigates possible cases of "genocide, war crimes, crimes
against humanity, and the crime of aggression." Thus, the list of available
courts narrows to those that possess the competence to hear a specific issue,
as specified in treaty obligations. If numerous courts have competence,
states will likely select the one they believe will serve their interests best
(Busch 2007).

Second, the function of third parties within legal approaches does not vary.
The statutes that govern international courts establish uniform procedures

that all cases submitted to it follow. The court then adheres to these procedures. Even arbitration, which has a more ad hoc flavor than adjudication (see
below), follows a standard process; indeed, the preamble to the 1899 Hague
Convention for the Pacific Settlement of International Disputes, along with
the Permanent Court of Arbitration (PCA) it created, suggests that the convention intended to achieve exactly this goal.

Finally, legal approaches seek to be unbiased, applying and interpreting
international law while remaining blind to the particular disputants involved
in any case. They achieve this via constitutional and procedural means. The ICJ
illustrates this well. It consists of fifteen independent judges elected separately,
but in parallel, by both the UN General Assembly and the Security Council, for
nine-year terms. The election process omits the veto of Permanent Members of
the Security Council, so as to prevent major states from dominating the court
(see especially ICJ Statutes, Article 10). It also substantially dilutes the entire
Security Council's influence over the court by requiring that *both* the General
Assembly *and* the Security Council elect each judge, within elections distinct
to each body. Once successfully elected, each judge then takes an oath to be
impartial and conscientious (Article 20), and may not "exercise any political or
administrative function, or engage in any other occupation of a professional
nature" (Article 16). As a last bastion against bias, any disputing state that does
not have one of its own judges sitting on the court may appoint one to sit for
any cases involving it that the court hears. Even when the court deliberates,
disputants ensure that their interests are at least considered. Other court
statutes similarly prioritize legal independence and, therefore, an unbiased
process.

The final characteristic that sets legal approaches apart from negotiation
and mediation involves the enforcement of settlements. Enforcement concerns plague all interstate agreements. Without a powerful, central authority
to ensure compliance, there is always a risk that a state will renege on its
commitments and, consequently, exploit its counterpart. Enforcement is a
greater concern with legal approaches than with other conflict management
approaches, however. Whereas negotiation and mediation allow disputants
to decide whether to accept a settlement, legal approaches remove this
autonomy. Moreover, cases that go through a legal process are likely to defy
easy settlement. States, as a general rule, prefer to retain control over the
management and outcome of their disputes, prompting them to try negotiation and mediation before legal approaches (see Gent and Shannon 2010;
Mitchell and Owsiak 2018). Thus, when a disagreement enters the legal process, we know disputants have halted voluntary concessions, even though
settling their disagreement demands such concessions. A legal approach can
subsequently dictate settlement terms and, therefore, the concessions each
party must make. If a lack of concessions sets the legal process in motion,
however, then any outcome a legal approach produces will fall short of at

least one disputant's preferred settlement terms, increasing the likelihood that this disputant will not cooperate with the settlement's implementation. Were international legal approaches to contain a mechanism for enforcing their settlements, this lower voluntary implementation rate would be moot. Unfortunately, they lack such a mechanism.

Arbitration versus Adjudication

Two specific tools fall under the broad heading of international legal approaches: arbitration and adjudication. These differ in some key characteristics, but each is dedicated to solving disputes on the basis of international law. We consequently discuss them together as "legal approaches" throughout this book, and many scholars do the same (e.g., Gent and Shannon 2010; Huth et al. 2011). Nonetheless, it is worth exploring their similarities and differences more explicitly.

Arbitration occurs when states agree to refer their disagreement to a third party, ask that third party to settle the disagreement (subject to provided constraints), and promise at the time of that referral to abide by the third party's award. The process begins with a *compromis* or its equivalent. A *compromis* outlines the issues under dispute, identifies the specific arbiter(s) to hear the case (or how those arbiters will be selected), establishes any powers granted to or constraints placed upon the arbiter's process or award (e.g., requesting that the arbiter focus on interpreting specific legal documents), and handles logistical matters (e.g., where to meet, what language to use, and so on). It may be either a distinct document or embedded within a treaty. The dispute settlement of the UNCLOS, for example, handles most key features of a stand-alone *compromis*. Depending on the exact terms of the *compromis*, arbitration therefore changes form slightly on a case-by-case basis. This quality gives arbitration a moderate ad hoc flavor and situates it between mediation (which is entirely ad hoc) and adjudication (which uses standing legal bodies and pre-set processes). Disputants retain more control over the conflict management process in arbitration than in adjudication because the courts that employ adjudication typically follow pre-established, uniform procedures that empower them to seek the evidence they wish to consider. Disputants hold less control than in mediation, however, since, once it is started, the disputants cannot voluntarily end the arbitration process.

Adjudication is the process most people associate with legal approaches. A disputant seeking adjudication applies to an international court (i.e., submits its case), and the court then hears arguments from the disputants, deliberates, and issues an award. In this process, the disputants cede additional control over the dispute's management—and not merely through the pre-set bodies and process guidelines noted above. Independent judges generally constitute a court, removing the possibility that disputants can select exactly which individuals hear its case. Similarly, although courts examine the interstate law specifically adopted by the disputants (e.g., bilateral treaties), they also consider other instruments of international law, including international custom (i.e., practices accepted as law), general legal principles (as recognized by states), and, where necessary, legal decisions and teachings (ICJ Statutes, Article 38). Disputants therefore lack the ability to constrain courts as they can arbiters.

Despite these differences, arbitration and adjudication generally look very similar in the international system. Both follow a similar process, which begins when one or more disputants initiate it. Generally speaking, all disputants cooperatively initiate arbitration, while only one (i.e., the claimant) initiates adjudication; yet this is not a hard-and-fast rule. Roughly 10% of applications to the ICJ occur via a "special agreement" (i.e., a joint application, or *compromis*-like document; see Mitchell and Owsiak 2018); similarly, arbitration processes may originate with one aggrieved state. How the process begins does not therefore distinguish arbitration and adjudication fully from one another.

Upon receiving an application, the legal body moves in one of two directions. If there is a respondent—that is, the disputants are not co-applicants—then the legal body asks the respondent to reply to the charges leveled against it. Respondents can question the jurisdiction of the legal body at this time. If they do, then the process enters a phase designed to answer that particular question. The legal body hears written and oral arguments from each side, after which it deliberates and decides whether it possesses or lacks the jurisdiction to hear the case. A negative finding leads to a case's dismissal (i.e., terminating the process); a positive finding moves the case to the next phase: deliberation "on the merits" (i.e., the substantive issues under dispute). If disputants are co-applicants to the process, then the legal body skips this jurisdictional issue and proceeds directly to arguments on the merits.

When considering the merits of the case, the legal body first receives written arguments before entertaining oral arguments from each disputant. It then closes the argument phase of the process, moves into deliberation (usually in private, or *in camera*), and issues its award. This award is binding on the disputants, who are obligated to implement it even though they may not agree with the award's terms and no formal enforcement mechanism exists. Some legal bodies permit the subsequent appeal of an award (e.g., the WTO Dispute Settlement Mechanism), but many do not, as there exists no higher legal body to which disputants might appeal. ICJ awards, for example, cannot be appealed (ICJ Statutes, Article 60); although disputants can ask the ICJ to revise its award, the court has so far rejected every request to do so (Mitchell and Owsiak 2018). The PCA follows a similar procedure to the ICJ. Thus, in general, legal awards are final once given.

Forms of International Courts

World politics is increasingly judicialized. As Alter notes, judicialization means that "citizens, organizations, and firms see law as conferring upon them rights, ... and politicians conceive of their policy and legislative options as bounded by what is legally allowed" (2014: 335). These rights require legal processes that define, interpret, and defend them, and the number of legal bodies available to aggrieved disputants has grown substantially in the last forty years. In some sense, this trend is both a cause and an effect of judicialization. The expansion of international legal commitments, international legal bodies, and the legal awards derived from these bodies has increased actors' awareness of their rights. This, in turn, has created greater demand for legal processes, necessitating the establishment of additional legal bodies. As this process perpetuates, the number of legal bodies rises.

Figure 7.1 illustrates this trend using data from the Project on International Courts and Tribunals (PICT) and Alter (2014). During the period 1816–2011, these data together track the number of international judicial bodies—that is, a permanent body of independent judges that follows predetermined rules of procedure to issue binding awards that adjudicate disputes involving a least one state or international organization (e.g., courts like the ICJ). The data also include quasi-judicial bodies, those that may lack one of the

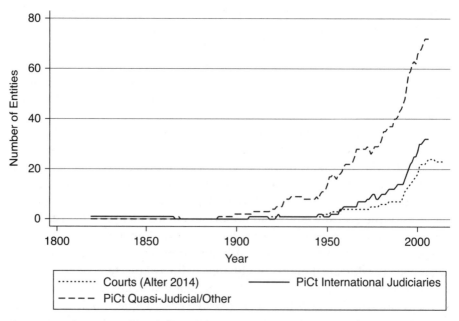

Figure 7.1 International Legal Bodies, 1816–2011
DATA SOURCES: The Project on International Courts and Tribunals (PICT); Alter (2014).

defining characteristics noted for judicial bodies (e.g., the Permanent Court of Arbitration, the Committee on the Elimination of All Forms of Discrimination against Women, and the [now extinct] European Commission on Human Rights). The number of international legal bodies expanded markedly in the post-World War II period, and especially after the end of the Cold War. Prior to 1919, only two international judicial bodies had existed: the African Slave Trade Mixed Tribunals (1819–66) and the Central American Court of Justice (1908–18). Quasi-judicial bodies fared similarly. By 1945, two judicial and ten quasi-judicial bodies existed; by 1990, these numbers had increased to fourteen and forty-three respectively; and by 2004, they had risen further to thirty-two and seventy-two respectively. This exponential trend may have leveled off by 2011. Alter's (2014) data, for example, suggests stability in the number of judicial bodies after 2001. Whether that trend holds in the future and for how long, however, remains to be seen.

What the above data do not illustrate are the key characteristics that differentiate judicial bodies from one another: membership, scope, standing, and procedure (see also Koremenos et al. 2001). First, every international judicial body requires state membership before a state can enter its legal processes, meaning that states must agree (usually via a treaty) to participate in the body. Nonetheless, not all states can belong to every legal body. General membership organizations (e.g., the ICJ, the International Centre for the Settlement of Investment Disputes, the WTO, or the International Criminal Court) allow any state to join. In contrast, regional membership organizations—for example, the Court of Justice of the Andean Community, the Court of Justice of the African Union, and the European Court of Human Rights (ECHR)—require member states to be within a particular region. The PICT data suggest that Europe and Africa contain a relatively high number of judicial bodies, while Asia contains almost none. China's reluctance to cede sovereignty to international judicial bodies, as well as its desire to control events within its sphere of influence, may explain this trend—something that, to a lesser extent, also corresponds with US behavior in the Americas.

Second, courts vary in the issues they hear. Some possess general jurisdiction (e.g., the ICJ), allowing them to hear any interstate dispute submitted to them. Others specialize more narrowly on trade, investment, human rights, or post-conflict justice (e.g., the WTO or the ECHR). Third, courts differ in who has standing, or can apply to and appear before the court. The ICJ, for example, only grants standing to states (ICJ Statutes, Article 34). The ECHR, in contrast, gives standing to both states and individuals, although the vast majority of its cases involve an individual applying for the court's assistance to correct a state's alleged transgressions. States, in other words, are almost always the respondents in ECHR cases, whereas individuals are the claimants. The ICC reverses these roles. Its prosecutor, a signatory state, or the UN Security Council can begin an investigation into an *individual's* alleged crimes; states can therefore only be claimants, while individuals are always the respondents.

Finally, courts differ somewhat in their procedures as well. Most require an aggrieved actor or all disputing parties to initiate proceedings (see above). An exception lies with the ICC, whose prosecutor can initiate an investigation against an individual believed to have committed genocide, crimes against humanity, war crimes, or crimes of aggression. After initiation, courts then diverge in the degree of their adversarial process. Some, such as the ICJ or the PCA discussed earlier, follow a less adversarial, albeit still contentious, process, while others function more like domestic trial courts, containing pre-trial, trial, appeal, and sentencing phases (e.g., the International Criminal Tribunal for the former Yugoslavia).

The Logic of Legal Approaches

Conflict management generally originates from three interrelated premises: (a) because disagreement is an endemic characteristic of systems in which actors are interdependent, the goal is not to eradicate conflict, but to channel its management into non-violent processes; (b) although disagreement should be expected, *persistent* disagreements create more costs than benefits—not only directly for the disputants, but also indirectly for others within the interdependent system; and (c) disputants cannot always settle their own disagreements. Legal approaches respond to these premises by creating unique, (semi-)permanent actors and processes, rather than more ad hoc ones, that take control over the settlement of a disagreement away from the disputants and hand it to a third party. Moreover, to prevent disputants from simply continuing their disagreement regardless of this third party's involvement, this process is also binding on disputants. Ideally, this means that states could compel one another to use a legal approach (when applicable), despite objections; at a minimum, however, it requires that once the legal approach starts, states cannot unilaterally back out of either it or the settlement it produces.

To create an international legal process, states initially looked to the judicial parallels found in domestic systems. Nevertheless, they immediately encountered a logical challenge: if states are independent, sovereign, and equal in stature in the international system, then no process can be truly binding on them. No authority, in other words, can compel states to abide by a legal process. Skirting this challenge produced the institutionalization of legal approaches that we witness over time. For some time, states used arbitration, which affords them greater control than adjudication (see above), on an entirely ad hoc basis. The transaction costs associated with these ad hoc legal processes, however, encouraged them to formalize arbitration. They therefore established a standing body, the Permanent Court of Arbitration (1899), to create an available supply of arbiters and to serve as registrar to arbitration cases; this reduced the need to start each arbitration process from scratch, while still preserving some of the ad hoc qualities of arbitration (e.g., determining the exact issue to be settled, selecting the arbiter, and restricting the arbiter's powers).

Despite these advances, two logical problems persisted. First, initiating the legal process still required the disputing states' permission. In the domestic realm, this would be equivalent to asking a respondent whether they agree to being sued in court; most respondents would reply negatively. If the approach depends on securing a positive response to begin with, then it shuts down in the majority of cases. Thus, the ideal that states sought to achieve—namely, that they could settle interstate disagreements over the objection of disputing states—remained elusive. Second, and relatedly, states face competing incentives: to bind other states, but remain unbound themselves. These incentives derive from states wanting predictability in other states' behavior, while maximizing their own autonomy.

A (partial) solution to these problems crystalized slowly with the emergence, organization, and expansion of international courts. The first step was to ask states to recognize a court's jurisdiction, subject to various conditions that the states themselves could specify. Under the 1922 Statutes and Rules of the Permanent Court of International Justice (PCIJ), for example— as well as the current Statutes of the ICJ—states *can* recognize the court's jurisdiction via: a special agreement; any separate treaty or convention they signed (dealing with any matters); or a declaration in which they explicitly accept the court's compulsory jurisdiction in any or all of four legal matters— treaty interpretation, international law (broadly understood), the violation of international obligations, and reparations for such violations (Article 36 in both documents). They also are able to condition their recognition of the court temporally or based on other members' reciprocal recognition of the court's jurisdiction. Through this process, states intend to bind one another *ex ante*. That is, they attempt to secure acceptance of the court's jurisdiction before the need for the court arises. If it does, the case then moves directly into the legal process, even if one of the states later raises objections to that process.

This version of the solution, although an improvement over prior arrangements, contains a Trojan horse: states can either opt out of or circumscribe the court's jurisdiction, and they can change their mind about the court at any time. This cuts two ways. Drafters may have intended it to make the court more attractive to signatories by permitting them to make a non-permanent commitment (Helfer 2013). Nevertheless, this also allows states to abandon the court when it acts contrary to their interest. When, for example, Nicaragua initiated proceedings against the United States at the ICJ in 1984, the US argued that the court could not hear the case. It first attempted (days before the case filing) to negate its standing acceptance of the court's jurisdiction, at least in cases involving Central American countries during the period 1984–86 (United Nations 1984). This attempt failed, after which the court heard arguments, decided it had jurisdiction to hear the case, and moved forward. The United States then withdrew entirely from the case proceedings and terminated its acceptance of the ICJ's jurisdiction altogether in 1985 (United Nations 1985). It has never re-accepted the court's jurisdiction since, and indeed remains phobic of *any* international court's jurisdiction. Behavior such as this threatens to undermine the foundation on which legal approaches operate.

The World Trade Organization embodies the next iteration of a solution to this problem: compelling signatories to participate and assigning self-enforcing consequences for not doing so. Under the WTO's precursor, the General Agreement on Tariffs and Trade (GATT), a signatory state could refer any unresolvable disagreement over the treaty's content to a panel, which would hear the matter and issue a report. The difficulty, however, lay in GATT's consensus default. While panels could be initially convened, the organization only adopted the panels' reports if no signatory including the respondent *objected* to the adoption. Because most respondents would prefer not to be involved in a legal process, this, in effect, left drafted "awards" (i.e., panel reports) that the organization never formally issued. The World Trade Organization fixed this. It not only granted signatories the right to a panel, but also reversed the consensus requirement; the organization now adopts a panel report unless consensus dictates that it *not* do so. Once these reports are adopted, aggrieved states can then retaliate against transgressors who injure them; whether they do so, however, is another matter (Busch and Reinhardt 2003).

In general, states struggle with identifying the dividing line between ceding too little and ceding too much sovereignty to legal processes. The exact placement of this line continues to be (re)drawn. Evidence to this effect appears in the protests that often accompany legal approaches. These protests occur frequently and take numerous forms, even as legal approaches generally anticipate and account for them procedurally. At the ICJ, for example, it is common for the respondent state to argue that the court lacks jurisdiction to hear the case (based on the logic outlined above; see, e.g., Kenya's objections to the ICJ's involvement in its ongoing maritime dispute with Somalia). Ultimately, a court generally has the final authority to decide whether it has jurisdiction, at which point the case continues along the established procedural path (see Statutes, Article 36). Nonetheless, international courts remain reluctant to push the boundaries of their jurisdiction too far, lest they lose state support; even the ICJ dismisses 27% of the cases it receives on the grounds that it lacks jurisdiction (Mitchell and Owsiak 2018).

A second protest type involves a disputant refusing to participate in legal proceedings altogether. China adopted this stance in the South China Sea arbitration initiated by the Philippines in 2013. As the 2016 award from this arbitration notes: "China did not participate in the constitution of the Tribunal [i.e., selecting the arbiters], it did not submit a Counter-Memorial in response to the Philippines' Memorial, it did not attend the Hearings on Jurisdiction or on the Merits [i.e., the substance of the case], it did not reply to the Tribunal's invitations to comment on specific issues of substance or procedure, and it has not advanced any of the funds requested by the Tribunal toward the costs of the arbitration." China's non-participation extended to correspondence as well: It "rejected and returned" all correspondence the Tribunal sent it, with a note that China "does not accept the arbitration" (South China Sea Arbitration 2016: para. 116).

Circumventing these protests proves critical to the logic of legal approaches. Accordingly, legal approaches often contain guidelines for how to proceed despite an intransigent disputant. The ICJ Statutes, for example, stipulate that if one disputant refuses to participate the other may ask the court to rule in its favor (Article 53). Similarly, non-participation does not halt the Permanent Court of Arbitration's process; arbitration simply proceeds without the absent disputant, as it did in the South China Sea Arbitration. These statutes attempt to preserve the crucial characteristic of legal approaches: that they bind disputants to the process and its outcome, even as self-interest motivates disputants to abandon it.

When Do Parties Choose Legal Options?

Legal approaches require disputing parties to cede control over both the process and outcome of their dispute's management. Nevertheless, they find this cession attractive under certain conditions. First and foremost, disputants may need to *resolve* their dispute, rather than *manage* it. Both actions hold value. In the midst of conflict, for example, obtaining a ceasefire that limits violence may be necessary before serious negotiations over a permanent resolution to the dispute can occur. Management therefore plays a crucial role, but risks treating only the symptom, rather than the underlying cause, of conflict. To address this underlying cause, parties must shift attention specifically to conflict resolution.

Legal approaches excel at resolution, but will be inappropriate for management short of that. When non-binding conflict management (i.e., negotiation or mediation) fails to resolve a dispute, it is often because the process depends on disputants' voluntary participation and they cannot themselves reach a resolution. They therefore settle for a short-term gain instead (e.g., a partial agreement or a *modus vivendi*). In contrast, legal approaches, once started, produce a final award that serves as a resolution of the contested issues under international law, largely because the process lies outside of the disputants' control. Enforcement concerns may persist after the award, but resolution terms result from the legal process regardless of whether these concerns exist. The challenge, however, is that legal approaches require a substantial amount of time to decide whether jurisdiction exists, hear arguments, deliberate, and issue an award. This renders them inappropriate for more pressing needs such as halting violence.

Numerous considerations motivate the need for a resolution of disputed issues. Conflict is costly, not just in time and resources, but also psychologically. Rivalries illustrate this dynamic best. A rivalry occurs when two states view one another as threats, competitors, and enemies (Colaresi et al. 2007). These sentiments increase hostility in the interstate relationship and lead the rivals to orient their foreign policy apparatus toward confronting one another. The apparatus then institutionalizes the relationship and encourages states to invest significantly in defending themselves against, or attacking, their rivals. Breaking out of this dynamic is hard. It often requires rivals to resolve their most salient, disputed issues—most notably territorial issues (Goertz et al. 2016). The mistrust that develops from a relationship based on hostility, however, undermines any non-binding resolution attempts; each rival worries the other will take advantage of it. A legal process allows states to circumvent this mistrust because settlement no longer depends on them alone. Indeed, rivals are more than 300% more likely to resolve their territorial issues via legal approaches than their non-rival counterparts (Huth et al. 2011).

The impetus for resolution may also derive from the need to produce a legal outcome. Occasionally, laws conflict or lack sufficient detail to preclude disagreements, at which point disputants need a court to sort the matter out legally—not just in their own case, but also for the purposes of building a broader consensus internationally. In the South China Sea, for example, multiple overlapping maritime claims require clarity about how to define key geographic features, since how this is done alters parties' legal claims to the disputed areas. "Low-tide features," "rocks," and "islands" entitle states to different distributions of territory under the UNCLOS; it therefore matters how one legally classifies a given geographic feature—a concern that has broader legal applicability than to the case at hand. When such situations arise, legal approaches become necessary. They are the only conflict management tool capable of building, interpreting, and re-enforcing international law. In accordance with this, scholars find that legal uncertainty about how to resolve a territorial dispute produces a roughly 200% increase in the likelihood of a legal approach being used (Huth et al. 2011).

Beyond these considerations, states may enter legal processes specifically to avoid responsibility for a dispute's outcome. As we have seen in previous chapters, conceding in a highly contentious dispute may produce audience

costs for a democratic or non-democratic leader, if the constituency supporting them believes that concessions run counter to the state's interests (Bueno
de Mesquita et al. 2003). A third party who controls not only the process but
also the settlement terms offers leaders political cover from these domestic
audiences (Gent and Shannon 2010). The leader can reluctantly agree to the
process, receive the award, and implement its terms, all while grumbling a
little if necessary to placate domestic audiences. Democratic leaders may be
more susceptible to such audience costs; consistent with this position, scholars find that democracies with a weak legal claim (states that do not expect to
fare well in a legal process, but strongly respect the rule of law) are over 300%
more likely than other states to find themselves in legal processes.

The foregoing discussion risks painting legal approaches as ideal for conflict
resolution, yet they come at numerous costs. We have already noted the greatest of these: legal approaches require states to cede control over their dispute's
management and outcome to a third party (Gent and Shannon 2010; Owsiak
and Mitchell 2019). For actors accustomed to being the highest authority in
their domain, and absent an international authority that sits above states,
this loss of control may prove too costly. States therefore often restrict legal
bodies' jurisdiction. For example, even though the UNCLOS contains legal
approaches designed to manage disagreements over the convention's content,
states can prevent these approaches from handling their most contentious
issues, namely disputes over sovereignty and military activities (UNCLOS,
Article 298). China, among others, has a declaration on file with the UN that
does exactly this.

A second cost, again already noted, concerns the time-consuming nature of
legal processes, which play out over a longer time frame than do non-binding
approaches. The ICJ process, for example, takes approximately four years from
the initial application to an award on the merits (Mitchell and Owsiak 2018).
The WTO estimates that its cases take approximately one year—a shorter,
though still significant, period of time for those anxious for a resolution.
Enforcement concerns, a third cost, compound matters. Although these
concerns arise repeatedly in interstate politics, contentious legal processes
exacerbate them. One party will likely be unhappy with an award. More powerful disputants may therefore (try to) avoid legal approaches altogether, and
they often do (Huth et al. 2011). Those that cannot, however, may not abide by
an award's terms (e.g., the US in the Nicaragua case or China in the 2016 South
China Sea Arbitration). A disputant that waits patiently for a legal award may
consequently learn that the award does not bring resolution. Moreover, even
if it does, enforcement of the award may cost it more than the benefits the
award provides (e.g., retaliation under the WTO, which requires the retalia-
tor to impose the allotted penalties and bear the attendant economic costs
involved in doing so).

BOX 7.1 Border Dispute Between Benin and Niger

Case: Benin–Niger Frontier Dispute
Date of Conflict Management: 2002–05
Disputing Parties: Benin and Niger (co-applicants)
Third Party: International Court of Justice
Outcome: Success

Neighboring states often struggle to define the jurisdiction of their sovereignty post-independence, especially when colonial documents lack precision. The Benin–Niger dispute exhibits this characteristic. Although colonial documents specified that the Benin–Niger boundary resided in the Mekrou and Niger rivers, they did not clarify whether the boundary followed the thalweg—that is, the main navigational channel—or the median line of the river. French practice may have employed the thalweg, but a British–French agreement in 1906 specified the median line as the boundary (Brownlie 1979). Interpretation of where this line lay left sovereign jurisdiction over islands in the river unclear, including Lété, a fertile island with a permanent population of about 2,000 people (Brownlie 1979).

Benin and Niger tried to resolve the issue bilaterally for many years. In 1994, they established a Joint Commission to delimit the border, but it failed to do so. The 1994 agreement, however, contained a clause committing them to peaceful dispute resolution, and in accordance with this clause, they agreed jointly to send the case to the International Court of Justice. In particular, they asked the ICJ to decide: (a) the boundary in the River Niger, (b) ownership of islands in the Niger, including Lété, and (c) the boundary in the River Mekrou. The ICJ award in 2005 responded to these specific points. It delimited both river boundaries, finding that the boundary in the River Niger generally followed the main navigable channels, while that in the River Mekrou adhered to the median line. It also assigned ownership of twenty-five islands to each of the disputants, with Lété going to Niger.

We classify this case as a success for two reasons. First, the parties complied with the ruling (Mitchell and Owsiak 2018). Second, the court clarified the legal ambiguities resulting from colonial legal documents. Such matters *should* appear before a legal body because awards are needed in cases like this to build, interpret, and re-enforce international law. The ICJ therefore not only settled an interstate dispute, but also fulfilled the larger function expected of it in the international legal system (see also Allen 2006).

Is Legal Dispute Resolution Effective?

Whether one finds legal approaches effective depends on how one defines the term. The effectiveness of legal approaches may lie more with award compliance than with reaching an award in the first place. Legal approaches, once started, reach a resolution in accordance with specified procedures; so a legal body reaching the end of its process is a low bar by which to judge its effectiveness. Compliance with awards therefore offers not only a different indicator of effectiveness, but also a more appropriate one for such approaches.

Legal processes will exert direct and indirect compliance effects on states. A direct effect occurs when a state changes its behavior after receiving an award from a legal process in which it participated. For example, after the Swiss Federal Council arbitrated the Colombia–Venezuela border dispute in 1922, and helped demarcate the border in 1922–24, neither side disputed their land border again (Huth and Allee 2002; Ireland 1938). Compliance with awards is the norm rather than the exception, despite the fact that legal approaches lack a mechanism to enforce their awards. For example, disputant states comply with over 90% of ICJ awards involving territorial, river, or maritime issues (Mitchell and Owsiak 2018: 454), and with over 80% of rulings issued by the WTO's Dispute Settlement Mechanism (Reich 2017).

The reasons for these high compliance rates remain open to debate, with scholars and critics offering four possible explanations (Mitchell and Owsiak 2018). First, self-interested states may benefit from a reputation for respecting international law (Guzman 2008). Because the international system lacks an enforcement mechanism, "good" and "bad" reputations allow states to predict one another's future behavior. These predictions are critical. Cooperation will be in everyone's best interest, but it only succeeds if actors do not take advantage of one another. Reputation allows states to identify the likely cooperators, in order to forge mutually beneficial agreements, while also avoiding the exploiters (see also Axelrod 1984).

Second, skeptics argue that states largely permit legal bodies to hear cases when they are willing to comply with a potential award in those cases. This selection effect would remove many possible instances of non-compliance. Although it appears plausible, existing evidence undermines this argument. For example, in ICJ cases we frequently observe one disputant questioning the jurisdiction of the court during the proceedings, even though they later comply with the court's award (Mitchell and Owsiak 2018). If compliance were generally decided before application to the court, these protests should be relatively infrequent. Similarly, if this skeptical argument held merit, we might expect legal approaches to handle less salient disputed issues, yet they frequently hear territorial disputes—arguably the most salient disputes facing states, since they touch upon sovereignty.

Third, key characteristics of either the disputants or the cases themselves could theoretically drive high compliance rates. Democratic states, for example, may comply more frequently with awards than non-democratic states, because the former hold the rule of law and judicial independence as core domestic political values. Finally, setting aside the issue of how cases enter the legal process (see above), "tougher" or more complex cases might generate a disproportionate amount of non-compliance. Scholars who examine these claims uncover mixed evidence (Mitchell and Owsiak 2018). Contrary to expectations, democratic pairs of states comply *less* often with ICJ awards in territorial disputes than their counterparts. Case complexity, on the other hand, may inform compliance. The ICJ takes nearly twice as long to hear cases that result in non-compliance as to hear those with which states comply. Assuming that case duration reflects complexity, this suggests that non-compliance disproportionately follows legal awards attempting to resolve the more complex cases.

In addition to the direct effects that compliance demonstrates, legal approaches may exert indirect effects on states as well, especially if judicialization leads politicians to "conceive of their policy and legislative options" as legally bounded (Alter 2014: 335). Indirect effects occur when a state changes its behavior without an award because it is (or might be) a disputant to a legal process that has not yet ended (or begun). Three situations create such indirect effects, all of which involve states operating "in the shadow" of legal processes. The first occurs when states involved in a legal process see the outcome toward which that process is moving and consequently decide to negotiate with renewed urgency. Doing so allows them not only to recoup the control they ceded to the legal process, but also grants them greater flexibility in crafting settlement terms than a court relying on its interpretation and application of international law alone. Moreover, if they achieve an outcome before the legal process ends, they simply request that the court dismiss their case. Nearly 18% of ICJ cases and 60% of WTO cases end this way (Mitchell and Owsiak 2018; Busch and Reinhardt 2003).

A second situation arises when states are party to an existing dispute that a legal body *might* hear at any time. This can incentivize reaching a successfully negotiated outcome before one of the disputants has the opportunity to apply to a legal body. The presence of a strong legal claim within a territorial dispute, for example, raises the likelihood of bilateral negotiation by 150–400%, producing terms more favorable to the disputant with that legal claim (Huth et al. 2013). Disputants know who would fare better in court and use this information to settle without the court's direct assistance. Similarly, under the UNCLOS, disputing states can refer unresolved maritime disputes to various legal bodies for an award. Were states involved in a maritime claim to know which legal body will likely hear their case, and the terms that body generally follows in its awards (i.e., the case law of the legal body), it might behave *as if* it had a pending court case (Mitchell and Owsiak 2018). In these examples, legal claims and case law function as focal points, allowing disputants to locate possible settlement terms more successfully in a bilateral setting (Schelling 1960). The disputants' incentive, as above, is to resolve the dispute at hand, even though it has not yet entered a legal process.

Finally, after observing a prior award, states may believe they are susceptible to a similar award and adjust their behavior before a dispute even arises. In the context of the ECHR, for example, empirical evidence supports this idea (Helfer and Voeten 2014). After witnessing human rights awards involving other states, numerous states change their domestic laws to align with those awards. Critics may see this latter effect as unique to the European experience, or as the result of an interstate court that hears disputes between citizens and states. We concur that such an effect will likely be rarer in pure interstate disputes, as states will argue that their dispute's circumstances are unique. Nonetheless, it remains a possible mechanism by which legal processes can extend a larger shadow over international conflict management. Such shadows enhance the efficacy of legal processes by helping resolve cases outside the courtroom for a variety of reasons.

BOX 7.2 South China Sea Arbitration

Case: South China Sea Arbitration
Date of Conflict Management: 2013–16
Disputing parties: Philippines (claimant) v. China (respondent)
Third Party: Tribunal constituted under the Permanent Court of Arbitration
Outcome: Failure

In 2013, the Philippines asked an arbitration Tribunal constituted under the UNCLOS treaty to declare that: (a) the UNCLOS limits China's entitlements to maritime space; (b) China founds its entitlements on "rocks" or "low-tide elevations," rather than "islands," which negates many of its claimed entitlements; and (c) China "unlawfully interfered with the exercise of the Philippines' sovereign rights and freedoms under UNCLOS and other rules of international law." These three broad points yielded fifteen specific issues (Reed and Wong 2016; Schoenbaum 2016).

China refused to participate in the proceedings altogether. Given this protest, the Tribunal first entertained the question of its jurisdiction. It interpreted China's position to be: (a) that the dispute concerned sovereignty, which lies beyond the scope of the UNCLOS; and (b) that even if the UNCLOS applied, the dispute involved maritime delimitation, which its declaration (on file with the United Nations) specified that legal approaches could not decide. After considering these matters, including the Philippines' position, the Tribunal decided it indeed had jurisdiction to hear the case, and responded to both of China's perceived objections. First, it proposed that it could address the Philippines' request without deciding the issue of sovereignty over any disputed areas. Second, it argued that the issues the Philippines raised might subsequently affect maritime delimitation, but that addressing these issues did not in itself constitute "maritime delimitation."

The proceedings on the merits continued in China's absence. In the award that followed, the Tribunal almost always disagreed with what it understood the Chinese position to be, issuing legal rulings on fourteen of the fifteen points raised by the Philippines. Most notably, the award, *inter alia*: (a) argues that China's "nine-dash line"—a mapped area to which China claims historic rights—affords China no entitlements under the UNCLOS; (b) determines that China's construction of artificial islands, as well as some of its fishing activities, violates the UNCLOS; (c) classifies numerous geographic features as "high-tide" or "low-tide," (d) defines "rocks" under the UNCLOS for the first time; and (e) clarifies that "fully entitled islands" must independently sustain either economic activity or a permanent community over a lengthy period of time (for a detailed legal discussion of the award, see Reed and Wong 2016).

Labeling the case as a success or failure depends on one's perspective. Broadly speaking, the Tribunal clarifies the legal classification of many reefs and shoals in the South China Sea. This may be a long-term success in a highly intractable, multiparty dispute; use of the award's terms in future conflict management cases will tell. Indeed, it may have already provoked China into clarifying what it intends its nine-dash line to be (Reed and Wong 2016). Nonetheless, we classify this award as a failure for three reasons. First, although it was technically legally binding on both disputants, China rejected the outcome immediately (Reed and Wong 2016). Second, it failed to secure China's participation in its proceedings. Finally, some legal scholars question the Tribunal's ruling, arguing that it not only created the impression of unfairness, but also was "incorrect and unwise" in how it decided on certain issues (e.g., China's nine-dash line; see Schoenbaum 2016; for a more positive view, see Reed and Wong 2016). Enforcement remains doomed under these conditions, making it impossible for the award to resolve the dispute successfully.

Conclusion

Throughout this chapter, we have explored the role legal approaches play in international conflict management. Our discussion yielded a handful of summary conclusions, including:

- Legal approaches to conflict management differ from negotiation and mediation in three ways. First and foremost, they are *binding* on disputants; once started, a disputant cannot unilaterally back out of either the conflict management process or the settlement award it produces. Second, legal approaches require the participation of *specialized, unbiased* third parties. They hinge, in particular, on third parties that possess the legal knowledge and authority necessary to build, interpret, and re-enforce international law fairly. Finally, enforcement concerns are more pronounced following legal awards, given that disputants often (partially) participate non-voluntarily in them.
- Arbitration and adjudication constitute the two specific tools that fall under the broader category of legal approaches. These tools share many similarities when operating in interstate disputes, particularly in how cases proceed from application to award. Nonetheless, there are notable differences. Arbitration retains a more ad hoc flavor than adjudication, which grants disputants greater control over the conflict management process and outcome (e.g., the ability to select the arbiter and specify the factors that arbiter should consider when making its decision). Adjudication, in contrast, relies on standing courts that pre-date the dispute and adhere to a more rigid, predetermined process.
- The number of international legal bodies has increased exponentially since 1980. These bodies differ in membership, scope (i.e., the issues they can hear), and procedure (e.g., who has standing). Some regions (e.g., Europe or Africa) possess more legal bodies than others (e.g., Asia).
- Legal approaches operate on the logic that conflict resolution sometimes requires disputants to transfer control over a dispute's outcome entirely to a third party. International history shows that states struggle with transferring such control; in particular, it reveals a tug-of-war between states' desire to create such a process and their desire to retain autonomy and sovereignty.
- Disputants choose legal options for numerous reasons. They may seek a permanent resolution to their conflict, so that the costs of conflict end. Unable to achieve this outcome on their own, they turn to a legal body whose process, once initiated, pushes toward an outcome independent of their voluntary participation. Alternatively, some disputants want a legal body to clarify international law, not just in their own case, but

for future ones as well. Finally, by taking responsibility for a dispute's outcome, legal bodies provide disputants with political cover from the domestic backlash that might accompany the resolution of highly salient issues.

- The effectiveness of legal approaches might be measured in two ways: in terms of their direct and indirect effects. Compliance with awards serves as an indicator of the former, and the empirical record shows high compliance rates with many legal bodies' rulings (e.g., the ICJ and the WTO). Indirect effects might stem from the "shadow of legal bodies"; that is, as states observe the development of case law, the threat of litigation may motivate them to negotiate more successfully before legal cases are filed or heard, or to change their behavior before potential cases arise.

8

Peace Operations:
Peacekeeping and Peacebuilding

As Somalia descended into civil war in the early 1990s, the first of several international peace operations deployed to the country. These operations were tasked with addressing a series of problems within what has been described as a "complex emergency," including widespread violence, refugees, starvation, and human rights violations. Such challenges illustrate the fact that the core conflict management goal of limiting armed conflict is often intertwined with other concerns that arise in contemporary civil conflict. Moreover, the short-term and long-term outcomes of the various Somali operations provide evidence of both successes and failures, with life-saving humanitarian aid delivered even as the basis for durable peace and stability remained elusive.

The previous chapters on conflict management approaches moved from active military involvement to less coercive and more traditional third-party roles. Here, we return to approaches that are more operational (i.e., actively involved on the ground), rather than separated from the conflict at hand. Peace operations, as with military interventions (see Chapter 3), involve the deployment of troops. Nevertheless, the configurations, purposes, and activities of peacekeepers distinguish them from regular military operation forces. We discuss these differences in detail below; most notably, the peacekeeping soldier is lightly equipped (with limited firepower and capability) and part of a much smaller operation, with personnel numbering a few thousand (the average is under 6,000 for UN operations), as opposed to several hundred thousand (as was the case in the First Persian Gulf War).

Although the term "peacekeeping" is used to cover a panoply of activities, there are some distinctions between peacekeeping in its original or traditional form and what are now referred to as peacebuilding operations. We first turn to understanding these two forms of peace operations—the term that we use to encompass both forms.

Traditional Peacekeeping versus Peacebuilding

Modern peace operations date to the Suez Crisis in 1956, when the United Nations first deployed armed forces following a ceasefire between Egypt and Israel, although unarmed observers had performed similar functions previously in the Middle East and South Asia, starting in the late 1940s. Traditional peacekeeping involves the stationing of a small number of lightly armed troops or observers to separate the combatants—generally following a ceasefire, but before an agreement exists that resolves the underlying, disputed issues.

Peacekeeping operations are based on the so-called "holy trinity" of host-state consent, impartiality, and a minimum use of force (Bellamy et al. 2010). Host-state consent means that the country on whose territory the peacekeepers are deployed must grant permission for that deployment. This is consistent with the sovereign rights that states have within their own borders. It also means that permission can be withdrawn, as when Egypt asked the United Nations Emergency Force (UNEF I) peacekeepers to leave prior to the 1967 Arab–Israeli War. Although other, non-state parties to the conflict do not have to grant consent, they often do so by supporting or signing a ceasefire agreement that provides for the peacekeeping force.

While deployed, peacekeepers should also be impartial, carrying out their tasks without prejudice for or against any of the disputants. Peacekeepers therefore do not alter the balance of forces between the combatants. This impartiality should not be confused with neutrality. Peacekeepers, for example, will impartially report ceasefire violations by whoever commits them, even if repeatedly by only one side. In contrast, neutrality implies taking no position on controversies between or actions against the protagonists, even if the mandate calls for it. Finally, peacekeepers use minimum force, typically engaging in military action only in self-defense; that is, their rules of engagement are very limited, which yields forces of far smaller size and lighter arms than standard military forces.

Since the end of the Cold War, peace operations have increasingly incorporated objectives beyond the supervision of ceasefires, primarily in response to the needs of civil war contexts. The term "peacebuilding" has been used to capture many of these functions, which often extend beyond the peace operation itself (for a conceptual discussion, see Jenkins 2013; Barnett et al. 2007). The purpose of peacebuilding (minimally) is to prevent the recurrence of conflict. Rather than simply halt violence, however, some peacebuilding activities are predicated on a long-term conflict management strategy that addresses the root causes of the conflict. Creating or supporting non-violent conflict management mechanisms (e.g., functioning national judiciaries), facilitating and monitoring elections, repatriating refugees, providing humanitarian assistance, and strengthening government institutions—including assistance with local security and law enforcement—constitute activities consistent with this goal, although they might also serve other goals, such as the promotion of liberal values (Diehl and Druckman 2018). Other activities not formally connected with the operation may also be undertaken (e.g., fostering economic development or building civil society institutions).

Most conceptions of peacebuilding envision it occurring after some type of peace settlement between warring parties, rather than in the post-ceasefire/pre-settlement phase typical of traditional peacekeeping's deployment. They typically also deploy to a civil context, following an intrastate war, significant ethnic conflict, or even within a failed state. These characteristics demand not only the deployment of more troops than their traditional cousin, but also different types of personnel, including civilian police and other staff members. As a result of this complexity, peacebuilding operations frequently coordinate with other actors—for example, non-governmental organizations (NGOs), such as the Red Cross, or other international organizations, such as the World Bank.

The terms peacebuilding and state-building (or nation-building) are sometimes used interchangeably. Generally, state-building focuses more on building or restoring government authority. It stresses the security and institutional aspects of governance in the post-conflict context. Dealing with these aspects might be a prerequisite for peacebuilding, but is not synonymous with it. Rather, peacebuilding deals more with social, economic, and humanitarian elements: human rights, economic justice and development, humanitarian assistance, and reconciliation (Richmond and Franks 2009). Whereas state-building prioritizes stabilization, peacebuilding concentrates on societal change. For example, NATO forces in Afghanistan have emphasized strengthening local security forces, whereas UN peacekeepers in Haiti have worked on promoting sustainable development and human rights observance.

Peacebuilding operations might also relax some aspects of the holy trinity of traditional operations. For example, they could enter a conflict without the full consent or cooperation of the host state or other warring parties. In the case of a failed or near-failed state (e.g., Somalia), no central authority may exist to grant consent. In other circumstances, peacekeepers may deploy over the objections of the government, or at least well short of its full cooperation (e.g., Sudan). Impartiality and rules of limited engagement might also be compromised when the peacebuilding missions must pacify an area; for example, peacekeepers in Mali have been deployed to respond to an "asymmetric threat" from terrorist and separatist groups and have had to use offensive military force to achieve their mission.

In practice, contemporary peace operations typically involve some traditional peacekeeping elements as well as some peacebuilding functions. As noted below, the exact mixture of missions and associated functions varies considerably depending on the operation.

The Logic of Peace Operations

If traditional peacekeepers are relatively small in number and lightly armed, how do they prevent a recurrence of conflict between more numerous and heavily armed combatants? Most notably, they seek to limit violence in a conflict zone primarily by deploying troops as an interposition or buffer force that separates the combatants following a ceasefire. The size, rules of engagement, and military capacity of these forces are, however, insufficient to stop a determined party from attacking its opponent; Israeli forces, for example, quickly broke through peacekeeping lines (United Nations Interim Force in Lebanon [UNIFIL]) in southern Lebanon during the 1982 invasion. Nonetheless, by separating combatants physically, peacekeepers prevent the accidental engagement of opposing armies, thereby inhibiting minor incidents that could escalate to renewed war. They also deter deliberate cheating on ceasefire agreements: physically separating the protagonists facilitates the detection of violations, provides early warning of any attack, and therefore decreases any tactical advantages from surprise attacks. The accurate identification of aggressors is also likely to produce international condemnation, especially when that aggression targets the peacekeepers themselves. The costs to international reputation and the possibility of sanctions, combined with the decreased likelihood of quick success, are designed to be sufficient to deter any renewal of violence (Fortna 2008). In these ways, peacekeepers offer the kind of "credible commitment" referenced in Chapter 2: disputants can trust the peace operation to perform these functions in an even-handed fashion, where they would otherwise mistrust ceasefire promises from their enemies.

Traditional peacekeeping is also predicated, at least in part, on promoting an environment suitable for conflict resolution. Peacekeepers do not engage in diplomatic initiatives themselves, although other personnel from the sponsoring organizations (e.g., the UN) may do so. Rather, they are thought to create the conditions conducive to the hostile parties resolving their differences. Several rationales for this thought exist. First, a cooling-off period, evidenced by a ceasefire, can lessen hostilities and build some trust between the protagonists. This increases the likelihood both that the protagonists will turn to diplomacy and that their efforts will succeed. Second, in times of armed conflict, leaders and domestic audiences become both habituated and psychologically committed to the conflict, and some segments of the population profit politically and economically from the fighting. Before diplomatic efforts can succeed, these processes must be curtailed or interrupted, something with which a well-maintained ceasefire can assist.

The ways in which peacebuilding operations are designed to work vary substantially according to the particular "missions" that accompany a given peace operation. Missions are subsumed under operations and involve coherent categories of tasks designed to achieve given purposes or mandates; for example, election supervision and promoting democracy are missions for some peace operations, and could involve tasks such as supervising the voter registration process and monitoring polling sites on election day. In addition, some missions—such as disarmament, demobilization, and reintegration (DDR)—require a credible commitment (see Chapter 2); groups will be unwilling to give up their weapons without the monitoring and guarantee of third-party peacekeepers. In other cases, efforts to support the rule of law and protect human rights are mandated to a peace operation. For example, the African Union–UN Hybrid Operation in Darfur (UNAMID) was charged with these responsibilities, which it undertook by monitoring, mentoring and building the capacity of local police forces and supporting community-oriented policing.

Although diverse in their specific tasks, all peacebuilding missions desire to prevent the renewal of violence in a twofold manner. One element involves dealing with the underlying causes of conflict: if the issues in dispute can be resolved, then the likelihood of violence occurring again will be reduced. A peace agreement often resolves the contentious issues, and peacebuilding efforts are part of the agreement's implementation plan. The second element has a longer-term focus. Bettering the conditions of a post-conflict society through improved services, democratic accountability, and institution building will make new and serious disputes are less likely to arise, and if they do, they can be managed by the new norms and mechanisms put in place by the peacebuilding operation.

Patterns in Peace Operations

By some estimates, there have been just over 200 peace operations since the end of World War II (Diehl and Balas 2014). In this section, we unpack some of the broader historical trends in peace operations, focusing on their frequency over time, the kinds of conflicts to which they have been deployed, the types of operational missions performed, and where they are likely to occur. These trends show that peace operations have become more numerous, more complex, and more focused on civil conflict.

Trends in Frequency

Although it is now standard practice to consider peacekeeping as one item on the menu of conflict management choices for international organizations, it was not always that way. The history of peace operations can roughly be divided into four historical eras (for detailed descriptions, see Diehl and Balas 2014). The so-called "golden age of peacekeeping" (1956–78) commenced with the deployment of the United Nations Emergency Force (UNEF I) after the Suez Crisis, which ushered in a number of UN operations that supervised ceasefires in some longstanding interstate conflicts. This was followed by the so-called "Lost Decade" (1979–88), during which no new peace operations were authorized and many believed that peacekeeping had become passé. This latter view proved incorrect, as the end of the Cold War in the late 1980s and early 1990s marked the beginning of an era that involved a dramatic expansion in the number of new operations, which took on a series of "peacebuilding" missions in addition to traditional ceasefire-monitoring roles. Operations in Somalia and Haiti illustrate this trend. The legacy of this era remains with us in the contemporary period, but peacekeeping has expanded further since the turn of the century, with more "robust" missions involving greater use of military force and deployments in contexts of ongoing conflict, as opposed to post-ceasefire environments. Indeed, UN peace operations have increasingly been authorized under Chapter VII of the UN Charter dealing with the use of force, in contrast to earlier missions authorized by Chapter VI, which centers on the peaceful settlement of disputes (Howard and Dayal 2018).

As Figure 8.1 demonstrates, the first forty years of peace operations were characterized by an infrequent resort to this approach. Only twenty-eight peace operations began between 1945 and 1988, an era that includes the "golden age" and "Lost Decade" periods noted above. These were, and sometimes continue to be, largely UN operations that perform traditional missions, such as supervising ceasefires with a relatively small number of troops. Hot spots such as the Middle East have received the most attention. The end of the 1980s then represented a major inflection point, as peace operations increased dramatically in number and in geographic range. Between 1989 and 2016, 172 operations started. This represents a rate of more than six new operations per year, although many are related to one another and deploy to the same conflict (e.g., numerous operations to Haiti, beginning in 1993).

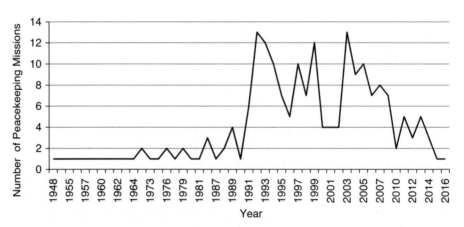

Figure 8.1 New Peacekeeping Missions, 1948–2016
Data Source: Diehl and Druckman (2017).

The length of peace operations varies tremendously. On average, an operation lasts 5.69 years—although operations range from a few months to more than seven decades (the UNTSO mission in the Middle East and the UNMOGIP force monitoring the ceasefire in Kashmir between India and Pakistan) (Diehl and Druckman 2017). Post-Cold War peacekeeping has tended to involve multiple and consecutive operations sent to the same conflict—each of which is of limited duration—rather than a single operation that stays in place for an extended time. The multiple operations sent to the former Yugoslavia exhibit this characteristic.

Trends in Conflict Types

Early in their history, peace operations were largely confined to conflicts between states. The UN, for example, sent the first observation missions to monitor ceasefires in the Arab–Israeli (United Nations Truce Supervision Organization [UNTSO]) and India–Pakistan (United Nations Military Observer Group in India and Pakistan [UNMOGIP]) rivalries respectively. This pattern continued through the 1970s, with internal issues drawing attention only as they intersected with decolonization concerns, as was the case both in Western New Guinea (United Nations Temporary Executive Authority (UNTEA)/United Nations Security Force in West New Guinea [UNSF]) and in the Congo (United Nations Operation in the Congo [ONUC]).

The dramatic expansion of peace operations into conflicts that have an exclusive or significant intrastate (i.e., internal) component began in the 1990s, largely in response to the increase in civil conflict noted in Chapter 2. Thereafter, intrastate operations have constituted almost 90% of new operations, whereas previously they were a minority. Since 2000, the only operation sent to a purely interstate conflict was the one deployed following the Ethiopian–Eritrean War (United Nations Mission in Ethiopia and Eritrea [UNMEE]). Even this interstate war, however, originated in the internal secessionist conflict less than a decade earlier that resulted in Eritrean independence.

Trends in Operational Missions

Originally, peace operations were intended to perform a single primary mission: supervising ceasefires between disputants. More recently, however, peacekeeping has evolved to include a wide variety of other missions. For example, within the UN context during the period 1948–2015, there are clear patterns and dramatic changes over time in mission mandates, including ceasefire monitoring as well as ten other missions, such as election supervision and those that fall under the peacebuilding rubric (e.g., promoting the rule of law).

Peace operation mandates generally correspond to the goals of a given operation. Table 8.1 lists the range of different missions carried out by peace operations.

Among UN peace operations, only about 17% are confined to one mission. In other words, almost 83% are tasked with more than one mission. The average number of missions is 4.17, and therefore peace operations are being assigned multiple roles in achieving the goals of promoting international peace and security. A small set of operations are even asked to do a majority of the missions on the list (Diehl and Druckman 2018), such as MINUSMA (United Nations Multidimensional Integrated Stabilization Mission in Mali) with ten missions.

Peace operations changed dramatically with the end of the Cold War, most notably by the increase in the number of new operations authorized by the UN Security Council, as reflected in Figure 8.1. Accompanying this is a 130% increase in the number of missions assigned to peace operations. In the Cold War period (operations initially authorized before 1991), peace operations averaged 2.11 missions, whereas post-Cold War operations (authorized in 1991 and thereafter) had a mean of 4.88 missions. In a related fashion, operations deployed in interstate conflicts had 1.73 missions on average, whereas those with a civil conflict component averaged more than double that: 4.84 missions for civil wars and 4.00 missions for internationalized civil wars respectively (Diehl and Druckman 2018).

Table 8.2 indicates that traditional peacekeeping missions involving observation and monitoring of ceasefires remain the most common, present in almost 80% of peace operations. Nevertheless, many other missions appear one-quarter to one-half of the time. Only preventive deployment and pacification/coercion missions are rare. The former does not occur because of the difficulties associated with early warning systems in the United Nations, whereas the latter mission goes beyond "robust" peacekeeping and is more often taken by multilateral or unilateral national military forces than by peacekeepers. Into the twenty-first century, there has also been a shift toward stabilization missions, consistent with state-building, and away from other purely peacebuilding concerns (Baranyi and Powell 2008).

Where Do Peace Operations Occur?

Peace operations do not deploy to all conflicts, but rather to a small subset, even as their numbers have increased over time. Organizations, for example, are more likely to authorize and deploy operations in high-severity and protracted conflicts (Gilligan and Stedman 2003), suggesting that the international community uses peace operations to address the biggest threats to international peace and security. Nevertheless, this also means that peace operations may struggle to succeed, as they are deployed to contexts with the least prospects

Table 8.1 Peace Operation Mission Types

- Traditional Peacekeeping/Ceasefire Monitoring: the stationing of troops as an interposition force following a ceasefire to separate combatants and promote an environment suitable for conflict resolution.

- Humanitarian Assistance: the transportation and distribution of life-sustaining food and medical supplies, in coordination with local and international NGOs, to provide for the basic needs of threatened and internally displaced peoples.

- Election Supervision/Promotion of Democracy: observation and monitoring of a democratic election following a peace agreement among previously warring internal groups and/or institution-building to promote political participation and democratic culture.

- Preventive Deployment: stationing troops in an area that has not yet experienced violence to deter the onset or prevent the spread of violent conflict from other areas.

- Disarmament, Demobilization, and Reintegration (DDR): some or all of three sets of activities, including the collection, documentation, control, and disposal of small arms, ammunition, explosives, and light and heavy weapons from combatants and often from the civilian population and/or the supervision of troop withdrawals; the formal and controlled discharge of active combatants from armed forces and groups; and the process by which ex-combatants acquire civilian status and gain sustainable employment and income. These generally follow a peace agreement that ends a civil war.

- Pacification/Coercion: quelling civil disturbances, defeating local armed groups, and forcibly separating belligerents through the proactive use of military force to establish or reestablish "peace."

- Human Rights/Protecting Threatened Populations: the establishment of safe havens, "no-fly" zones, and guaranteed rights of passage for the purpose of protecting or denying hostile access to threatened civilian populations or areas of a state, as well as specifically protecting designated groups from attack or human rights abuses.

- Local Security/Law and Order: the maintenance of law and order in cities and towns, including the physical protection of civilians in their everyday activities and policing of those areas, sometimes in conjunction with indigenous forces.

- Rule of Law/Civil Society: assisting in the establishment of legal processes and institutions for the maintenance of order and the peaceful resolution of disputes and/ or the creation or encouragement of NGOs that promote citizen dialogue and input into government functions.

- Local Governance: the provision of standard government services and facilitation of indigenous government institutions to provide such services.

- Restoration/Reconciliation: providing mechanisms for changing attitudes among former disputants, redressing past grievances and crimes, and enhancing cooperation among former enemies.

SOURCE: Diehl and Druckman (2018).

Table 8.2 Distribution of Peace Operation Mission Types, 1948–2015

Mission Type	Count	% Total
Traditional	55	78.57
Humanitarian Assistance	36	51.43
Election Supervision/Democratization	32	45.71
Preventive Deployment	1	1.43
DDR	39	55.71
Pacification/Coercive Peace Keeping	2	2.86
Human Rights Protection/Protect Threatened Groups	25	35.71
Local Security/Law and Order	38	54.29
Promoting Rule of Law/Civil Society	22	31.43
Local Governance/Government Services	18	25.71
Restoration/Reconciliation	24	34.29

DATA SOURCE: Diehl and Druckman (2018).

for success. In contrast, operations are less likely when the target state is allied with or is itself a major power (Mullenbach 2005), although several peace operations in the Middle East are exceptions (e.g., between Israel and Egypt). Finally, no evidence indicates that operations are more likely in secessionist conflicts, non-democracies, former colonies of UN Security Council members, or states with high primary commodity exports (Gilligan and Stedman 2003), as conventional wisdom might suggest.

At the subnational level (that is, within a country), peacekeepers deploy to the areas of greatest need—where the most severe violence occurs. These tend to be major urban areas. That said, there is often a lag time between the onset of that most serious violence and the deployment of the peacekeeping troops (Ruggeri et al. 2016). In the post-Cold War era, Sub-Saharan Africa has been the primary locus for peace operations, a shift away from an earlier concentration on the Middle East and elsewhere (Diehl and Balas 2014).

Accounting for Trends

As described above, peace operations have become more numerous, have been confined primarily to civil conflicts, and thus have been tasked to perform a broader set of missions beyond ceasefire monitoring. They have also become more likely to be carried out by agents other than the United Nations (see the following section). What accounts for these dramatic changes, many of which have taken place following the end of the Cold War?

Balas et al. (2012) explored a demand-side perspective that argues that peace operations responded to a shift in the kinds of conflicts facing the global community (specifically, a change from predominantly interstate conflicts to internal ones—see Chapter 2 on conflict trends), a general increase in conflicts of all varieties, and an increase in the number of more comprehensive, negotiated agreements that terminate those conflicts. Thus, one explanation is that the international community has responded to a change in the environment and adapted peace operations accordingly.

There is mixed support, however, for the demand-side argument. The number of civil conflicts has indeed increased with the end of the Cold War, and there was a decline in the number of interstate wars, at least for the decade of the 1990s. Nevertheless, the general trend toward the increase in armed conflict that was apparent in the immediate post-Cold War period has dissipated and then reversed in the twenty-first century.

Changes in conflict patterns do not explain the disproportionate increase in the rate of intervention by the UN and regional organizations. That is, the likelihood of a peace operation being sent to a given conflict is now greater, *ceteris paribus*, than in previous eras. Even as armed conflict—the demand for intervention in the form of peace operations—has been reduced in the last decade or more, peace operation creation has maintained its high rate. Particularly important is the scope and intensity of conflicts, not merely their raw numbers. Civil conflicts increasingly have negative externalities, or spillover effects, on neighboring states, threatening international peace and security as well as providing impetuses for the international community to act; such effects include refugee flows, cross-border fighting, and even genocide.

A more substantial cause may lie within the increased prevalence of comprehensive, negotiated agreements that terminated civil conflicts. These agreements appeared far more frequently in the post-Cold War world (see Joshi et al. 2015). This suggests that disputants may have requested more peacebuilding activities as part of their peace agreements. The expansion of peace operation missions and the increase in peace operations generally are not merely functions of the opportunities available to the international community, but also of its willingness and capacity to take action, and in a more expansive fashion.

There is now greater capacity for multiple organizations to meet any changes in demand. As new peace operations have skyrocketed in the last twenty-five to thirty years, it is unrealistic for any single organization to assume responsibility for them. At the same time, regional (e.g., EU) and sub-regional (e.g., Economic Community of West African States [ECOWAS]) organizations have moved beyond their founding economic purposes to include conflict management. As a result, peace operations are now carried out by multiple actors (see the section below on agents).

The rise in the number of missions and peace operations can be linked to substantial shifts in three related international norms: sovereignty, democratization, and humanitarian intervention. During the Cold War, before a traditional peacekeeping operation could be deployed, host-state consent was required. That traditional notion held that sovereignty was nearly absolute: what happened inside state borders was solely the domain of national governments. More recently, exceptions to state sovereignty have been carved out and the idea that the international community has a vested interest in, and can play a role in, internal matters has been increasingly accepted (a similar point is made in Chapter 3). Post-Iraq examples include the continuing involvement in fighting the Taliban in Afghanistan and incursions into Syria to destabilize the Assad regime.

Democratization has also influenced intervention behavior and a commitment to democratic principles, strengthened in the wake of the Cold War. Since 1989, when disputants sign agreements to end conflicts that request a peace operation, they often ask the operation to accept tasks associated with democratization, such as monitoring elections (for example, in Angola, Liberia, Mozambique, and Namibia) or facilitating rule of law changes associated with the emergence of a new, democratic entity (for example, in East Timor). In short, as the norm of democratization strengthened after the Cold War, disputants have been encouraged to build democratic states, and organizations have offered to expand their mandates to include such associated peacebuilding tasks.

Finally, there has been the rise of the norm of humanitarian intervention. This norm encourages the international community to intervene in the event of humanitarian disasters and widespread human rights violations (see Chapter 3). Of course, in the case of failed states, no sovereign barriers to intervention exist, although there has not been an expectation of an affirmative response by the global community until recently. Peace operations have been sent to areas without the full cooperation of the legally sovereign state (for example, Kosovo Force [KFOR]; see Box 3.2), or where no functioning government existed (for example, United Nations Operation in Somalia [UNOSOM I]). Both illustrate a shift in international norms that allows for a more expansive role for peace operations.

Agents of Peace Operations

The UN deployed a peace observation operation in 1948 after the first Arab–Israeli war. Over the next forty years, the UN remained the predominant, traditional peacekeeping agent. Regional organizations had yet to be formed or were relatively weak in their delegated powers or material capabilities. This, along with the number of operations, changed dramatically starting in the late 1980s and into the twenty-first century. As indicated in Table 8.3, the UN still carries out a significant proportion of operations (just under 40%), but now regional organizations undertake about half. The most

Table 8.3 Peace Operations by Sending Agencies, 1946–2016

Agency	Number of peace operations
United Nations	79
European Union	33
Multinational Peace Operations	20
Organization for Security and Cooperation in Europe (OSCE)	16
Organization of African Unity (OAU)/African Union (AU)	14
North Atlantic Treaty Organization (NATO)	13
Organization of American States (OAS)	7
Economic Community of West African States (ECOWAS)	5
Commonwealth of Independent States (CIS)	3
League of Arab States (LAS)	2
Southern African Development Community (SADC)	2
Commonwealth Secretariat	2
UN/Regional Hybrid Peace Operations	2
Economic Community of Central African States (ECCAS)	1
Economic and Monetary Community of Central Africa (CEMAC)	1
Pacific Islands Forum (PIF)	1

SOURCE: updated from Diehl and Balas (2014).

active regional organizations include the European Union, the Organization for Security and Cooperation in Europe, NATO, and the Organization of African Unity/African Union. Multinational operations, those carried out by ad hoc collections of states, constitute the remaining operations (just over 10%).

One major difference between traditional peacekeeping and peacebuilding is the number and variety of actors involved in carrying out missions. In the former, soldiers exclusively or primarily carry out the duty of monitoring ceasefires. In contrast, other actors supplement or supplant soldiers in many peacebuilding activities (e.g., other agencies of the UN or regional organizations). For example, the UN Department of Humanitarian Affairs coordinates humanitarian assistance. The World Bank provides loans to promote economic development, whereas the International Monetary Fund assists post-conflict states with short-term financial adjustments. Moreover, NGOs are critically important to peacebuilding efforts. Many have been in place in a country prior to and during the civil conflict there. In the conflict's aftermath, they work both with and independently of other actors.

UN peace operations are authorized by the UN Security Council, and as such require support from at least nine of the fifteen members of the Council, and no opposition from the permanent five members. The mandate of an operation is specified in the authorizing resolution. Operations are typically approved for six-month periods, subject to renewal. There is considerable variation in the organization, conduct, and frequency of regional peace operations. The most obvious differences are the institutional capacities for conducting such operations, which condition all other aspects of their policy and performance. The ability of regional organizations to play significant roles is largely conditioned by the authority granted to them by their members. In some cases, no security institution at all exists in a region, foreclosing the possibility of peace operations except by an ad hoc multinational coalition of regional states. For example, the north Asian region has no regional organization to handle conflict management. In other parts of Asia, the institutions are relatively weak. Until recently, the African Union (primarily its predecessor, the Organization of African Unity) was structurally weak, often no more than a forum for a yearly meeting of heads of state on that continent. The AU has more recently expanded its activities to include election monitoring and peace operations, including the deployment of forces to Sudan (African Union Mission in Sudan [AMIS]).

At the other extreme of the continuum is the European region, which has multiple institutions for dealing with security. These have overlapping memberships and complementary roles. Of longest-standing importance is NATO, which traditionally handled the duties for collective security and collective defense. At the end of the Cold War, its missions were modified, and it now functions as a peacekeeper in Bosnia, Kosovo, and Afghanistan. In some cases, there are "joint" operations involving multiple agents. These take several forms: sequential, in which one organization hands over duties or provides bridges to another operation; those occurring in parallel to each other; and finally "hybrid" operations, in which there is integration between two organizations (Balas 2011); the African Union–UN operation (UNAMID) in Darfur is an example of the latter.

Are Peace Operations Effective and Under What Conditions?

Do peace operations prevent the renewal of conflict and promote peacebuilding? If they do, are there some conditions that are more conducive to this success than others? In this section, we address these questions, although the evidence is much clearer for traditional peacekeeping functions than it is for peacebuilding activities.

Do Peacekeeping and Peacebuilding Work?

Traditional operations' success at armed conflict varies widely. The longstanding Multinational Force and Observers (MFO) in the Sinai, for example, has successfully monitored the peace between Israel and Egypt since late 1981, no doubt aided by the Camp David Accords between the former enemies. In contrast, the United Nations Interim Force in Lebanon (UNIFIL) was helpless as rocket fire from Palestinian camps rained over the heads of peacekeepers into Israel, followed by Israeli retaliatory raids. UN peace operations also could not deter Israeli invasions of Lebanon in 1982 and 2006. Relying less on anecdotes or individual cases, the evidence suggests, however, that peace operations are effective at maintaining ceasefires, although this outcome is not necessarily complete or universal.

Fortna (2008) offers a detailed analysis, comparing conflicts to which peace operations deployed with those to which they did not. Overall, she finds that peace lasts longer when peace operations deploy; depending on contextual factors (e.g., time period), Fortna notes that peace operations reduce the renewal of warfare by 30% to 95%. The MFO illustrates such an outcome, although the opposite outcome appears in the United Nations Assistance Mission for Rwanda (UNAMIR); these operations are discussed in more detail in Boxes 8.1 and 8.2. Finally, Ruggeri et al. (2017) find that conflict episodes last for shorter periods when peacekeepers go to particularly conflict-prone locations inside a country; whether they deter the onset of local conflicts, however, remains less clear. Without peacekeepers, though, a substantial risk exists that the conflict will spread to a neighboring, rival state (Beardsley and Gleditsch 2015).

The outcomes of peacebuilding activities become more difficult to discern. Not only do fewer studies of these impacts exist, but the outcomes of interest are long-term; thus, the results of more recent peacebuilding efforts are not yet fully apparent. Furthermore, peacebuilding involves a variety of activities, and general assessments of an operation will be difficult because success might be apparent for some missions (e.g., election supervision) and not others (e.g., promoting the rule of law). Despite these challenges, there are some indications of a mixed record of success.

Doyle and Sambanis (2006) consider the aftermath of all civil wars that began in the twentieth century. They first examine whether armed conflict was renewed. Broadly, peacebuilding was more successful in the presence of UN peace operations than not (also confirmed by Collier et al. 2006). In particular, UN peace operations delay, and in some cases prevent, the renewal of violent conflict; this mirrors the findings on traditional peacekeeping above.

The findings are considerably murkier with respect to promoting democracy. Doyle and Sambanis (2006) conclude that political participation and other indicators of democratization showed positive movement in the aftermath of peacebuilding operations. Other studies are more cautious about the results of peacebuilding. Sisk (2008) finds ambiguous evidence that peace must precede a successful transition to democracy and notes that such peace efforts sometimes undermine the quest for stable democracy. Most pessimistic are Richmond and Franks (2009), who are highly critical of the "liberal" peace-building strategy that prioritizes democratization and free market economic growth. In five case studies, they give credit to peace operations for "negative peace" (i.e., preventing the renewal of warfare). Nevertheless, they note that state security rather than human security has been achieved. Democratic institutions emerged, but these created serious political conflict. Furthermore, rule of law initiatives privileged some societal elites or failed in the face of a weak judicial system.

There is some consensus that peacebuilding does not necessarily promote economic growth. Although a few operations promoted prosperity, others were clear failures (Paris 2004). Still other studies found no evidence for post-war economic growth in the shadow of peace operations (Doyle and Sambanis 2006).

When Do Peacekeeping and Peacebuilding Work Best?

The research results summarized in the previous section suggest that peace operations, on average, limit violence and, to some extent, promote peace-building success. Nevertheless, such a conclusion does not apply to every peace operation, as there are successes and failures among different kinds of operations and across historical eras.

The conditions for peace operation success (and failure) can broadly be divided into three categories (Diehl and Balas 2014). The first set of factors, "operational," includes those associated with the organization and execution of peace operations. In effect, these factors lie largely within the control of the operation itself, or at least within the purview of the authorizing agency. The second set of conditions, "contextual," refers to those elements associated with the conflict. Finally, "behavioral" aspects derive from the reactions of belligerents and key third-party actors.

Operational

The peacekeeping operation itself has limited control over its actions; the timing of its deployment and its mandate are determined by the organizing agent, which in turn is determined by the membership of the organization or coalition. Research suggests that the UN holds no inherent advantage over regional arrangements with respect to conflict management (Boehmer et al. 2004). Some regional organizations might be ill-equipped to conduct peace operations, but the trade-off between UN and regional-sponsored operations is not necessarily determinative of success. The most one may be able to say is that a peace operation carried out by a certain regional grouping may experience serious problems. The alternatives, however, are not guarantors of success and are still subject to other influences that determine the operation's fate.

Despite the relative importance of contextual and behavioral factors discussed below, there are some operational elements that are important for traditional peacekeeping and peacebuilding success. Most notable for the former is the size of the peacekeeping operation (Hultman et al. 2013). Broadly, the larger the number of personnel in the peacekeeping operation, the better able it is to prevent the renewal of violence and, in particular, to limit civilian casualties. If peacekeepers inhibit conflict by monitoring ceasefires and deterring surprise attacks, it is perhaps not surprising that a larger force performs better; such a force is better able to cover a wider area, thereby detecting violations and deterring would-be aggressors. Unfortunately, many peace operations lack optimal troop numbers, as the perceived costs of larger operations and the unwillingness of members to contribute personnel constrain authorizing organizations. Beyond sheer size, the diversity of the force in terms of national troop composition is also associated with operation success, specifically in reducing civilian deaths (Bove and Ruggeri 2016).

Box 8.1 Traditional Peacekeeping Success and Failure

Case: The United Nations Assistance Mission for Rwanda (UNAMIR)
Date of Conflict Management: 1993–96
Disputants: Rwandan Government and Rwandan Patriotic Front
Third Party: United Nations
Outcome: Failure

The first phase of the UNAMIR deployed in the aftermath of the 1993 Arusha Accords between the Rwandan government and the Rwandan Patriotic Front (rebel movement). This agreement sought to end the civil war and facilitate a transitional period of government reform and, ultimately, national elections. UNAMIR began as a traditional operation, whose primary mission was to (a) supervise the ceasefire, (b) monitor the border between Rwanda and Uganda, and (c) oversee both the handing over of illegal weapons and the return of refugees. It operated under the classic holy trinity of consent, impartiality, and self-defense rules of engagement. Thus, eighty-one military observers were initially deployed in 1993, only growing to less than 3,000 in subsequent months.

The downing of a plane carrying the President of Rwanda triggered chaos in the country, including a campaign of genocide against the Tutsi population by the extremist Hutu elements then controlling the government. UNAMIR was unable to deter or stop the carnage, and estimates of the resulting fatalities range from 300,000 to 800,000. The peace operation effectively collapsed in 1994 when the UN Security Council reduced the force's size to 270 individuals, even though it was also tasked with humanitarian relief and working for a new ceasefire.

The second phase of the UNAMIR operation took place in the two months after the genocide. It was charged with addressing humanitarian concerns and providing security for personnel from an international war crimes tribunal. Although the force strengthened significantly to over 7,000 (including 5,000+ soldiers) and successfully delivered some humanitarian aid, violence persisted in various pockets around the country. Despite these latter achievements, many consider UNAMIR to be one of the worst UN peacekeeping failures in history, especially given the genocide's death toll.

The reasons UNAMIR failed comport well with those identified in the earlier sections on success and failure. Peace operations have difficulty separating combatants and monitoring ceasefires in civil wars. In Rwanda, non-state actors, operating without uniforms or official control, conducted most of the killing, and it was almost impossible for the peacekeeping force to distinguish between Hutu and Tutsi, or combatant and non-combatant. Operating in the urban environment of Kigali, the peacekeepers also could not adequately separate the armed militias from the civilians they were supposed to protect. Moreover, the peacekeeping force was poorly designed to enforce the ceasefire, even if contextual conditions were good. The small force could not adequately patrol the large country; reducing the force size—whether to save money or because leading UN states lacked the political will to continue—only made things worse. It was also ill-equipped to take enforcement action against the perpetrators of violence even if the rules of engagement had been relaxed.

Case: Multinational Force and Observers (MFO)
Date of Conflict Management: 1982–present
Disputants: Egypt and Israel
Third Party: Multinational collection of states
Outcome: Success

The Arab–Israeli rivalries are some of the most enduring in the world, and have been the focus of UN peacekeeping efforts several times. A major breakthrough occurred in 1979, when Israel and Egypt signed a peace agreement that, in part, provided for a withdrawal of forces in the Sinai around the Egyptian–Israeli border. That agreement envisioned a UN peacekeeping force to monitor the withdrawal and supervise the ceasefire (there had been two previous ones stationed there). Yet political disagreements in the Security Council and Israel's suspicion of the UN prevented the latter from authorizing another operation. As an alternative, a multinational coalition of twelve (mostly, but not exclusively, Western) states therefore constituted the force.

Deployed in 1982, the MFO remains in place today, with largely the same mandate as it had originally. It monitors the ceasefire and reports on any illegal stationing or movement of troops and border personnel in the area. It also ensures freedom of navigation through the Strait of Tiran. Thus, this operation has a very traditional mission consistent with the "holy trinity" elements described above.

By all accounts, the mission is a success. Egypt and Israel have not gone to war again, despite a history of four previous wars. Indeed, the number of hostile incidents in the Sinai has been minimal. There are several factors accounting for this success. First, the MFO deployed *after* a peace agreement, thus allowing it to monitor a ceasefire in which the belligerents resolved some disputed issues. Accordingly, both states have cooperated with the force and have strong interests in not renewing the conflict. Supervising a ceasefire between only two state parties (for most of its existence) and along a defined border/ceasefire line also makes the peacekeeping job easier. This is supplemented by the geographic advantages of the deployment area being sparsely populated and mostly desert area; such characteristics allow the peacekeepers to detect prospective violations more quickly and easily than would be the case in an urban area.

Recent problems for the MFO have arisen not from the state parties, but from Islamic State (ISIS) affiliates operating in the area. Egyptian government troops and ISIS forces have battled in the Sinai, with MFO soldiers sometimes caught in the cross-fire. MFO is not charged with dealing with this threat, but it does somewhat complicate its ability to perform its primary functions.

Beyond structural elements such as size are organizational adaptions and strategies; these are most often explanations for failure rather than useful in identifying conditions for success, especially with respect to peacebuilding operations. Howard (2008) emphasizes adaption in operations that come from information collection and analysis in post-conflict societies, coordination between different peacebuilding actors, and the ability to work well with local disputants, especially in terms of managing small disagreements so that they do not escalate. Such "learning" is determined, in part, by the effectiveness of the bureaucracy, emphasizing functions in the UN Secretariat, for example, rather than field actions taken by peacekeeping commanders. This is often difficult for international organizations in general (Barnett and Finnemore 2004). One of the characteristics of failed peacebuilding is poor coordination between the various actors involved (Richmond and Franks 2009), thus precluding one important source of learning.

On the one hand, the UN still lacks the regional expertise and many of the resources for analysis that are necessary for the management and adaptation of a peace operation; this deficiency persists despite recommendations by previous UN reports to address these problems (Benner et al. 2011). Political considerations can inhibit learning and this can have a deleterious effect on performance. Nevertheless, political considerations can also provoke learning in some cases, and Benner et al. (2011) cite how past failures with building police institutions as well as gender concerns have prompted the UN to reassess its policies and institute new procedures and strategies.

Perhaps most fundamental is the orientation or organizational "culture" of the peace operation that determines the strategies undertaken. No aspect of peacebuilding has come under greater criticism than its neoliberal orientation in promoting democracy and aggregate economic growth. The attempt to rebuild states on the Western model, often in a one-size-fits-all fashion (Richmond and Franks 2009), has often been ineffective; in particular, holding early elections has proved to be a failure when economic stability and security have not been in place. The institutions of democracy have been prone to backsliding, as can be observed from Cambodia to Bosnia. The mismatch between peacebuilding and the needs of the area of deployment is also evident at the micro or local level. In her case study of the United Nations Mission in the Congo (MONUC), Autesserre (2010) blames the dominant peacebuilding culture within the UN for failures to promote conflict resolution in Congolese society. Specifically, she criticizes the UN for holding an incorrect, top-down view of conflict, with an emphasis on the superstructures of regional and global sources of tension. This view led the peace operations and associated bureaucratic personnel to ignore local actors and processes in promoting conflict resolution. Local governance, not peacebuilding governed by external elites, is said to be associated with sustainable peace (Goetze 2017; Tschudin and Trithart 2018).

Similarly, the values and orientations of the peacebuilding personnel are also not reflective of those that they serve or the local conditions on the ground (Autesserre 2014). Those who work on peacebuilding missions that deal with promoting the rule of law, humanitarian assistance, and enhancing local capacity often do not understand local traditions and practices. The strategies they use and the institutions they promote come from Western models of development and governance that don't necessarily work in other contexts.

This mismatch between strategy and local context is most evident in debates over how and whether peacebuilding operations should promote democracy relative to promoting economic stability. Paris (2004) decries the world community's attempts to build democracy and stability too quickly and without adequate resources. He also thinks that domestic institutions need to be properly strengthened before peacebuilding can succeed. The war-proneness of democratizing states (Mansfield and Snyder 2005) is also a condition that seems to complicate any attempts at peacebuilding. Paris advocates promoting economic policies that moderate rather than exacerbate conflicts and ensuring that the state has effective security institutions and competent bureaucracies. Supplementing these are civil society organizations that can unite different parts of society and mitigate factors that promote conflict. Similarly, Doyle and Sambanis (2006) argue that local capacity, defined in terms of local economic health and resources, is also strongly related to success. Paris cautions against democratic elections being conducted too soon in the peacebuilding process, a point echoed by Autesserre (2010). There needs to be some opportunity for reconciliation and stability. Plans for elections and governing systems must also be carefully considered. Doyle and Sambanis note that ethnically divided societies already pose a difficult context for peacebuilding. Political stalemates resulting from elections or other democratic processes inhibit progress toward stability and development. The Implementation Force (IFOR) efforts in Bosnia and Croatia have helped limit the renewal of civil war, but broader peacebuilding (e.g., the repatriation of refugees) has been stifled by elections that have handed power to ethnically polarized parties.

Contextual or Environmental Factors

Peace operations must deal with the circumstances of the conflict, some of which might inhibit success. As noted above, peace operations tend to be deployed in conflicts that are more serious than average, which means that halting or preventing violence will be challenging. Nevertheless, there is still considerable variation among the contexts of operations, with the key interrelated dimensions being the kind of war, the phase of operational deployment, and the geography of the conflict.

Perhaps the most important contextual distinction is whether the conflict is civil or interstate. Generally, traditional peacekeeping experiences more problems in conflicts that have an internal conflict component, as compared to those purely between two or more states (Diehl 1994; Jett 2000). This is an especially ominous finding, in that peace operations have increasingly shifted to civil conflict contexts in the post-Cold War era. Also note that peacebuilding operations almost by definition take place in civil conflict contexts. Civil conflicts often involve more than two identifiable conflicting groups; by definition, an internationalized civil war (e.g., Lebanon, Congo) involves more than two actors. In contrast, interstate disputes have been overwhelmingly between only a pair of states. As the number of actors in the dispute increases, so too does the likelihood that one or more of them will object to a ceasefire and the provisions for the deployment of peace forces; they may also take military action against other actors or the peacekeeping soldiers. As noted in Chapter 2, a greater potential for "spoilers" exists in civil conflicts than interstate ones as well. Compounding this, participants in a civil conflict, being from the same state and often not wearing military uniforms (indeed, sometimes not being traditional military or paramilitary units at all), are hard to identify and less subject to control by commanders, making it difficult to monitor them or separate them from the civilian population.

Peace operations have also been judged to be more effective according to the timing of deployment in certain phases of conflict, which is closely related to the kinds of missions that they perform (Diehl 1994; McQueen 2002). Phases of conflict can roughly be divided into pre-violence, ongoing violence, post-ceasefire, pre-settlement and post-peace agreement. There has only been one operation in the pre-violence phase (the UN operation in Macedonia), and therefore there is no basis yet for generalizations, although some commentators posit that traditional peacekeeping might be well suited to such preventive operations. Research indicates that peacekeepers have problems during active hostilities, the second phase of conflict. So-called "robust" missions during this phase of the conflict typically involve some enforcement actions. Unless peacekeepers are given enhanced military capacity and have an overwhelming advantage over local forces, difficulties are likely to arise. Thus, peacekeeping soldiers in Bosnia (United Nations Protection Force [UNPROFOR]) were unable to pacify many areas, and the civil war continued largely unabated.

Peace operations generally receive credit for conflict abatement in the post-ceasefire, pre-settlement phases. Thus, traditional peacekeeping forces in the Middle East, such as the United Nations Disengagement Observer Force (UNDOF) on the Golan Heights, have been successful in promoting stability. The consensus seems to be that traditional missions are most effective in the fifth conflict phase, after the disputants have signed a peace agreement (not merely a ceasefire), and the force is charged with assisting in the implementation of that agreement (Heldt 2001; Diehl 1994). Still, success in this phase relates more to the ability to prevent the reoccurrence of war than it does to a host of other missions associated with peacebuilding.

Another contextual factor concerns the geographic configuration of the conflict and the accompanying peace operation deployment (Diehl 1994). If an operation is charged with supervising an election or with monitoring the aftermath of a broad civil war (as was the case with MONUC in the Congo), this may mean being responsible for an entire country. Even with an extremely large peace force, this is largely impractical; for example, the Congo is 2,267,599 sq km and shares borders with nine other states as well as having a maritime border. Congo's limited transportation system further complicates the ability of an international force to monitor activities there. Large size is not the only barrier to effective peace missions. Topography can also affect monitoring capacity. An open terrain and a lightly populated area are conducive to the detection of improper activity by disputants. If the parties believe that they can get away with violations, then sniper fire, smuggling, and other actions will be more likely to occur. Accordingly, the open desert terrain of the Sinai (where MFO operates) or the sparsely populated areas of the Golan Heights (where UNDOF functions) seem ideal geographically for detecting movement. In contrast, the dense jungles of the Congo or the high-traffic area of southern Lebanon (where UNIFIL operates) make it difficult to monitor activities.

Equally important, disputants must be prevented from direct engagement with one another. This is almost impossible in certain contexts. Urban environments, whether in Beirut, Kigali, or Mogadishu, are very difficult to monitor because of the large and heterogeneous populations moving about the area. An identifiable international border is clearly preferred. Yet civil wars often have no identifiable ceasefire lines. UN forces in Lebanon and outside Srebrenica in Bosnia could not stop rocket attacks from sailing over their heads.

For peacebuilding operations, the contextual factors that promote success are not necessarily the same as those described above as inhibiting the renewal of violence. Low levels of hostility, as with more traditional peace operations, assist peacebuilding missions. Nevertheless, the factors promoting peacebuilding success in tasks beyond violence limitation can be difficult to discern. Peacebuilding is a long-term process, and it is difficult to identify correlates of success for a process that is still incomplete in most cases.

An element of the conflict environment important for peacebuilding is the degree to which basic government services (e.g., water, electricity) are provided in the deployment and related areas. The supply of such services will, in part, define the goals and scope of the mission at the outset. If these services are not being provided or they exist at inadequate levels, then the mandate and responsibilities of the operation are likely to be expanded; the time and material resources required will also be greater. The status of those services will also influence the success of an operation—as they improve, or if they already exist at adequate levels, the peace operation will be able to promote stability and move ahead with other missions. In failed states and in areas that have experienced significant destruction from conflict, the provision of basic services such as water, electricity, medical care and fire protection might have been disrupted. A peace operation will need to devise plans to narrow the gap between the level of desired services and the current provision, and this may involve both allocating its own resources and working with other actors (e.g., local authorities, NGOs) to ensure delivery.

Even if basic services are operational, there may be some concern about which actors are providing them. If it is the host government, then the peace operation's role is more limited. If NGOs (e.g., Doctors without Borders) or private entities are the providers, there may need to be some transitional arrangements in which local authorities eventually assume responsibility. Most dangerous might be provision by local militias or political groups.

Although having these services is desirable, there is the risk that such actors may establish parallel and alternative government structures that threaten long-term stability and national government authority. Such services may also be withheld at times for political purposes. Black market provision of services such as fuel is sometimes more desirable than their total absence, but this creates alternative authorities, encourages criminal activity and corruption, and may hamper the reestablishment of legitimate service provision in the future.

Along with cooperation and the provision of services, a key element of a functioning society is its infrastructure—the condition of the roads, ports, pipelines, electrical grids, and communication systems. Again, if these are degraded in the host state, it will become part of the peace operation's responsibilities to improve them, either alone or with the assistance of local authorities and international development actors (e.g., the World Bank, NGOs); in the short and medium term, such conditions are not malleable. Problems with infrastructure also complicate the ability of the peace operation to complete other mission tasks. For example, poor or non-existent roads (as in the Congo) make it nearly impossible to get food and medical supplies to refugees or displaced populations.

Behavioral Factors

Most of the other factors identified by analysts have concerned the behavior of actors in the conflict, those directly involved as well as third parties. The cooperation of the primary disputants (McQueen 2002; Pushkina 2006) in traditional operations is thought to be the most critical for peace operation success. Yet such claims run the risk of a tautology: if success is defined by a lack of violence between the disputants, then lack of violence between the disputants cannot be considered a causal factor. As the peace operation evolves, one or more of the disputants may be disadvantaged by the maintenance of the status quo in a traditional mission or by elections and changes in society during a peacebuilding one. At that stage, the interests of such parties will no longer be to support the operation but rather to renew violence. In southern Lebanon following the kidnapping of an Israeli soldier in 2006, Israel launched attacks on Hezbollah strongholds and beyond; they included attacks against UNIFIL, with conflicting accounts as to whether this was intended or not. Largely successful elections in Angola in 1992 led to a renewal of violence when the losers in the election, forces loyal to Jonas Savimbi and his UNITA movement, reignited the civil war thereafter.

Beyond the primary disputants, most relevant are the actions of neighboring states (Pushkina 2006) or interested major powers (Bratt 1997). Third-party states can influence the success of a peace operation in several ways. Most obviously, they can directly intervene militarily in a conflict, causing a renewal of the fighting or jeopardizing the safety and missions of the operation (see Chapter 3). This was the case in the Congo when several states in the region joined the fighting in support of different armed groups and in pursuit of securing resources such as diamonds. More subtly, third-party states might supply arms and other assistance to one of the disputants (or to a subnational actor—see below) thereby undermining the peace force's ability to limit violence. Support from the former Yugoslavia provided to fellow Serbs had this effect in the Bosnia civil war. Third parties might also bring diplomatic pressure to bear on one of the actors, such that they are more or less disposed to support the presence of the peace operation (Bratt 1997; Jett 2000; Diehl 1994). In particular, major powers are the key players in leading international organizations, such as the International Monetary Fund and the World Bank, which will be critical in providing assistance to states during later phases of peacebuilding operations. Without the support of leading states, such assistance is not likely to be forthcoming.

Third-party states are not the only relevant actors, as many operational deployments are subject to the behavior of subnational actors (see, e.g., Norton 1991). These include ethnic groups, competing political movements, terrorist organizations, and non-governmental organizations. The actions of these groups can be especially important when peace forces are thrust into areas of internal instability (Diehl 1994; Bratt 1997; Jett 2000). In some cases, subnational actors may actually control a larger geographic area than the recognized government. Unlike third-party states, however, subnational actors affect peace operations primarily by direct actions of support or opposition. For example, the Young Patriots group started riots in Côte d'Ivoire in 2006, targeting UN personnel and forcing the operation to relocate personnel and staff away from the affected areas.

If local groups and authorities cooperate in various peace operation activities, there are several benefits to the operation. First, some local resources (e.g., transportation, personnel) might be leveraged to complete tasks, thereby lessening the burden on the peace operation agency and/or freeing up resources for allocation to other tasks. Second, cooperation in peace operation activities creates "ownership" on the part of local authorities and the population. This makes it more likely that the operation's efforts will be regarded as legitimate and therefore sustainable in the long run after the peacekeepers are withdrawn.

The corresponding problems and risks from lack of cooperation are probably greater than any benefits accrued from cooperation. Local groups or officials can undermine or even block peacebuilding efforts. For example, rebuilding infrastructure often requires getting the necessary permits from local authorities. A water treatment plant could easily be sabotaged by a group opposed to assisting a rival ethnic group or clan. In any peacebuilding activity, the goal is ultimately to turn operations over to local authorities; if they are unwilling to assume responsibilities or hostile to them, the prospects for long-term success are dim.

Overall, the key concerns with respect to third-party and subnational group cooperation are (1) their preferences and interests, and (2) the resources they command (Diehl 2000). If the peace operation does not serve the interests of third parties, this is likely to generate opposition to the force. Yet this opposition alone is not sufficient to jeopardize success. These parties must have significant resources that can be brought to bear against the mission. Such resources include political influence with key actors and the local population in the area of deployment. The ability to intervene militarily or supply weaponry to those opposed to the operation may also be critical.

Box 8.2 Peacebuilding Success and Failure

Case: United Nations Stabilization Mission in Haiti (MINUSTAH)
Date of Conflict Management: 2004–17
Disputants: Haiti government and various internal groups
Third Party: United Nations
Outcome: Primarily failure with limited successes

Multiple peacekeeping operations have been deployed to Haiti in the last three decades. These have responded to instability in the country, nearly failed state apparatuses, and crushing poverty among its population. In 2004, armed conflict broke out, and insurgents gained control of Haiti's north. They next threatened President Aristide, who consequently resigned and fled into exile. The UN deployed MINUSTAH to restore order for a new transitional government, replacing (most recently) a multinational force and following four other UN peace operations there. The operation's mandate therefore initially concerned security sector reform (e.g., DDR and reform of the Haitian National Police). It was also charged with human rights protection and election supervision, and later expanded its mission to include reconstruction (e.g., infrastructure rebuilding) and recovery efforts (e.g., humanitarian assistance) in the aftermath of the 2010 earthquake.

That the operation lasted over thirteen years and has now been followed by another UN peace operation is indicative of the problems that MINUSTAH encountered and the difficulties of peacebuilding in general. The peace operation prioritized local security, and early on it failed to integrate former paramilitary soldiers into the national police, since the local population viewed this with suspicion. The operation also failed to prevent large numbers of murders and sexual assaults. Indeed, peacekeepers may have exacerbated the situation. Peacekeepers from multiple national contingents were accused of sexual misconduct, and a 2010 outbreak of cholera among the population was traced to the Nepalese peacekeeping contingent. Although there has been some stabilization and improvement of conditions during MINUSTAH, the county remains terribly poor and lacking good development prospects.

Some of MINUSTAH's failures can be attributed to the context it faced. Haiti was and is very low on any development scale, and would present a monumental challenge even to the best-resourced of peacebuilding efforts. Nevertheless, the "security first" approach was not only ineffective, but also failed to deal with the underlying social and economic divisions that fueled violence and complicated peacebuilding efforts. The major earthquake in 2010 hurt too, setting back initial efforts and necessarily re-prioritizing the mission to focus on humanitarian aid. As this demonstrates, external shocks can overwhelm even the best peace operations and are devastating to those that already have serious problems.

Case: The United Nations Mission in Sierra Leone (UNAMSIL)
Date of Conflict Management: 1999–2005
Disputants: Sierra Leone government and Revolutionary United Front (RUF)
Third Party: United Nations
Outcome: Success after initial failure

Sierra Leone experienced almost a full decade of civil war during the 1990s. Various diplomatic efforts could not quell the violence nor could several peacekeeping and observer operations (the Economic Community of West African States Monitoring Group [ECOMOG] and the United Nations Observer Mission in Sierra Leone [UNOMSIL]). Finally, the warring parties signed the Lomé Peace Accord, in which they requested an expanded peacekeeping mission to help implement its provisions.

UNAMSIL had not only the traditional task of monitoring the ceasefire, but also some peacebuilding missions including DDR, supporting elections, and delivering humanitarian assistance. The mandate was subsequently expanded to include providing local security and assisting the government in maintaining order. The initial deployment did not go well. UNAMSIL's peace force initially had 6,000 personnel, who were supposed to be assisted by the larger ECOMOG; yet within two months, Nigeria, which provided 90% of the latter's troops, withdrew its soldiers. The RUF also did not cooperate with the peace operation in rebel-controlled areas; they refused to disarm and even kidnapped and held hostage 500 peacekeepers. At the outset, this operation possessed all the earmarks of a failure.

The UN overcame these problems through a combination of factors, which reveal the reasons for its past failure and for its newfound success. Liberia, a neighboring state, pressured the RUF to release the hostages and support the peace agreement, while the United Kingdom helped reform the army. New talks between the rebels and the government led to another peace agreement, which this time held. The UN Security Council both increased the number of peacekeepers several times (ultimately ending with a force of over 17,000) and permitted UNAMSIL to use military force, in one of the first moves toward more "robust" peace operations. Finally, UNAMSIL also made internal adjustments to improve its efficiency. As a result of these factors, the mission withdrew in late 2005, with the civil war over and a stable elected government in place; war has not returned, diamond smuggling has been minimized, and subsequent elections suggest stability in the country.

UNAMSIL began under less than ideal conditions: a civil war, an unco-operative combatant, and a sub-optimally sized force. It reversed these conditions, and its success can be attributed to both the cooperation of the disputing parties and the assistance of third-party states. The presence of a peace agreement helped, but only after it was revised to broaden support. Finally, the large troop contingent allowed the force to act as an effective deterrent and patroller of the country.

Conclusion

Peace operations have become a vital part of conflict management approaches for international organizations, from which we can draw the following conclusions:

- Peace operations have evolved into two overlapping types: traditional peacekeeping and peacebuilding. The former focuses primarily on monitoring ceasefires, occurs in both interstate and intrastate conflict, and is characterized by the "holy trinity" (host-state consent, impartiality, and minimum use of force). The latter undertakes a wider variety of missions, takes place primarily in civil conflicts, and often loosens the restraints of the holy trinity.
- Peace operations have increased dramatically in number (especially since 1990), have increasingly been deployed to civil conflicts, and have performed more and newer missions over time (e.g., election supervision, promoting the rule of law). These trends are best explained not only by an increase in conflicts, but also by increased organizational capacity and changes in international norms.
- Peace operations tend to be deployed to the most serious conflicts, and whereas the United Nations conducts a plurality of them, regional

organizations have become progressively more involved in authorizing and directing peace operations.

- Peace operations are generally effective in preventing the renewal of violence. It is less clear that they are able to promote a series of peace-building missions, including increasing democratization and stimulating economic growth, the areas that have received the most scholarly attention.
- Peace operation success is influenced by how the operation is organized and conducted (force size, adaption, strategies), a series of contextual factors (conflict type, phase of deployment, geography), and the behavior of the belligerents and key third-party actors.

9

The Intersection of Conflict Management Approaches

We have thus far significantly reduced the complexity in our discussion of conflict management approaches by adopting two assumptions. First, the previous chapters assumed that the various approaches do not *interact*; that is, they do not influence one another. We therefore highlighted each approach's key characteristics, logic, and effectiveness independent of one another. If, however, using one approach alters the logic or effectiveness of another, this can be problematic. Greig and Diehl (2005) offer an illustration of this problem: they find that mediation loses effectiveness during a traditional peacekeeping operation because peacekeepers reduce violence and freeze the status quo, thereby removing a hurting stalemate and, consequently, some of the disputants' motivation to engage in conflict management. Although third parties probably do not intend this to happen, when it does occur it may therefore promote changes in how they manage conflicts. Second, even when considering a single, given approach, we often did not consider whether actors might use that approach numerous times within the same conflict, as for example when repeated mediations addressed heightened tensions between Turkey and Cyprus in 1996–97 or Burkina Faso and Mali in 1985–86 (on the latter, see Figure 9.1; Bercovitch and Fretter 2004). This assumption, too, can cause us to miss important effects. The likelihood of resolving disputed issues, for example, partially depends on the disputants' pattern of interactions. Repeated conflict management may consequently increase or decrease the likelihood of peace, depending on whether it fosters a better or worse relationship between the disputing parties (Hopmann 1996; Greig and Diehl 2006).

There are good reasons to relax the above assumptions. The logic underlying various approaches suggests that interactive effects exist, and indicates what we should expect to happen when they do. The assumptions themselves are also admitted oversimplifications that prove unrealistic in practice. Few international disputes receive conflict management at all, yet of those that do, nearly 73% experience more than one conflict management effort (Bercovitch and Fretter 2004; see also Owsiak 2014). Moreover, 77% of the disputes that see conflict management efforts will experience multiple *approaches*; that is, negotiation *and* mediation will occur, as opposed to merely one or the other (Bercovitch and Fretter 2004). To pretend that these various efforts—designed to manage the same conflict—are completely independent of one another seems a difficult position to sustain. Disputants and third parties should be aware of previous efforts to manage a given conflict, and should use those earlier efforts when deciding on what approaches to use next.

Mindful of such considerations, we shift our analytic attention in this chapter to the trajectory (or path) of conflict management approaches as they evolve throughout a given dispute. The trajectory concept suggests that these paths are not only descriptive, but also meaningful. Early efforts to manage a conflict inform later ones.

Conflict Management Trajectories

We typically encounter the term "trajectory" in physics, referring, for example, to the trajectory of bullets or rockets. In these contexts, a trajectory describes the path an object travels through space and time. That path derives from the aggregation of individual data points representing where the object appears in both time and space. It also reflects another key property: the current position of the object (at time t) depends on where it was at an earlier moment (at time $t-1$). Thus, the trajectory explains where the object has been at each point in the past, identifies where it is currently, and predicts where it is likely to go (subject to its current position and the various forces operating on it). The focus lies not on the object, but on its path of travel.

The same trajectory concept can be applied to international conflict management within a given dispute (Owsiak 2014). Constructing these conflict management trajectories (hereinafter simply trajectories) requires two bits of information: measurements in "space" and "time." Rather than conceiving of space as geographic, however, trajectories organize conflict management approaches along a unified "cost" (or control) dimension (for reference, see Table 2.2). Negotiations, for example, afford disputants a significant degree of control. As one moves from mediation to legal approaches to humanitarian intervention to peace operations to sanctions and then to military intervention, the disputants lose sequentially more control over the conflict management process and outcome. This same shift grants a third party increasingly greater control (e.g., legal approaches versus mediation) and imposes greater management costs on them (*ceteris paribus*). These properties allow us to collapse and organize the myriad conflict management approaches along a single, unified dimension: a cost/control "space" (see *y*-axis, Figure 9.1). The time at which a disputant or third party uses an approach then constitutes the temporal dimension, permitting us to order the use of approaches chronologically within a given dispute (see *x*-axis, Figure 9.1). We then have both the spatial and temporal measurements necessary to chart a dispute's conflict management trajectory.

Our theoretical discussion gains clarity through an illustration. Figure 9.1

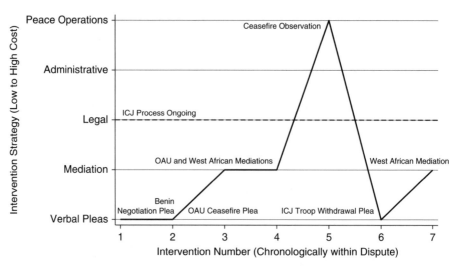

Figure 9.1 Conflict Management Trajectory in the Burkina Faso–Mali Dispute, 1985–1986
Data Source: Frazier and Dixon (2006).

depicts the conflict management trajectory for the militarized dispute between Burkina Faso and Mali in 1985–86, while Box 9.1 supplies the detailed historical events underlying this trajectory. The figure demonstrates a few general observations about trajectories well. First, a trajectory focuses on the *path* of conflict management and that path's evolution during a conflict, rather than the individual conflict management attempts that constitute that path. Preceding chapters discussed myriad conflict management approaches, asking questions such as: when is mediation successful? The trajectory concept reframes this question. To see why, consider the information presented in Figures 9.1 and Box 9.1. Benin asks Burkina Faso and Mali to reach a ceasefire (the first approach used in the conflict; $x=1$), and the Organization of African Unity (OAU) facilitates one a few days later ($x=2$). Did Benin's statement produce the intended result? The OAU's mediated ceasefire ($x=2$) immediately breaks down. Was the OAU successful because it obtained a ceasefire or unsuccessful because that ceasefire did not hold? The International Court of Justice (ICJ) demanded a ceasefire well after the West African states obtained one that held ($x=6$). Does this mean the ICJ succeeded, or were its actions "too late" to matter? Various approaches together halted violence in this dispute, but did not resolve any of the underlying issues. Does that mean the approaches collectively failed?

In contrast to these questions, the trajectory concept poses different and broader ones. It first asks: what constitutes the dispute? The Burkina Faso–Mali militarized encounter begins in 1985, but the issue underlying that dispute—contested border territory—pre-dates both states' independence. If *issue* contestation and resolution is the focus, then the dispute runs from 1960 (i.e., independence) to 1986 (i.e., the ICJ ruling that resolved the territorial dispute). The militarized episode, however, constitutes a sub-dispute in its own right; conflict management in this episode aimed not to resolve the underlying issues (as the ICJ was already in the process of doing that), but rather to halt the violence. Thus, although the issue underlying the violence concerned disputed territory, the immediate issue at hand was the violence itself. Framed this way, the dispute runs from the outbreak of violence in December 1985 to the resumption of "normal" relations in January 1986 (as depicted in Figure 9.1 and Box 9.1).

BOX 9.1 Example of a Conflict Management Trajectory

Case: Burkina Faso–Mali Frontier (Territorial) Dispute
Date of Conflict Management: 1985–86 and following
Disputing Parties: Burkina Faso and Mali
Third Parties: Benin, the Organization of African Unity (OAU), the West African Economic Community (ECOWAS), and the International Court of Justice (ICJ)
Outcome: Overall success, with some intermittent failures

Burkina Faso and Mali began disputing mutual border territory upon independence, having inherited unclear borders from the French. The disputed territory contains the only fresh water in the region, making it valuable not only for basic necessities, but also for agricultural and pastoral activities (Day 1987).

In October 1983, the two states jointly agreed to submit their border dispute to the ICJ. Yet, as the ICJ's process unfolded, the conflict occasionally flared up, notably in December 1985, when Burkina Faso officials entered the disputed territory with armed forces to take a census of its nationals residing there. Mali accused these officials of occupying four villages and forcing the inhabitants to accept Burkina Faso identity cards. Mali therefore responded with force on 25 December, attacking the border villages to end the occupation. This caused a multi-day militarized skirmish: the "Christmas War." Details of the skirmish remain sparse, but both parties reportedly attacked one another, became targets of attacks, and repeatedly struggled to secure a lasting ceasefire.

The conflict spurred a series of conflict management efforts (for a visual depiction of these efforts as a trajectory, see Figure 9.1). Libya may have mediated a Burkina Faso troop withdrawal from the disputed area once violence broke out on 25–26 December. If so, it failed to reduce hostilities. On the 26th, Benin urged the disputants to negotiate, while the OAU encouraged them to pursue a ceasefire. Libya and Nigeria then successfully mediated such a ceasefire on 28–29 December (under OAU auspices); unfortunately, it did not hold, and hostilities resumed. A team of West African states (Ivory Coast, Mauritania, Senegal, Niger, Togo, and Benin) next secured another ceasefire around 30 December and deployed an observer mission to foster compliance with the ceasefire's terms. To cement this last ceasefire, Burkina Faso also petitioned the ICJ, which was still hearing its case, to impose provisional measures. The court issued these measures on 10 January, asking all parties to withdraw their troops, observe the existing ceasefire, avoid actions that might escalate the dispute, and return to the pre-conflict situation in the disputed areas (ICJ No. 86/2). The ceasefire held, and West African states orchestrated "warm talks" involving smiles, handshakes, and hugs between leaders of the disputing states on 17 January. This officially ended the immediate, militarized disagreement.

The ICJ subsequently issued its judgment in the case on 22 December 1986. Both parties have complied with this judgment (Mitchell and Owsiak 2018).

To ask whether a conflict management process succeeded requires one to define its goals, and these, in turn, depend on how one defines the dispute. It also depends on whether an approach must *immediately* achieve a goal or can work, in sequence and tandem, with other approaches. The West African ceasefire mediation ($x=4$, Figure 9.1) succeeds, in part, because these states also deploy a peace operation to observe compliance with the ceasefire ($x=5$). Although the later West African mediation effort ($x=7$) secures smiles, handshakes, and hugs between leaders of the disputing states, its ability to do so almost certainly derives from the ceasefire's persistence (see Box 9.1). Indeed, even the efforts of other third parties could have contributed to this final mediation's success. The OAU mediation effort familiarized disputants with what mediation would look like in this dispute, clarified the interests of other African states, and demonstrated those states' commitment to ending the violence (Greig and Diehl 2006). It set the stage for further third-party assistance. The ICJ's provisional measures, although arriving late, may also have reinforced the ceasefire, the persistence of which fostered the conditions needed for a final diplomatic settlement to the militarized dispute (i.e., the ICJ's later award, with which the disputing states complied).

Trajectories therefore shift the focus from individual approaches to the *constellation* of approaches that foster effective conflict management, including their sequence, timing, and interaction. This does not imply that individual approaches hold no value; on the contrary, we can only chart a trajectory with them. Nevertheless, trajectories offer additional value to our understanding of international conflict management. Rather than focus on one approach, a trajectory includes the entire menu of approaches and considers why third parties select from the menu when and as they do. Similarly, research typically examines conflict management undertaken by either states *or* inter-governmental organizations (IGOs). Trajectories unify these actors under one umbrella too, allowing *any* third party to join the efforts. Different character-istics and interests guide these various actors' choices, but all seek to manage a conflict, however defined. Each third party's efforts therefore comprise part of the trajectory, regardless of that third party's specific character.

This latter point leads to a second observation: individual third-party efforts inform one another, a premise that Figure 9.1 supports. Whether a state, an IGO, or a non-governmental organization, those managing a conflict are aware of other efforts to manage that same conflict. Moreover, this awareness informs their decision about what to do next. The simplest illustration tracks the same third party over time in a given dispute. In the Burkina Faso–Mali dispute, for example, a coalition of West African states mediated a ceasefire (x=4) and then, days later, deployed a peace operation to observe the implementation of that ceasefire (x=5). To claim that the coalition was unaware of its mediation when the peace operation deployed or that these approaches did not inform one another is untenable; the mediation produced the peace operation. Another, less temporally proximate example involves the ICJ. It issued intermediate pro-visions toward the end of the dispute (x=6), but had been working on resolving the contested territorial issues before, during, and after the militarized dispute depicted in Figure 9.1 (this is the dotted horizontal line running throughout the figure). The court would be aware of its various efforts, especially because these occurred concurrently. Finally, connections across actors exist as well. Members of the West African coalition belonged to the OAU; when Libya and Nigeria led the OAU mediation (x=3), it seems plausible that these other OAU members knew about it and that this informed their later mediation effort (x=4). In fact, the breakdown of the earlier OAU ceasefire likely created the impetus for the West African mediation to deploy an observation mission after achieving its own ceasefire, to ensure that it held.

A third observation about trajectories concerns shape. At a basic level, we can describe how conflict management evolved over the course of the dispute (see Owsiak 2014 for a typology of trajectory shapes). In this case, third parties tried less costly approaches first (e.g., Benin's plea), and cycled through suc-cessively more costly ones (e.g., mediation and then peace operations) as the earlier efforts failed. Once the violence stopped, they then shifted back to low-cost strategies (e.g., the ICJ intermediate provisions and further mediation). The trajectory concept asserts that a *causal* explanation for this path exists; Owsiak (2014) has proposed two such models so far—a cost minimization and a learning one—although these have yet to be tested in published research. We return to these theoretical ideas in the final section of this chapter.

Approach Compatibility: Complements and Contradictions

The trajectory concept suggests two broad questions. We address the first in this section, namely how do different approaches complement and contradict each other? Numerous possibilities exist. Rather than supply an exhaustive list of these, we highlight a handful of the most notable.

First, negotiations prove the most flexible of any approach, compatible logically with any other approach at any time. Every disputant wants as much control as possible over its dispute's management and outcome; this protects its interests best. When, however, disputants cannot reach a mutually satisfactory outcome on their own, they cede control over conflict management—willingly (e.g., mediation) or unwillingly (e.g., sanctions)—to a third party. This presupposes that negotiation occurs *before* other conflict management approaches; indeed, documents such as the United Nations Charter and the UN Convention on the Law of the Sea (UNCLOS) support this expectation. It also suggests that disputants can return to negotiation at any time, even after a third party begins conflict management. Disputants cede control to a third party for a specific purpose: to receive help in managing the effects of conflict (e.g., reducing or ending violence) or resolving the issues that drive it. If they can subsequently achieve these goals independently of the third party, then the third party's purpose and involvement necessarily fade. In effect, the disputants "reclaim" the control they previously granted to third parties.

Two specific approaches seem inconsistent with this reclamation, but only at face value. The first concerns legal approaches (arbitration and adjudication), which begin when disputants agree to allow a third party to decide how to resolve their conflict and (*ex ante*) to abide by that third party's decision. Because of its binding characteristic, it would seem that disputants cannot reclaim their autonomy from a legal process, as doing so threatens to undermine the legal approach itself (see Chapter 7). In some sense, this is true, but it confuses unilateral reclamation with multilateral reclamation. The former occurs when an individual disputant attempts to back out of a legal approach to which it is bound and whose direction it does not like. China exhibited this behavior in its 2013–16 South China Sea arbitration with the Philippines, seeking to avoid arbitration despite its commitments under the UNCLOS. Such actions are antithetical to the logic of legal approaches, for if a disputant can renounce a legal approach when it does not get its way, the binding characteristic and, therefore, the value of legal approaches in conflict management necessarily evaporates.

What we propose here, however, is a multilateral reclamation of the conflict management process, one in which all disputants pursue a *mutually acceptable* agreement as the legal approach proceeds. This can be useful in two general scenarios. On the one hand, a crisis flare-up might demand immediate attention while the legal actor hears, deliberates, and decides a case. International courts and arbiters require years to rule on a case (see, e.g., McLaughlin Mitchell and Owsiak 2018), and intervene in conflicts that disputants cannot resolve themselves. These intractable conflicts can therefore easily produce militarized or diplomatic crises, even in the years during which the legal process operates. Should this occur, an immediate need arises: to halt or limit violence. The 1985–86 Burkina Faso–Mali trajectory illustrates this need well; a militarized dispute occurred during the years that the ICJ worked to resolve the underlying issues, and this dispute required rapid, short-term conflict management. Disputants *can* request the legal actor to intervene in such crises, but it can do little to halt the hostilities. Instead, like the ICJ in the Burkina Faso–Mali dispute, it will encourage disputants to reach a ceasefire and negotiate on short-term arrangements, buying the legal process time to finish its work. Negotiations help reduce violence in these instances.

On the other hand, disputants might continue negotiating about how to resolve the underlying issues as the legal approach continues. Scholars label this "bargaining in the shadow of the court" (see, e.g., Mitchell and Owsiak 2018; Mnookin and Kornhauser 1979). Armed with the knowledge that a legal ruling will occur, disputants gain renewed motivation to find a way to prevent such a ruling. That might seem counterintuitive, but recall that legal approaches employ international law to settle disputes. Any legal ruling must be consistent with previous legal rulings (or reconcile discrepancies) and interpret and apply international legal principles to the case at hand. Disputants, however, can craft settlement terms that are far more flexible and perhaps more favorable to their interests. If they succeed, they then withdraw their case from the legal process. Approximately 19% of ICJ cases end with such withdrawals, often precisely because the disputants reach an agreement outside of the court (Mitchell and Owsiak 2018).

Coercion—sanctions and intervention—may also seem inconsistent with negotiations. Nevertheless, this incompatibility proves more theoretical than practical. Disputants often negotiate during armed conflict. Weaker actors (e.g., rebel groups) hesitate to end armed conflict before negotiations secure certain minimal goals, as the armed conflict creates bargaining leverage for them at the negotiating table. The strong and weak alike also negotiate ceasefires to create a more non-violent environment in which more comprehensive negotiations can occur. These ceasefire negotiations, by definition, occur during armed conflict. Finally, using a similar logic to rebel groups, third parties might employ coercion to increase the likelihood that negotiations will occur and succeed. Sanctions against Iran and North Korea have operated this way. Third parties promise to lift sanctions once a mutually acceptable, negotiated agreement emerges. The sanctions offer third parties the bargaining leverage to facilitate such an outcome.

Regardless of the approach a third party might employ, it is simpler for disputants to work out their own solutions if they can, and the results may be more durable. Because negotiations lie entirely within disputants' control, they can resort to these at any time, regardless of third-party behavior; negotiations are therefore easier to coordinate logistically than other approaches. In addition, any involved third party will have its own interests, whether a preference for a particular substantive outcome (e.g., how exactly a given territory should be divided) or for peace generally (Princen 1992). These interests motivate third-party involvement in the first place. Thus, a third party will require its interests to be included in the conflict management process—a requirement that complicates reaching an agreement, since it becomes more challenging to find an agreement that satisfies all involved parties' interests simultaneously as the number of these parties increases (Hopmann 1996). Although a third party can reward settlement or punish non-settlement to increase the likelihood of a settlement being reached, that settlement may be unstable. The rewards and punishments encourage disputants to behave in ways they otherwise would not. When the rewards and punishments end, so too might the settlement built on them. Negotiators working independently of third parties do not face this kind of manipulation or, therefore, this type of instability.

A second compatibility between approaches concerns mediation, which also remains consistent with any other approach at most times (but see the exceptions below). This is especially the case for facilitative mediation, in which the mediator seeks to foster communication between disputants and provide logistical support for any meeting between them (e.g., a neutral meeting space). In such cases, mediation operates as a facilitated negotiation, and therefore shares the complementarities noted above for negotiations. When mediators adopt a more directive mediation strategy instead—one in which they propose substantive solutions or offer rewards for settlement (or punishment for non-settlement)—the complexity of finding a solution increases and the unstable settlement problem (noted above) emerges.

There are two exceptions to mediation's versatility, the first of which involves combining mediation with coercive approaches. Disputants participate voluntarily in mediation and can, in theory, end their involvement at any time. Coercion, in contrast, compels a disputant to do something it would otherwise not do voluntarily. One can therefore coerce a disputant into mediation or into a mediated agreement, but this violates the voluntary tenet of mediation, at least in some capacity. Of course, coercion violates the voluntary aspect of negotiations too. There is a key difference, however. Disputants retain full control over the negotiation process and outcome. In contrast, when coercion pushes mediation, a third party compels disputants to cede control over their dispute to a third-party mediator; in other words, they involuntarily lose control.

A disputant that freely chooses to mediate and one that chooses to mediate in the face of coercion are therefore not identically motivated. Coercion can attempt to alter motivations, but its overall effect on mediation largely depends on whether and for how long it does so. Coercion that causes disputants to reevaluate the benefits of a mediated agreement, for example, may increase the motivation for a settlement, while coercion aimed merely at getting disputants to the bargaining table may do little to incentivize reaching an agreement (see Richmond 1998). The use of coercion to support mediation may therefore be challenging—particularly if the coercer and (would-be) mediator are the same third party, since disputants may conclude that the coercive mediator might exercise a heavy hand to restrict disputant autonomy further during the mediation process. In the end, though, the verdict on compatibility between mediation and coercion depends on the order in which the approaches are sequenced—a point to which we return in the next section.

The second exception mixes mediation with peace operations. A peace operation usually deploys after disputants reach a ceasefire or other (often, preliminary) settlement. In this sense, mediation *before* a peace operation remains compatible with and facilitates that operation. This does not necessarily mean, however, that disputants will have fully resolved their contested issues when the peacekeepers arrive. In such cases, conflict management will be necessary during the peace operation to achieve such a resolution. This opens a space for further mediation, but it may not be a large one. Peace operations tend to freeze the status quo, remove the urgency for settlement that armed conflict creates (i.e., eliminate a hurting stalemate), and normalize non-settlement. These factors combine to undermine the chances that mediation will succeed in the shadow of a peace operation (Greig and Diehl 2005). Compatibility therefore ultimately depends once again on the sequencing of approaches.

A third (in)compatibility, generally speaking, mixes coercive and non-coercive approaches: coercive approaches can encourage non-coercive conflict management. When actors employ coercion (military intervention or sanctions), they typically do so with the intent of forcing disputants to the negotiating table. NATO, for example, bombed the Serbs in the 1990s to encourage Milosevic to abandon his use of force and pursue peaceful conflict management instead (Albright 2003). Similarly, recent sanctions against Iran and North Korea aim(ed) to alter how attractive each found the pursuit of a nuclear weapons program. To escape the sanctions, the international community required Iran and North Korea to re-engage diplomatically with it. Cases such as these underscore the expectation that coercive approaches facilitate non-coercive ones, moving a conflict toward resolution.

The logic linking these two types of approaches rests on a rational-actor assumption. It asserts that, whatever goals an actor might pursue, they will choose the "least (or less) costly" path to pursue them. Such a path may involve militarized conflict, and when it does, this perspective advocates raising the costs associated with such conflict to change disputant behavior. If engaging in militarized conflict hurts an actor more than they are prepared to accept, then they will adopt a non-militarized approach instead. This explains why third parties punish militarized action and reward non-militarized action (or both); coercion paradoxically begets peace.

There are two difficulties with this underlying logic. First and foremost, imperfect information, indivisible issues, and credible-commitment problems impede rational decision-making (Fearon 1995). Disputants do not possess perfect information about the superiority of one another's military forces, intelligence, strategy, or resolve (i.e., the costs an actor is willing to incur in pursuit of its goal). This uncertainty yields miscalculations. Misperception then complicates matters further. The psychology involved can be complex (Jervis 1988), but in general actors overestimate their own abilities and under-estimate those of their adversaries, suggesting they will fight long after a rational actor would have stopped. Coercion may therefore need to be extreme in order to shift a disputant's preference from a violent to a non-violent pur-suit of its goals. Without crossing this extreme threshold, it may never achieve the shift to non-violence, suggesting that there are conditions under which coercive and non-coercive approaches may be inconsistent with one another.

Additional instances of incompatibility derive from the remaining two dif-ficulties. Indivisible issues, for example, preclude the possibility of mutually acceptable settlement terms. In such cases (e.g., the status of and sovereignty over Jerusalem), a compromise solution does not exist. One might be created via issue linkage (i.e., adding more issues to the negotiation), side payments (i.e., compensating actors for compromise on the indivisible issue, perhaps with gains on another issue), or creativity (Fearon 1995). Coercion alone, how-ever, is unlikely to secure it. Similarly, credible-commitment problems occur when a disputant fears that a settlement will significantly alter its power, thereby rendering it vulnerable to its adversary. Rebel groups, for example, worry that disarmament, often a necessary step in civil war termination, weakens them relative to the government, which still possesses arms. Israel similarly worries that a nuclear Iran will constitute a fundamentally more powerful threat to its existence. Although some approaches can help guaran-tee the weaker actor's position in cases like these (e.g., a peace operation that observes compliance with settlement terms after civil war; Walter 2002), this is not always true. No guarantee will satisfy Israel that a nuclear Iran poses no threat to it. Moreover, if present, the *guarantee* secures the settlement; coercion itself does not. This, combined with the unstable outcomes it can produce (through time-inconsistency problems; see above), renders coercion unhelpful to long-term conflict management in many cases.

Finally, humanitarian interventions fall within a gray zone. The Responsibility to Protect movement advocates international intervention when states cannot or will not secure citizens' basic human rights. To conduct such an operation, however, one needs either the support of the state in which the conflict occurs, or the willingness to violate state sovereignty. The former proves unlikely in many cases; a government under attack from domestic groups often tries to repress that dissent, and will view international intervention as supporting the dissenters. In addition, violating state sovereignty creates incompatibilities with other approaches. When the international community deploys a humanitarian mission that violates a state's sovereignty, that state may be less amenable to other conflict management approaches. Believing external actors to threaten it now too, it may instead adopt a hardline stance that eschews, or at least remains suspicious of, other third-party involvement.

Guidelines: What to Choose and When

Given that approaches interact and affect one another, a second question emerges: under what conditions should a policymaker seeking peace choose a given approach? No simple answer to this question exists, largely because, as this book demonstrates, numerous factors alter the prospects of conflict management. For example, many approaches require both disputant and third-party participation; the demand for and supply of conflict management must therefore align. The demand for conflict management derives from conflict characteristics (e.g., whether a hurting stalemate exists) and disputant characteristics (e.g., the relationship and history between the disputants). The supply of conflict management, in contrast, depends on the interests of third parties. A failure to align disputant interests, third-party motivations, and conflict characteristics often explains why conflict management fails to appear in certain cases (e.g., Rwanda in 1994), why conflict management efforts end without resolving a conflict (e.g., United Nations Emergency Force I in the Middle East), and why conflict management efforts seem not to match the needs of the conflict itself (e.g., sanctions, but little else, against Syria during its recent civil war).

Despite such challenges, we can assume a demand–supply alignment and derive a series of guidelines that address the motivating question of this section. First, doing nothing is an option, but one that should not be adopted lightly. International conflict carries costs (e.g., fatalities or the destruction of homes, natural resources, and economic activity) and negative externalities (e.g., refugee flows or conflict spillover). These will be borne most heavily by disputants and states in the immediate vicinity of the original conflict; yet there may be wider effects as well (e.g., human displacement, threats to development, and economic losses). Although early conflict management can mitigate these effects, many actors will feel no *immediate* need to help. This results from international peace being a public good. If any actor secures it, all enjoy it. A "wait and see" policy therefore develops, being broken only when the costs mount high enough to trigger an interested party to assist. What might have been a less costly conflict management effort (e.g., mediation) then becomes a more expensive one (e.g., a peace enforcement operation).

A wait-and-see policy may prove helpful if it can create a hurting stalemate. For this to happen, disputants must fight long enough to experience significant costs and, as a result, recognize both that militarized conflict is unlikely to achieve their goals and that non-violent conflict management strategies could be a better option (Zartman 2000). This provides disputants with the motivation and urgency to abandon militarized conflict. Third parties that forestall such a hurting stalemate risk starting a conflict management trajectory that atrophies; indeed, the failure of mediation to secure a settlement during an ongoing peace operation may result from this dynamic (see, e.g., Cyprus; Greig and Diehl 2005). As an outsider, however, it is difficult to know whether disputants are trending toward a hurting stalemate, whether one is near at hand, or, if one exists, how long it will last. Moreover, as one waits, the costs of conflict mount. The human and economic toll rises, and the hostility between the disputants deepens. This encourages them to view past conflict as sunk costs, thereby increasing their commitment to fighting and rendering the conflict less amenable to third-party management efforts. Waiting for a stalemate may therefore be imprudent or undesirable, although some third parties may use the absence of a hurting stalemate to justify their desire to avoid conflict management altogether.

A second guideline focuses on costs: To facilitate peace at the lowest possible price, begin with a low-cost approach. If this fails to achieve the desired goal, then employ a more costly approach, repeating the process until the goal is met (e.g., negotiation and mediation, followed later by legal approaches or coercion; see Figure 9.1). Such a strategy carries numerous advantages. Recall that the costs of conflict management approaches increase (or decrease) as disputants cede more (or less) control over the process and outcome to third parties. Starting with "low-cost" strategies (e.g., negotiation) and then substituting successively more costly approaches if necessary (e.g., mediation, followed by legal approaches, and so on) will maximize disputant flexibility and motivation, while limiting the costs that both disputants and third parties must pay. It also theoretically facilitates more durable outcomes. Disputants with greater involvement in the design of a settlement, and the autonomy to accept it, are not only more likely to implement that agreement without assistance, but are also more likely to develop a better relationship. A time-inconsistency problem may still arise, but this should occur less often than if third parties have manipulated the disputants' calculus to achieve a settlement. And improved relations may make the management of future disputes easier.

This overall strategy appears within many domestic legal systems for the same reasons as those noted here. If a dispute arises among neighbors they will typically first try to manage it between themselves. If this fails, a third party might then mediate (e.g., other neighbors, a homeowners' association, or, increasingly, a community mediator). Should this fail too, the neighbors may then take recourse to legal processes. If they cannot implement a settlement from within one of these phases, they call on law enforcement to coerce compliance. This process minimizes the total costs associated with a conflict's management by only involving a successively more costly approach (e.g., the legal system or law enforcement) when a less costly approach fails.

The process can work similarly in international conflicts, and we see some evidence that it does. Third parties, for example, generally allow disputants to attempt negotiation before getting involved. When they do assist, third parties then rely first on less costly approaches (e.g., mediation or arbitration), before attempting more costly ones (e.g., sanctions). They also purposely sequence a more costly approach to follow and support a less costly one. Mediation, for example, typically secures agreement about what terms a subsequent peace operation will help to enforce. This often yields success (see, e.g., Burkina Faso–Mali or the NATO mission supporting the Dayton Peace Accord in Bosnia), at least in terms of limiting violence. In contrast, sequencing in the other direction—from a more costly to a less costly approach—more often fails. A peace operation, sanctions, or intervention can create time-inconsistency problems or remove a hurting stalemate, each of which undermines attempts to fully settle the issues under dispute.

A third guideline stresses learning. Each conflict presents partly unique circumstances (e.g., disputants, issues, and third parties), the combination of which yields a distinct conflict fingerprint. Interested parties might therefore need to adapt as the conflict unfolds. For example, if mediation can secure a ceasefire, but that ceasefire fails to hold, third parties know that mediation can achieve *something* in pursuit of peace. West African states realized this in the Burkina Faso–Mali dispute, so they mediated again after the initial, OAU-mediated ceasefire failed; yet they also knew they needed more than mediation to quell the violence and therefore combined mediation with another approach (a peace operation) to support the ceasefire. These combined actions halted the violence. As this demonstrates, third parties might pay careful attention to which approaches inch them closer to or further away from their intended goal(s) and why. This allows them to repeat what works and adapt what does not.

Our fourth guideline asks policymakers to consider allowing conflict management and conflict resolution to proceed in parallel. Legal approaches, for example, aim to resolve the underlying issue under dispute (e.g., a maritime border's placement), but are not equipped to handle the symptoms associated with that dispute (e.g., outbreaks of militarized violence). Whereas active conflicts demand immediate, quick action to limit violence, legal approaches require time to unfold as the legal process plays out. Thus, legal processes can succeed at issue resolution (through their binding characteristic), but need other approaches to support them to mitigate short-term, violent outbursts.

This idea of parallel tracks can be seen in the Burkina Faso–Mali dispute (Figure 9.1 and Box 9.1). It extends, however, beyond the legal/non-legal divide. Legal approaches can excel at issue resolution, and to the extent that they are underused relative to other approaches, we advocate that they play a bigger role in conflict management. Beyond this narrow suggestion, however, lies a larger one. Issue resolution and violence mitigation are two distinct, reinforcing goals. Resolving issues removes the motivation for violence, whereas violence mitigation creates a hospitable environment in which substantive negotiations over the contested issues can occur. Policymakers often consider these to be a single dimension: stop the violence first, then address the issues. This may be impossible or unnecessary. Both can proceed in parallel. Moreover, because they address different goals, parallel tracks might require distinct third parties, processes, and therefore trajectories. Policymakers might therefore consider more carefully whether such parallel tracks can be created, which third parties should operate within each, and how both the tracks and the various conflict management efforts can support one another as they work toward a more peaceful world.

Conclusion

Throughout this chapter, we have relaxed the assumption that conflict management approaches and efforts operate independently of one another. This led naturally to an exploration of how approaches interact. The resultant discussion produced a handful of conclusions that offer preliminary insights into this question, including:

- To understand how approaches interact, we must shift our analytic attention from the individual approach to the conflict management trajectory. This necessarily combines all disputant behavior, third-party types (e.g., states, IGOs, and NGOs), and approaches within one analytical framework. In so doing, we can not only chart trajectories in past disputes but also investigate how individual approaches affect one another in greater detail.
- The trajectory concept forces analysts to define a dispute and conflict management success more carefully. All disputes contain underlying, contested issues. Nonetheless, these issues are not acute in all disputes. Some trajectories therefore focus on issue resolution, whereas others stress the cessation of violence; whether efforts "succeed" depends on what

drives the dispute and what conflict managers intend to achieve. Moreover, individual efforts that seem to fail in the immediate term (e.g., a mediated ceasefire that does not hold, or provisional measures that arrive late in a trajectory) may contribute to a broader success. Only focusing on trajectories allows us to consider such possibilities.

- Conflict management approaches complement and contradict one another in myriad ways. Negotiations and mediations prove particularly versatile, being compatible with all other approaches most of the time. In contrast, coercive approaches will frequently undermine non-coercive ones; they violate the basic logic of many non-coercive strategies (most notably, mediation and legal approaches), create time-inconsistency problems that can complicate settlement stability, and erode disputants' motivation for engaging in long-term conflict resolution.

- What approach to use and when are not easy questions to answer. We have proposed a few guidelines, however, that might inform such decisions. First, doing nothing may be a sound policy when early intervention threatens to forestall the hurting stalemate needed for successful conflict management. This, however, cannot become an excuse for inaction and must be balanced against the human and economic toll the conflict exacts. Second, conflict managers can start with less costly approaches first and employ successively more costly ones if and when the earlier efforts fail. This achieves peace for the lowest price. We note, though, that such a policy favors early conflict management, since waiting typically makes a bad situation worse (i.e., more costly along numerous human and economic dimensions). Third, conflict managers must learn from their collective efforts, reusing approaches that bring them closer to peace and adapting failed approaches to achieve more. Finally, where possible, conflict management and conflict resolution should proceed in parallel. These may require distinct third parties (and trajectories), but because each reinforces the other, pursuing one before or without the other creates opportunities to derail peace.

References and Suggested Readings

Aggestam, K. and Jönsson, C. (1997) (Un)Ending Conflict: Challenges in Post-War Bargaining. *Millennium* 26(3), pp. 771–93.

Albright, M. (2003) *Madam Secretary.* New York: Miramax.

Allen, S. (2006) Case Concerning the Frontier Dispute (Benin/Niger). *International and Comparative Law Quarterly* 55(3), pp. 729–42.

Alter, K. (2014) *The New Terrain of International Law.* Princeton: Princeton University Press.

Andreas, P. (2004) The Clandestine Political Economy of War and Peace in Bosnia. *International Studies Quarterly* 48(1), pp. 29–51.

Andreas, P. (2005) Criminalizing Consequences of Sanctions: Embargo Busting and Its Legacy. *International Studies Quarterly* 49(2), pp. 335–60.

Autesserre, S. (2010) *The Trouble with the Congo: Local Violence and the Failure of International Peacebuilding.* Cambridge: Cambridge University Press.

Autesserre, S. (2014) *Peaceland: Conflict Resolution and the Everyday Politics of International Intervention.* Cambridge: Cambridge University Press.

Aydin, A. (2012) *Foreign Powers and Intervention in Armed Conflicts.* Stanford: Stanford University Press.

Axelrod, R. (1984) *The Evolution of Cooperation.* New York: Basic Books.

Bakaki, Z. (2018) Do International Organizations Reduce the Risk of Crisis Recurrence? *Journal of Global Security Studies* 3(3), pp. 358–70.

Balas, A. (2011) It Takes Two (or More) to Keep the Peace: Multiple Simultaneous Peace Operations. *Journal of International Peacekeeping* 15(3–4), pp. 384–421.

Balas, A., Owsiak, A., and Diehl, P. (2012) Demanding Peace: The Impact of Prevailing Conflict on the Shift from Peacekeeping to Peacebuilding. *Peace & Change* 37(2), pp. 195–226.

Bapat, N. (2005) Insurgency and the Opening of Peace Processes. *Journal of Peace Research* 42(6), pp. 699–717.

Baranyi, S. (2009) *The Paradoxes of Peacebuilding Post-9/11.* Vancouver: UBC Press.

Baranyi, S. and Powell, K. (2008) Conclusion. In S. Baranyi, ed., *The Paradoxes of Peacebuilding Post-9/11.* Vancouver: UBC Press, pp. 293–316.

Barnett, M. and Finnemore, M. (2004) *Rules for the World: International Organizations in Global Politics.* New York: Cornell University Press.

Barnett, M., Kim, H., O'Donnell, M., and Sitea, L. (2007) Peacebuilding: What is in a Name? *Global Governance* 13(1), pp. 35–58.

Beardsley, K. (2008) Agreement without Peace? International Mediation and Time Inconsistency Problems. *American Journal of Political Science* 52(4), pp. 723–40.

Beardsley, K. (2009) Intervention Without Leverage: Explaining the Prevalence of Weak Mediators. *International Interactions* 35(3), pp. 272–97.

Beardsley, K. (2010) Pain, Pressure and Political Cover: Explaining Mediation Incidence. *Journal of Peace Research* 47(4), pp. 395–406.

Beardsley, K. (2011) *The Mediation Dilemma*. Cornell: Cornell University Press.

Beardsley, K. and Gleditsch, K. (2015) Peacekeeping as Conflict Containment. *International Studies Review* 17(1), pp. 67–89.

Bellamy, A. (2015) *The Responsibility to Protect: A Defense*. Oxford: Oxford University Press.

Bellamy, A. and Williams, P. (2012) Local Politics and International Partnerships: The UN Operation in Côte d'Ivoire (UNOCI). *Journal of International Peacekeeping* 16(3–4), pp. 252–81.

Bellamy, A., Williams, P., and Griffin, S. (2010) *Understanding Peacekeeping*. Malden, MA: Polity.

Benner, T., Mergenthaler, S., and Rotmann, P. (2011) *The New World of UN Peace Operations: Learning to Build Peace?* Oxford: Oxford University Press.

Bercovitch, J. (1989) International Dispute Mediation. In K. Kressel and D. Pruitt, eds, *Mediation Research: The Process and Effectiveness of Third-Party Intervention*. San Francisco: Jossey-Bass.

Bercovitch, J. (2002) Introduction: Putting Mediation in Context. In J. Bercovitch, ed., *Studies in International Mediation*. New York: Palgrave Macmillan, pp. 3–24.

Bercovitch, J. (2004) International Conflict Management Database. *Data and Coding Manual*. Available at: http://www.arts.canterbury.ac.nz/bercovitch/databases.shtml.

Bercovitch, J., Anagnoson, J., and Wille, D. (1991) Some Conceptual Issues and Empirical Trends in the Study of Successful Mediation in International Relations. *Journal of Peace Research* 28(1), pp. 7–17.

Bercovitch, J. and Fretter, J. (2004) *Regional Guide to International Conflict Management from 1945–2003*. Washington, DC: CQ Press.

Bercovitch, J. and Gartner, S. (2006) Empirical Studies in International Mediation. *International Interactions* 32(4), pp. 319–28.

Bercovitch, J. and Kadayifci-Orellana, A. (2009) Religion and Mediation: The Role of Faith-Based Actors in International Conflict Resolution. *International Negotiation* 14(1), pp. 175–204.

Bethell, L. (1966) The Mixed Commissions for the Suppression of the Transatlantic Slave Trade in the Nineteenth Century. *Journal of African History* 8(1), pp. 79–93.

Biersteker, T., Eckert, S., Tourinho, M., and Hudakova, Z. (2013) *The Effectiveness of United Nations Targeted Sanctions: Findings from the Targeted Sanctions*

Consortium. The Graduate Institute Geneva, Watson Institute for International Studies. Available at: https://repository.graduateinstitute.ch/record/287976/files/effectiveness_TCS_nov_2013.pdf.

Boehmer, C., Gartzke, E., and Nordstrom, T. (2004) Do Intergovernmental Organizations Promote Peace? *World Politics* 57(1), pp. 1–38.

Böhmelt, T. (2012) Why Many Cooks If They Can Spoil the Broth? The Determinants of Multi-Party Mediation. *Journal of Peace Research* 49(5), pp. 701–15.

Boutros-Ghali, B. (1995) *An Agenda for Peace.* New York: United Nations Publications.

Bove, V. and Ruggeri, A. (2016) Kinds of Blue: Diversity in UN Peacekeeping Missions and Civilian Protection. *British Journal of Political Science* 46(3), pp. 681–700.

Brahm, E. (2003) *Conflict Stages.* Beyond Intractability, Conflict Research Consortium, University of Colorado, Boulder. Available at: https://www.beyondintractability.org/essay/conflict_stages.

Bratt, D. (1996) Assessing the Success of UN Peacekeeping Operations. *International Peacekeeping* 3(4), pp. 64–81.

Bratt, D. (1997) Explaining Peacekeeping Performance: The UN in Internal Conflicts. *International Peacekeeping* 4(3), pp. 45–70.

Brochmann, M. and Hensel P. (2011) The Effectiveness of Negotiations over International River Claims. *International Studies Quarterly* 55(3), pp. 859–82.

Brownlie, I. (1979) *African Boundaries.* London: C. Hurst.

Bueno de Mesquita, B., Smith, A., Siverson, R., and Morrow, J. (2003) *The Logic of Political Survival.* Cambridge, MA: MIT Press.

Bueno de Mesquita, E. (2005) Conciliation, Counterterrorism, and Patterns of Terrorist Violence. *International Organization* 59(1), pp. 145–76.

Burton, J. (1987) *Resolving Deep-Rooted Conflict: A Handbook.* Lanham, MD: University Press of America.

Busch, M. (2007) Overlapping Institutions, Forum Shopping, and Dispute Settlement in International Trade. *International Organization* 61(4), pp. 735–61.

Busch, M. and Reinhardt, E. (2003) The Evolution of GATT/WTO Dispute Settlement. In J. Curtis and D. Ciuriak, eds, *Trade Policy Research.* Ottawa: Department of Foreign Affairs and International Trade, pp. 143–84.

Carneiro, C. and Apolinario, L. (2016) Targeted Versus Conventional Economic Sanctions: What is at Stake for Human Rights? *International Interactions* 42(4), pp. 565–89.

Chamberlain, D. (2017) A Non-Signal to Syria: Why the Strike May Not Shape Assad's Behavior. *Foreign Affairs,* April 14. Available at: https://www.foreignaffairs.com/articles/syria/2017-04-14/non-signal-syria.

Chandler, A. (2014) How the Pope Helped Bring the United States and Cuba Together. *The Atlantic,* December 17. Available at: https://www.the

atlantic.com/international/archive/2014/12/pope-francis-birthday-cuba-deal-castro-obama-letter/383854.

Chiozza, G. and Choi, A. (2003) Guess Who Did What: Political Leaders and the Management of Territorial Disputes, 1950–1990. *Journal of Conflict Resolution* 47(3), pp. 251–78.

Clausewitz, C. ([1832] 1982) *On War.* New York: Penguin.

Clayton, G. (2013) Relative Rebel Strength and the Onset and Outcome of Civil War Mediation. *Journal of Peace Research* 50(5), pp. 609–22.

Clifton, M., Bapat, N., and Kobayashi, Y. (2014) Threat and Imposition of Economic Sanctions 1945–2005: Updating the TIES Dataset. *Conflict Management and Peace Science* 31(5), pp. 541–58.

Clifton, M. and Schwebach, V. (1997) Fools Suffer Gladly: The Use of Economic Sanctions in International Crises. *International Studies Quarterly* 41(1), pp. 27–50.

Clinton, B. (2004) *My Life.* New York: Vintage.

Colaresi, M., Rasler, K., and Thompson, W. (2007) *Strategic Rivalries in World Politics.* Cambridge: Cambridge University Press.

Collier, P., Hoeffler, A., and Söderbom, M. (2006) *Post-Conflict Risks.* Centre for the Study of African Economies, University of Oxford. Available at: http://siteresources.worldbank.org/INTCONFLICT/Resources/PCP3797 CollierHoefflerSoderbom.pdf.

Corbetta, R. and Dixon, W. (2005) Dangers Beyond Dyads: Third-Party Participants in Militarized Interstate Disputes. *Conflict Management and Peace Science* 22(1), pp. 39–61.

Correlates of War Project (2008) *State System Membership List, v2008.* Available at: http://correlatesofwar.org/data-sets/state-system-membership.

Council of the European Union (2014) *Factsheet: EU Restrictive Measures.* Brussels. Available at: https://www.consilium.europa.eu/media/24503/135804.pdf.

Cox, D. and Drury, A. (2006) Democratic Sanctions: Connecting the Democratic Peace and Economic Sanctions. *Journal of Peace Research* 43(6), pp. 709–22.

Crescenzi, M., Kadera, K., McLaughlin Mitchell, S., and Thyne, C. (2011) A Supply Side Theory of Third Party Conflict Management. *International Studies Quarterly* 55(4), pp. 1069–94.

Crocker, C. (1992) *High Noon in Southern Africa: Making Peace in a Rough Neighborhood.* New York: W.W. Norton.

Crocker, C., Hampson, F., and Aall, P. (1999) *Herding Cats: Multiparty Mediation in a Complex World.* Washington, DC: United States Institute of Peace.

Crocker, C., Hampson, F., and Aall, P. (2001) A Crowded Stage: Liabilities and Benefits of Multiparty Mediation. *International Studies Perspectives* 2(1), pp. 51–67.

Cui, S. (2014) Conflict Transformation: The East China Sea Dispute and Lessons from the Ecuador–Peru Border Dispute. *Asian Perspective* 38(2), pp. 285–310.

Cunningham, D. (2006) Veto Players and Civil War Duration. *American Journal of Political Science* 50(4), pp. 875–92.

Cunningham, D. (2007) Chad. In K. DeRouen and U. Heo, eds, *Civil Wars of the World: Major Conflicts Since World War II*. Santa Barbara, CA: ABC-CLIO, pp. 235–48.

Cunningham, E. and Zakaria, Z. (2018) Turkey, Once a Haven for Syrian Refugees, Grows Weary of their Presence. *Washington Post*, April 10. Available at: https://www.washingtonpost.com/world/turkey-to-syrian-refugees-you-dont-have-to-go-home-but-dont-stay-here/2018/04/04/d1b17d8c-222a-11e8-94 6c-9420060cb7bd_story.html?noredirect=on&utm_term=.800507da8bf3.

Cunningham, K. (2011) Divide and Conquer or Divide and Concede: How do States Respond to Internally Divided Separatists. *American Political Science Review* 105(2), pp. 275–97.

Cunningham, K. (2013) Actor Fragmentation and Civil War Bargaining: How Internal Divisions Generate Civil Conflict. *American Journal of Political Science* 57(3), pp. 659–72.

Curran, D., Sebenius, J., and Watkins, M. (2004) Two Paths to Peace: Contrasting George Mitchell in Northern Ireland with Richard Holbrooke in Bosnia-Herzegovina. *Negotiation Journal* 20(4), pp. 513–37.

Dario, D. (2014) Peace Talks Between the FARC and Santos Government in Colombia. *BRICS Policy Center Brief* 4(2), pp. 4–15.

Day, A. (1987) *Border and Territorial Disputes*, 2nd edition. Harlow: Longman.

DeRouen, K., Bercovitch, J., and Pospieszna, P. (2011) Introducing the Civil Wars Mediation (CWM) Dataset. *Journal of Peace Research* 48(5), pp. 663–72.

Diehl, P. (1994) *International Peacekeeping*, 2nd edition. Baltimore: Johns Hopkins University Press.

Diehl, P. (2000) Forks in the Road: Theoretical and Policy Concerns for 21st Century Peacekeeping. *Global Society* 14(3), pp. 337–60.

Diehl, P. and Balas, A. (2014) *Peace Operations*, 2nd edition. New York: John Wiley & Sons.

Diehl, P. and Druckman, D. (2010) *Evaluating Peace Operations*. Boulder, CO: Lynne Rienner.

Diehl, P. and Druckman, D. (2017) Not the Same Old Way: Trends in Peace Operations. *Brown Journal of World Affairs* 24(1), pp. 249–60.

Diehl, P. and Druckman, D. (2018) Multiple Peacekeeping Missions: Analysing Interdependence. *International Peacekeeping* 25(1), pp. 28–51.

Doyle, M. and Sambanis, N. (2006) *Making War and Building Peace: United Nations Peace Operations*. Princeton: Princeton University Press.

Dreyer, D. (2012) Issue Intractability and the Persistence of International Rivalry. *Conflict Management and Peace Science* 29(5), pp. 471–89.

Drezner, D. (2000) International Organization Foundation Bargaining, Enforcement, and Multilateral Sanctions: When Is Cooperation Counterproductive? *International Organization* 54(1), pp. 73–102.

Drezner, D. (2003) The Hidden Hand of Economic Coercion. *International Organization* 57(3), pp. 643–59.

Drezner, D. (2015) Targeted Sanctions in a World of Global Finance. *International Interactions* 41(4), pp. 755–64.

Favretto, K. (2009) Should Peacemakers Take Sides? Major Power Mediation, Coercion, and Bias. *American Political Science Review* 103(2), pp. 248–63.

Fearon, J. (1995) Rationalist Explanations for War. *International Organization* 49(3), pp. 379–414.

Fearon, J. (1998) Bargaining, Enforcement, and International Cooperation. *International Organization* 52(2), pp. 269–305.

Fearon, J. (2004) Why Do Some Civil Wars Last so Much Longer than Others? *Journal of Peace Research* 41(3), pp. 275–301.

Filson, D. and Werner, S. (2002) A Bargaining Model of War and Peace: Anticipating the Onset, Duration, and Outcome of War. *American Journal of Political Science* 46(4), pp. 819–37.

Fink, C. (1968) Some Conceptual Difficulties in the Theory of Social Conflict. *Journal of Conflict Resolution* 12(4), pp. 412–60.

Fortna, V. (2008) *Does Peacekeeping Work? Shaping Belligerents' Choices After Civil War.* Princeton: Princeton University Press.

Fravel, T. (2008) *Strong Borders, Secure Nation.* Princeton: Princeton University Press.

Frazier, D. and Dixon, W. (2006) Third-Party Intermediaries and Negotiated Settlements, 1946–2000. *International Interactions* 32(4), pp. 385–408.

Fuhrmann, M. and Lupu, Y. (2016) Do Arms Control Treaties Work? Assessing the Effectiveness of the Nuclear Nonproliferation Treaty. *International Studies Quarterly* 60(3), pp. 530–9.

Galtung, J. (1969) Violence, Peace, and Peace Research. *Journal of Peace Research* 6(3), pp. 167–91.

Geddes, B. (1999) What Do We Know About Democratization After Twenty Years? *Annual Review of Political Science* 2(1), pp. 115–44.

Gent, S. and Shannon, M. (2010) The Effectiveness of International Arbitration and Adjudication: Getting Into a Bind. *Journal of Politics* 72(2), pp. 366–80.

Gent, S. and Shannon, M. (2011) Bias and the Effectiveness of Third-Party Conflict Management Mechanisms. *Conflict Management and Peace Science* 28(2), pp. 124–44.

Ghosn, F. (2010) Getting to the Table and Getting to Yes: An Analysis of International Negotiations. *International Studies Quarterly* 54(4), pp. 1055–72.

Gilligan, M. and Stedman, S. (2003) Where Do the Peacekeepers Go? *International Studies Review* 5(4), pp. 37–54.

Giumelli, F. (2015) Understanding United Nations Targeted Sanctions: An Empirical Analysis. *International Affairs* 91(6), pp. 1351–68.

Gleditsch, N., Nordkvelle, J., and Strand, H. (2014) Peace Research—Just the Study of War? *Journal of Peace Research* 51(2), pp. 145–58.

Goertz, G., Diehl, P., and Balas, A. (2016) *The Puzzle of Peace.* Oxford: Oxford University Press.

Goetze, C. (2017) *The Distinction of Peace*. Ann Arbor: Michigan University Press.

Greig, J. M. (2001) Moments of Opportunity: Recognizing Conditions of Ripeness for International Mediation Between Enduring Rivals. *Journal of Conflict Resolution* 45(6), pp. 691–718.

Greig, J. M. (2005) Stepping Into the Fray: When Do Mediators Mediate? *American Journal of Political Science* 49(2), pp. 249–66.

Greig, J. M. (2015) Rebels at the Gates: Civil War Battle Locations, Movement, and Openings for Diplomacy. *International Studies Quarterly* 59(4), pp. 680–93.

Greig, J. M. and Diehl, P. (2005) The Peacekeeping–Peacemaking Dilemma. *International Studies Quarterly* 49(4), pp. 621–46.

Greig, J. M. and Diehl, P. (2006) Softening Up: Making Conflicts More Amenable to Diplomacy. *International Interactions* 32(4), pp. 355–84.

Greig, J. M. and Diehl, P. (2012) *International Mediation*. Cambridge: Polity.

Greig, J. M. and Regan, P. (2008) When Do They Say Yes? An Analysis of the Willingness to Offer and Accept Mediation in Civil Wars. *International Studies Quarterly* 52(4), pp. 759–81.

Guzman, A. (2008) *How International Law Works*. Oxford: Oxford University Press.

Hartzell, C. (2016) Negotiated Peace: Power Sharing in Peace Agreements. In D. Mason and S. McLaughlin Mitchell, eds, *What Do We Know About Civil Wars?* Lanham, MD: Rowman & Littlefield.

Heldt, B. (2001) Conditions for Successful Intrastate Peacekeeping Missions. In *Euroconference*, San Feliu de Guixols, Spain.

Helfer, L. (2013) Flexibility in International Agreements. In J. Dunoff and M. Pollack, eds, *Interdisciplinary Perspectives on International Law and International Relations*. Cambridge: Cambridge University Press, pp. 175–96.

Helfer, L. and Voeten, E. (2014) International Courts as Agents of Legal Change: Evidence from LGBT Rights in Europe. *International Organization* 68(1), pp. 77–110.

Hoglund, K. and Svensson, I. (2009) Mediating Between Tigers and Lions: Norwegian Peace Diplomacy in Sri Lanka's Civil War. *Contemporary South Asia* 17(2), pp. 175–91.

Holbrooke, R. (1999) *To End a War: The Conflict in Yugoslavia—America's Inside Story—Negotiating with Milosevic*, revised edition. New York: Modern Library.

Hopmann, P. (1996) *The Negotiation Process and the Resolution of International Conflicts*. Columbia: University of South Carolina Press.

Hovi, J., Huseby, R., and Sprinz D. (2011) When Do (Imposed) Economic Sanctions Work? *World Politics* 57(4), pp. 479–99.

Howard, L. (2008) *UN Peacekeeping in Civil Wars*. Cambridge: Cambridge University Press.

Howard, L. and Dayal, A. (2018) The Use of Force in UN Peacekeeping. *International Organization* 72(1), pp. 71–103.

Hufbauer, G., Schott, J., and Elliott, K. (1990) *Economic Sanctions Reconsidered*, 2nd edition. Washington, DC: Institute for International Economics.

Hultman, L., Kathman, J., and Shannon, M. (2013) United Nations Peacekeeping and Civilian Protection in Civil War. *American Journal of Political Science* 57(4), pp. 875–91.

Hultman, L. and Peksen, D. (2017) Successful or Counterproductive Coercion? The Effect of International Sanctions on Conflict Intensity. *Journal of Conflict Resolution* 61(6), pp. 1315–39.

Huth, P. and Allee, T. (2002) *The Democratic Peace and Territorial Conflict in the Twentieth Century*. Cambridge: Cambridge University Press.

Huth, P., Croco, S., and Appel, B. (2011) Does International Law Promote the Peaceful Settlement of International Disputes? Evidence from the Study of Territorial Conflicts since 1945. *American Political Science Review* 105(2), pp. 415–36.

Huth, P., Croco, S., and Appel, B. (2013) Bringing Law to the Table: Legal Claims, Focal Points, and the Settlement of Territorial Disputes since 1945. *American Journal of Political Science* 57(1), pp. 90–103.

ICISS (International Commission on Intervention and State Sovereignty) (2001) Responsibility to Protect. Ottawa, ON: International Development Research Centre. Available at: http://responsibilitytoprotect.org/ICISS%20Report.pdf.

Ireland, G. (1938) *Boundaries, Possessions, and Conflicts in South America*. Cambridge, MA: Harvard University Press.

Jackson, V. (2016) Threat Consensus and Rapprochement Failure: Revisiting the Collapse of US–North Korea Relations, 1994–2002. *Foreign Policy Analysis* 14(2), pp. 235–53.

Jenkins, R. (2013) *Peacebuilding: From Concept to Commission*. New York: Routledge.

Jervis, R. (1988) War and Misperception. *Journal of Interdisciplinary History* 18(4), pp. 675–700.

Jett, D. (2000) *Why Peacekeeping Fails*. New York: St. Martin's Press.

Jie, C. (1994) China's Spratly Policy: With Special Reference to the Philippines and Malaysia. *Asian Survey* 34(10), pp. 893–903.

Jones, D., Singer, S., and Bremer, J. (1996) Militarized Interstate Disputes, 1816–1992: Rationale, Coding Rules, and Empirical Patterns. *Conflict Management and Peace Science* 15(2), pp. 163–213.

Joshi, M., Quinn, J., and Regan, P. (2015) Annualized Implementation Data on Comprehensive Intrastate Peace Accords, 1989–2012. *Journal of Peace Research* 52(4), pp. 551–62.

Joyner, C. (2015) The Responsibility to Protect: Humanitarian Concern and the Lawfulness of Armed Intervention. In B. Frederking and P. Diehl, eds, *The Politics of Global Governance*, 5th edition. Boulder, CO: Lynne Rienner, pp. 135–54.

Kacowicz, A. and Bar-Siman-Tov, Y. (2000) Stable Peace: A Conceptual Framework. In A. Kacowicz, Y. Bar-Siman-Tov, O. Elgström, and M. Jerneck, eds, *Stable Peace Among Nations*. Lanham, MD: Rowman and Littlefield, pp. 11–35.

Kantchevski, P. (2007) The Differences Between the Panel Procedures of the GATT and the WTO: The Role of GATT and WTO Panels in Trade Dispute Settlement. *Brigham Young University International Law and Management Review* 3(1), pp. 79–140.

Kaplow, J. (2016) The Negotiation Calculus: Why Parties to Civil Conflict Refuse to Talk. *International Studies Quarterly* 60(1), pp. 38–46.

Kelman, H. (1996) The Interactive Problem-Solving Approach. In C. Crocker, F. Hampson, and P. Aal, eds, *Managing Global Chaos: Sources of and Responses to International Conflict*. Washington, DC: United States Institute of Peace Press.

Kennedy, D. (2004) *The Dark Sides of Virtue: Reassessing International Humanitarianism*. Princeton: Princeton University Press.

Kirschner, S. (2010) Knowing Your Enemy: Information and Commitment Problems in Civil Wars. *Journal of Conflict Resolution* 54(5), pp. 745–70.

Kochan, T. and Jick, T. (2011) The Public Sector Mediation Process: A Theory and Empirical Examination. *Journal of Conflict Resolution* 22(2), pp. 209–40.

Koremenos, B., Lipson, C., and Snidal, D. (2001) The Rational Design of International Institutions. *International Organization* 55(4), pp. 761–99.

Krasner, S. and Weinstein, J. (2014) Improving Governance from the Outside. *Annual Review of Political Science* 17(1), pp. 123–45.

Kressel, K. and Pruitt, D., eds (1989) *Mediation Research: The Process and Effectiveness of Third-Party Intervention*. San Francisco: Jossey-Bass.

Kreutz, J. (2007) Colombia, 1978–Present. In K. DeRouen and U. Heo, eds, *Civil Wars of the World: Major Conflicts Since World War II*. Santa Barbara, CA: ABC-CLIO, pp. 267–90.

Kriesberg, L. (1992) *International Conflict Resolution*. New Haven: Yale University Press.

Kriesberg, L. (1997) The Development of the Conflict Resolution Field. In I. Zartman and J. Rasmussen, eds, *Peacemaking in International Conflict: Methods and Techniques*. Washington, DC: United States Institute of Peace Press, pp. 51–77.

Kritsiotis, D. (2000) The Kosovo Crisis and NATO's Application of Armed Force Against the Federal Republic of Yugoslavia. *International and Comparative Law Quarterly* 49(2), pp. 330–59.

Kuperman, A. (2015) Obama's Libya Debacle: How a Well-Meaning Intervention Ended in Failure. *Foreign Affairs*, March/April. Available at: https://www.foreignaffairs.com/articles/libya/obamas-libya-debacle.

Kydd, A. (2003) Which Side Are You On? Bias, Credibility, and Mediation. *American Journal of Political Science* 47(4), pp. 597–611.

Kydd, A. (2006) When Can Mediators Build Trust? *American Political Science Review* 100(3), pp. 449–62.

Kydd, A. and Walter, B. (2002) Sabotaging the Peace: The Politics of Extremist Violence. *International Organization* 56(2), pp. 263–96.

Lacy, D. and Niou, E. (2004) A Theory of Issue Linkage and Economic Sanctions: The Roles of Information, Preferences, and Threats. *Journal of Politics* 66(1), pp. 25–42.

Lake, D. and Rothchild, D. (1996) Containing Fear: The Origins and Management of Ethnic Conflict. *International Security* 21(2), pp. 41–75.

Larson, D. (1997) Trust and Missed Opportunities in International Relations. *Political Psychology* 18(3), pp. 701–34.

Lektzian, D. and Biglaiser, G. (2013) Investment, Opportunity, and Risk: Do US Sanctions Deter or Encourage Global Investment? *International Studies Quarterly* 57(1), pp. 65–78.

Lektzian, D. and Regan, P. (2016) Economic Sanctions, Military Interventions, and Civil Conflict Outcomes. *Journal of Peace Research* 53(4), pp. 554–68.

Lektzian, D. and Souva, M. (2007) An Institutional Theory of Sanctions Onset and Success. *Journal of Conflict Resolution* 51(6), pp. 848–71.

Linebarger, C. and Enterline, A. (2016) Third Party Intervention and the Duration and Outcomes of Civil Wars. In T. Mason and S. McLaughlin Mitchell, eds, *What Do We Know About Civil Wars?* Lanham, MD: Rowman & Littlefield, pp. 93–108.

Lounsbery, M. and Cook A. (2011) Rebellion, Mediation, and Group Change: An Empirical Investigation of Competing Hypotheses. *Journal of Peace Research* 48(1), pp. 73–84.

Lucena Carneiro, C. and Apolinário Jr, L. (2016) Targeted Versus Conventional Economic Sanctions: What is at Stake for Human Rights? *International Interactions* 42(4), pp. 565–89.

Lund, A. (2017) Syria's Fair-Weather Friends. *Foreign Affairs*, October 31. Available at: https://www.foreignaffairs.com/articles/syria/2017-10-31/syrias-fair-weather-friends.

Luttwak, E. (1999) Give War a Chance. *Foreign Affairs*, July/August. Available at: https://www.foreignaffairs.com/articles/1999-07-01/give-war-chance.

McQueen, N. (2002) *United Nations Peacekeeping in Africa Since 1960*. London: Pearson Education.

Mansfield, E. and Snyder, J. (2005) *Electing to Fight: Why Emerging Democracies Go to War*. Cambridge, MA: MIT Press.

Maoz, Z. (2004) Conflict Management and Conflict Resolution: A Conceptual and Methodological Introduction. In Z. Maoz et al., eds, *Multiple Paths to Knowledge in International Relations: Methodology in the Study of Conflict Management and Conflict Resolution*. Lanham, MD: Lexington Books, pp. 11–22.

Maoz, Z. and Siverson, R. (2008) Bargaining, Domestic Politics, and International Context in the Management of War: A Review Essay. *Conflict Management and Peace Science* 25(2), pp. 171–89.

Maoz, Z. and Terris, L. (2006) Credibility and Strategy in International Mediation. *International Interactions* 32(4), pp. 409–40.

Marinov, N. (2005) Do Economic Sanctions Destabilize Country Leaders? *American Journal of Political Science* 49(3), pp. 564–76.

Martin, C. (2002) Rewarding North Korea: Theoretical Perspectives on the 1994 Agreed Framework. *Journal of Peace Research* 39(1), pp. 51–68.

Mason, T., Weingarten, J., and Fett, P. (1999) Win, Lose, or Draw: Predicting the Outcome of Civil Wars. *Political Research Quarterly* 52(2), pp. 239–68.

Mattes, M. and Savun, B. (2009) Fostering Peace after Civil War: Commitment Problems and Agreement Design. *International Studies Quarterly* 53(3), pp. 737–59.

Matthaei, L. (1908) The Place of Arbitration in Ancient Systems of International Ethics. *Classical Quarterly* 2(4), pp. 241–64.

Maxmen, A. (2016) Sudan Sanctions Deprive "Whole Nation" of Health Care. *Foreign Policy*, January 14. Available at: http://foreignpolicy.com/2016/01/14/sudan-sanctions-deprive-whole-nation-of-health-care.

Melin, M. and Svensson, I. (2009) Incentives for Talking: Accepting Mediation in International and Civil Wars. *International Interactions* 35(3), pp. 249–71.

Meyer, A. (1960) Functions of the Mediator in Collective Bargaining. *Industrial and Labour Relations Review* 13(2), pp. 159–65.

Mitchell, C. (1995) The Right Moment: Notes on Four Models of Ripeness. *Paradigms* 9(2), pp. 38–52.

Mitchell, C. (2000) *Gestures of Conciliation: Factors Contributing to Successful Olive Branches*. London: Macmillan.

Mitchell, S. and Owsiak, A. (2018) The International Court of Justice. In R. Howard and K. Randazzo, eds, *Handbook of Judicial Behavior*. New York: Routledge, pp. 445–66.

Mnookin, R. and Kornhauser, L. (1979) Bargaining in the Shadow of the Law: The Case of Divorce. *Yale Law Journal* 88(5), pp. 950–97.

Morgan, C., Bapat, N., and Kobayashi, Y. (2014) Threat and Imposition of Economic Sanctions 1945–2005: Updating the TIES Dataset. *Conflict Management and Peace Science* 31(5), pp. 541–58.

Morgan, C. and Schwebach, V. (1997) Fools Suffer Gladly: The Use of Economic Sanctions in International Crises. *International Studies Quarterly* 41(1), pp. 27–50.

Muir, J. (2011) Syria Sanctions: Arab League Tightens Grip. BBC News. Available at: https://www.bbc.com/news/world-middle-east-15912376.

Mullenbach, M. (2005) Deciding to Keep Peace: An Analysis of International Influences on the Establishment of Third-Party Peacekeeping Missions. *International Studies Quarterly* 49(3), pp. 529–55.

Nasi, C. (2009) Colombia's Peace Processes (1982–2002). In V. Bourvier, ed., *Colombia: Building Peace in a Time of War*. Washington, DC: United States Institute of Peace, pp. 39–64.

Nilsson, D. (2008) Partial Peace: Rebel Groups Inside and Outside of Civil War Settlements. *Journal of Peace Research* 45(4), pp. 479–95.

Nilsson, D. (2010) Turning Weakness into Strength: Military Capabilities, Multiple Rebel Groups and Negotiated Settlements. *Conflict Management and Peace Science* 27(3), pp. 253–71.

Nilsson, D. and Kovacs, M. (2011) Revisiting an Elusive Concept: A Review of the Debate on Spoilers in Peace Processes. *International Studies Review* 13(4), pp. 606–26.

Norton, A. (1991) The Demise of the MNF. In A. McDermott and K. Skjelsbaek, eds, *Peacebuilding as Politics: The Multinational Force in Beirut, 1982–1984*. Miami: Florida International University Press, pp. 80–94.

Ott, M. (1972) Mediation as a Method of Conflict Resolution: Two Cases. *International Organization* 26(4), pp. 595–618.

Ottmann, M. and Vüllers, J. (2015) The Power-Sharing Event Dataset (PSED): A New Dataset on the Promises and Practices of Power-Sharing in Post-Conflict Countries. *Conflict Management and Peace Science* 32(3), pp. 327–50.

Owsiak, A. (2012) Signing Up for Peace: International Boundary Agreements, Democracy, and Militarized Interstate Conflict. *International Studies Quarterly* 56(1), pp. 51–66.

Owsiak, A. (2014) Conflict Management Trajectories in Militarized Interstate Disputes: A Conceptual Framework and Theoretical Foundations. *International Studies Review* 16(1), pp. 50–78.

Owsiak, A. and Mitchell, S. (2019) Conflict Management in Land, River, and Maritime Claims. *Political Science Research and Methods*, 7(1), pp. 43–61.

Palmer, D. (2001) Overcoming the Weight of History: "Getting to Yes" in the Peru–Ecuador Border Dispute. *Diplomacy & Statecraft* 12(2), pp. 29–46.

Palmer, G., D'Orazio, V., Kenwick, M., and Lane, M. (2015) The MID4 Dataset, 2002–2010: Procedures, Coding Rules, and Description. *Conflict Management and Peace Science* 32(2), pp. 222–42.

Pape, R. (1997) Why Economic Sanctions Do Not Work. *International Security* 22(2), pp. 90–136.

Paris, R. (2004) *At War's End: Building Peace After Civil Conflict*. Cambridge: Cambridge University Press.

Pearlman, W. and Cunningham, K. (2012) Nonstate Actors, Fragmentation, and Conflict Processes. *Journal of Conflict Resolution* 56(1), pp. 3–15.

Pedrosa de Sousa, R. (2014) External Interventions and Civil War Intensity in South-Central Somalia (1991–2010). *Cadernos de Estudos Africanos* 28(1), pp. 57–86.

Peksen, D. (2009) Better or Worse? The Effect of Economic Sanctions on Human Rights. *Journal of Peace Research* 46(1), pp. 59–77.

Pickering, J. and Kisangani, E. (2009) The International Military Intervention Dataset: An Updated Resource for Conflict Scholars. *Journal of Peace Research* 46(4), pp. 589–99.

Powell, R. (2006) War as a Commitment Problem. *International Organization* 60(1), pp. 169–203.

Princen, T. (1992) *Intermediaries in International Conflict*. Princeton: Princeton University Press.

Pruitt, D. (1997) Ripeness Theory and the Oslo Talks. *International Negotiation* 2(2), pp. 237–50.

Pruitt, D. (2002) Mediator Behavior and Success in Mediation. In J. Bercovitch, ed., *Studies in International Mediation*. New York: Palgrave Macmillan, pp. 41–54.

Pruitt, D. (2008) Back-Channel Communication in the Settlement of Conflict. *International Negotiation* 13(1), pp. 37–54.

Putnam, R. (1988) Diplomacy and Domestic Politics: The Logic of Two-Level Games. *International Organization* 42(3), pp. 427–60.

Pushkina, D. (2006) A Recipe for Success? Ingredients of a Successful Peacekeeping Mission. *International Peacekeeping* 13(2), pp. 133–49.

Quinn, D., Wilkenfeld, J., Smarick, K., and Asal, V. (2006) Power Play: Mediation in Symmetric and Asymmetric International Crises. *International Interactions* 32(4), pp. 441–70.

Quinn, J. (2007) Mozambique. In K. DeRouen and U. Heo, eds, *Civil Wars of the World: Major Conflicts Since World War II*. Santa Barbara, CA: ABC-CLIO, pp. 509–26.

Rathbun, B. (2012) *Trust in International Cooperation: International Security Institutions, Domestic Politics and American Multilateralism*. Cambridge: Cambridge University Press.

Reed, L. and Wong, K. (2016) Marine Entitlements in the South China Sea: The Arbitration Between the Philippines and China. *American Journal of International Law* 110(4), pp. 746–60.

Regan, P. (2000) *Civil Wars and Foreign Powers: Outside Intervention in Intrastate Conflict*. Ann Arbor: University of Michigan Press.

Regan, P. (2002) Third-Party Interventions and the Duration of Intrastate Conflicts. *Journal of Conflict Resolution* 46(1), pp. 55–73.

Regan, P., Frank, R., and Aydin, A. (2009) Diplomatic Interventions and Civil War: A New Dataset. *Journal of Peace Research* 46(1), pp. 135–46.

Regan, P. and Stam, A. (2000) In the Nick of Time: Conflict Management, Mediation Timing, and the Duration of Interstate Disputes. *International Studies Quarterly* 44(2), pp. 239–60.

Reich, A. (2017) *The Effectiveness of the WTO Dispute Settlement System: A Statistical Analysis*. European University Institute Working Papers, 2017/11. Available at: http://cadmus.eui.eu/bitstream/handle/1814/47045/LAW_2017_11.pdf.

Reykers, Y. (2017) EU Battlegroups: High Costs, No Benefits. *Contemporary Security Policy* 38(3), pp. 457–70.

Richmond, O. (1998) Devious Objectives and the Disputants' View of International Mediation: A Theoretical Framework. *Journal of Peace Research* 35(6), pp. 707–22.

Richmond, O. and Franks, J. (2009) *Liberal Peace Transitions: Between Statebuilding and Peacebuilding*. Edinburgh: Edinburgh University Press.

Rider, T. and Owsiak, A. (2015) Border Settlement, Commitment Problems, and the Causes of Contiguous Rivalry. *Journal of Peace Research* 52(4), pp. 508–21.

Roberts, A. (1993) Humanitarian War: Military Intervention and Human Rights. *International Affairs* 69(3), pp. 429–49.

Roberts, A. (1999) The So-Called Right of Humanitarian Intervention. Melbourne: Trinity College. Available at: https://www.trinity.unimelb.edu.au/getmedia/93b6f7c8-5ecc-412a-a225-a835de997d1c/TrinityPaper13.aspx.

Rogers, E. (1996) Using Economic Sanctions to Prevent Deadly Conflict. CSIA Discussion Paper 96–02. Cambridge, MA: Kennedy School of Government, Harvard University. Available at: https://www.belfercenter.org/publication/using-economic-sanctions-prevent-deadly-conflict.

Rubenzer, T. (2007) Nigeria. In K. DeRouen and U. Heo, eds, *Civil Wars of the World: Major Conflicts Since World War II*. Santa Barbara, CA: ABC-CLIO, pp. 567–58.

Ruggeri, A., Dorussen, H., and Gizelis, T. (2016) On the Frontline Every Day? Subnational Deployment of United Nations Peacekeepers. *British Journal of Political Science*, published online, June 1.

Ruggeri, A., Dorussen, H., and Gizelis, T. (2017) Winning the Peace Locally: UN Peacekeeping and Local Conflict. *International Organization* 71(1), pp. 163–85.

Rutkow, L. and Lozman, J. (2006) Suffer the Children? A Call for the United States Ratification of the United Nations Convention on the Rights of the Child. *Harvard Human Rights Journal* 19(1), pp. 161–90.

Ryckman, K. and Braithwaite, J. (2017) Changing Horses in Midstream: Leadership Changes and the Civil War Peace Process. *Conflict Management and Peace Science*, published online, October 5.

Sanchez, F. and Goodman, J. (2017) Venezuela's Maduro Vows to Punish Opponents for US Sanctions. *Chicago Tribune*, August 26. Available at: http://www.chicagotribune.com/business/sns-bc-lt–venezuela-crisis-20170825-story.html.

Savun, B. (2008) Information, Bias, and Mediation Success. *International Studies Quarterly* 52(1), pp. 25–47.

Schelling, T. (1960) *The Strategy of Conflict*. Cambridge, MA: Harvard University Press.

Schoenbaum, T. (2016) The South China Sea Arbitration Decision: The Need for Clarification. *AJIL Unbound* 110(1), pp. 290–5.

Segura, R. and Mechoulan, D. (2017) *Made in Havana: How Colombia and the FARC Decided to End the War*. New York: International Peace Institute.

Seybolt, T. (2010) Humanitarian Intervention and International Security. In *Oxford Research Encyclopedia of International Studies*. Oxford: Oxford University Press, pp. 1–23.

Shaw, M. (2017) *International Law*, 8th edition. Cambridge: Cambridge University Press.

Shin, G., Choi, S., and Luo, S. (2016) Do Economic Sanctions Impair Target Economies? *International Political Science Review* 37(4), pp. 485–99.

Shirkey, Z. (2018) Military Intervention in Interstate and Civil Wars: A Unified Interpretation. In *Oxford Research Encyclopedia of Politics*. Oxford: Oxford University Press, pp. 1–29.

Simmons, B. (1999) *Territorial Disputes and Their Resolution: The Case of Ecuador and Peru*. Washington, DC: United States Institute of Peace.

Sisk, T. (2008) *International Mediation in Civil Wars: Bargaining with Bullets*. New York: Routledge.

Slantchev, B. (2003) The Power to Hurt: Costly Conflict with Completely Informed States. *American Political Science Review* 97(1), pp. 123–33.

Smith, A. and Stam, A. (2003) Mediation and Peacekeeping in a Random Walk Model of Civil and Interstate War. *International Studies Review* 5(4), pp. 115–35.

South China Sea Arbitration (2016) Philippines v. China, Award. PCA Case No. 2013–19. Available at: https://www.pcacases.com/web/view/7.

Specia, M. (2018) How Syria's Death Toll is Lost in the Fog of War. *New York Times*, April 13. Available at: https://www.nytimes.com/2018/04/13/world/middleeast/syria-death-toll.html.

Spector, B. (2003) Negotiating with Villains Revisited: Research Note. *International Negotiation* 8(3), pp. 613–21.

Squires, N. (2014) How Much Does US–Cuba Thaw Owe to Pope Francis? *Christian Science Monitor*, December 18. Available at: www.csmonitor.com/World/Europe/2014/1218/How-much-does-US-Cuba-thaw-owe-to-Pope-Francis.

Sremac, D. (1999) *War of Words: Washington Tackles the Yugoslav Conflict*. Westport, CT: Praeger.

Stanley, E. and Sawyer, J. (2009) The Equifinality of War Termination: Multiple Paths to Ending War. *Journal of Conflict Resolution* 53(5), pp. 651–76.

Stedman, S. (1991) *Peacemaking in Civil Wars: International Mediation in Zimbabwe, 1974–1980*. Boulder, CO: Lynne Rienner.

Stedman, S. (1997) Spoiler Problems in Peace Processes. *International Security* 22(2), pp. 5–53.

Sullivan, P. and Koch, M. (2009) Military Intervention by Powerful States, 1945–2003. *Journal of Peace Research* 46(5), pp. 707–18.

Svensson, I. (2007) Bargaining, Bias and Peace Brokers: How Rebels Commit to Peace. *Journal of Peace Research* 44(2), pp. 177–94.

Svensson, I. (2009) Who Brings Which Peace? Neutral versus Biased Mediation and Institutional Peace Arrangements in Civil Wars. *Journal of Conflict Resolution* 53(3), pp. 446–69.

Tinsley, C., O'Connor, K., and Sullivan, B. (2002) Tough Guys Finish Last: The Perils of a Distributive Reputation. *Organizational Behavior and Human Decision Processes* 88(2), pp. 621–42.

Tir, J. and Karreth, J. (2018) *Incentivizing Peace: How International Organizations Can Help Prevent Civil Wars in Member Countries*. Oxford: Oxford University Press.

Toft, M. (2009) *Securing the Peace: The Durable Settlement of Civil Wars*. Princeton: Princeton University Press.

Toft, M. (2014) Territory and War. *Journal of Peace Research* 51(2), pp. 185–98.

Tostensen, A. and Bull, B. (2002) Are Smart Sanctions Feasible? *World Politics* 54(3), pp. 373–403.

Touval, S. (1982) *The Peace Brokers: Mediators in the Arab–Israeli Conflict, 1948–1979*. Princeton: Princeton University Press.

Touval, S. and Zartman, I. (1985) *International Mediation in Theory and Practice*. Boulder, CO: Westview Press.

Tschudin, A. and Trithart, A. (2018) The Role of Local Governance in Sustaining Peace. International Peace Institute. Available at: https://www.ipinst.org/wp-content/uploads/2018/02/1802_Local-Governance-and-Sustaining-Peace.pdf.

United Nations (1984) Declaration of the United States, 6 April 1984. Treaty Series 1354:452. Available at: https://treaties.un.org/doc/Publication/UNTS/Volume%201354/v1354.pdf.

United Nations (1985) Declaration of the United States, 7 October 1985. Treaty Series 1408:270. Available at: https://treaties.un.org/doc/Publication/UNTS/Volume%201408/v1408.pdf.

United Nations (2018) Operational Portal, Refugee Situations: Syria Regional Refugee Response. Available at: https://data2.unhcr.org/en/situations/syria#_ga=2.8626231.328370914.1540132285-39502455.1540132285.

Uppsala Conflict Data Program (2014) In *UCDP Conflict Encyclopedia*. Uppsala: Uppsala University.

Urlacher, B. (2011) Political Constraints and Civil War Conflict Resolution. *Civil Wars* 13(2), pp. 81–98.

US Department of the Treasury (2014) Announcement of Expanded Treasury Sanctions within the Russian Financial Services, Energy and Defense or Related Materiel Sectors. Available at: https://www.treasury.gov/press-center/press-releases/Pages/jl2629.aspx.

Vasquez, J. (2009) *The War Puzzle Revisited*. Cambridge: Cambridge University Press.

von Soest, C. and Wahman, M. (2015) Are Democratic Sanctions Really Counterproductive? *Democratization* 22(6), pp. 957–80.

Walch, C. (2016) Rethinking Ripeness Theory: Explaining Progress and Failure in Civil War Negotiations in the Philippines and Colombia. *International Negotiation* 21(1), pp. 75–103.

Wallensteen, P. and Grusell, H. (2012) Targeting the Right Targets? The UN Use of Individual Sanctions. *Global Governance* 18(2), pp. 207–30.

Walter, B. (2002) *Committing to Peace: The Successful Settlement of Civil Wars*. Princeton: Princeton University Press.

Walter, B. (2006) Building Reputation: Why Governments Fight Some Separatists but Not Others. *American Journal of Political Science* 50(2), pp. 313–30.

Walter, B. (2009) Bargaining Failures and Civil War. *Annual Review of Political Science* 12(1), pp. 243–61.

Watkins, M. and Lundberg, K. (1998) Getting to the Table in Oslo: Driving Forces and Channel Factors. *Negotiation Journal* 14(2), pp. 115–35.

Weiss, T. (1999) Sanctions as a Foreign Policy Tool: Weighing Humanitarian Impulses. *Journal of Peace Research* 36(5), pp. 499–509.

Weiss, T. (2016) *Humanitarian Intervention*, 3rd edition. Cambridge: Polity.

Wiegand, K. and Powell, E. (2011) Past Experience, Quest for the Best Forum, and Peaceful Attempts to Resolve Territorial Disputes. *Journal of Conflict Resolution* 55(1), pp. 33–59.

World Trade Organization (2015) WTO Disputes Reach 500 Mark. Available at: https://www.wto.org/english/news_e/news15_e/ds500rfc_10nov15_e.htm.

Wroughton, L. (2018) Exclusive: U.S. to Impose Arms Embargo on South Sudan to End Conflict—Sources. Reuters, February 2. Available at: https://www.reuters.com/article/us-usa-southsudan-arms-exclusive/exclusive-u-s-to-impose-arms-embargo-on-south-sudan-to-end-conflict-sources-idUSKBN1FM0ZE.

Yardley, J. and Pianigiani, G. (2014) Pope Francis is Credited With a Crucial Role in U.S.-Cuba Agreement. *New York Times*, December 17. Available at: http://www.nytimes.com/2014/12/18/world/americas/breakthrough-on-cuba-highlights-popes-role-as-diplomatic-broker.html.

Zartman, I. (1981) Explaining Disengagement. In J. Rubin, ed., *Dynamics of Third-Party Intervention: Kissinger in the Middle East*. New York: Praeger.

Zartman, I. (1995) *Elusive Peace: Negotiating an End to Civil Wars*. Washington, DC: Brookings Institution Press.

Zartman, I. (1997) Explaining Oslo. *International Negotiation* 2(2), pp. 195–215.

Zartman, I. (2000) Ripeness: The Hurting Stalemate and Beyond. In P. Stern and D. Druckman, eds, *International Conflict Resolution After the Cold War*. Washington, DC: National Academy Press.

Zartman, I. (2001) *Preventive Negotiation: Avoiding Conflict Escalation*. Lanham, MD: Rowman & Littlefield.

Zartman, I. (2002) Mediation by Regional Organizations: The OAU in Chad and Congo. In J. Bercovitch, ed., *Studies in International Mediation*. New York: Palgrave Macmillan, pp. 80–97.

Zartman, I. (2003) Ripeness. The Beyond Intractability Knowledge Base Project. Available at: http://www.beyondintractability.org/essay/ripeness/?nid=1029.

Zartman, I. (2007) The Timing of Peace Initiatives: Hurting Stalemates and Ripe Moments. In J. Darby and R. MacGinty, eds, *Contemporary Peacemaking: Conflict, Violence and Peace Processes*, 2nd edition. New York: Palgrave Macmillan.

Zartman, I. (2008) *Negotiation and Conflict Management*. New York: Routledge.

Zartman, I. and Berman, M. (1982) *The Practical Negotiator*. New Haven: Yale University Press.

Zartman, I. and Touval, S. (1996) International Mediation in the Post-Cold War Era. In C. Crocker, F. Hampson, and P. Aall, eds, *Managing Global Crises*. Washington, DC: USIP Press, pp. 445–62.

Zenko, M. and Friedman, R. (2011) UN Early Warning for Preventing Conflict. *International Peacekeeping* 18(1), pp. 21–37.

Zubek, J., D., Pruitt, R., Peirce, N., McGillicuddy, H. and Syna, H. (1992) Disputant and Mediator Behaviors Affecting Short-Term Success in Mediation. *Journal of Conflict Resolution* 36(3), pp. 546–72.

Index